Making Societies

The Historical Construction of Our World

William G. Roy

University of California, Los Angeles

PINE FORGE PRESS

Thousand Oaks, California • London • New Delhi

For information:

 Pine Forge Press
A Sage Publications Company
31 St. James Ave., Suite 510
Boston, Massachusetts 02116
E-mail: sdr@pfp.sagepub.com

Sage Publications Ltd.
6 Bonhill Street
London EC2A 4PU
United Kingdom

Sage Publications India Pvt. Ltd.
M-32 Market
Greater Kailash I
New Delhi 110 048 India

Printed in the United States of America

Library of Congress Cataloging-in-Publication Data

Roy, William G., 1946-
    Making societies: The historical construction of our world /
by William G. Roy.
        p.   cm. — (Sociology for a new century)
    Includes bibliographical references and index.
    ISBN 0-7619-8662-6 (pbk.: alk paper)
1. Knowledge, Sociology of.   2. Space and time.   3. Social groups.
4. Social classes.   I. Title.   II. Series.
HM651.R68   2001
306.4'2—dc21   00-012057

This book is printed on acid-free paper.

01   02   03   04   05   10   9   8   7   6   5   4   3   2   1

Acquiring Editor:	Steve Rutter
Editorial Assistant:	Ann Makarias
Production Editor:	Denise Santoyo
Editorial Assistant:	Cindy Bear
Designer/Typesetter:	Janelle LeMaster

Making Societies

Sociology for a New Century

A PINE FORGE PRESS SERIES

Edited by Charles Ragin, Wendy Griswold, and Larry Griffin

Sociology for a New Century brings the best current scholarship to today's students in a series of short texts authored by leaders of a new generation of social scientists. Each book addresses its subject from a comparative, historical, and global perspective and, in doing so, connects social science to the wider concerns of students seeking to make sense of our dramatically changing world.

To Alice,
for constructing an
enchanted reality

Contents

Illustrations

ABOUT THE AUTHOR

William G. Roy is Professor of Sociology at UCLA and author of *Socializing Capital: The Rise of the Large Corporation in America* (1997). He has won the Luckman Distinguished Teaching Award at UCLA and the Distinguished Contribution to Teaching Award from the American Sociological Association. His current research concerns American folk music, social movements, and race.

ABOUT THE PUBLISHER

Pine Forge Press is a new educational publisher, dedicated to publishing innovative books and software throughout the social sciences. On this and any other of our publications, we welcome your comments, ideas, and suggestions. Please call or write to:

Pine Forge Press
A Sage Publications Company
31 St. James Ave., Suite 510
Boston, MA 02116
617-753-7512
E-mail: sdr@pfp.sagepub.com
Visit our World Wide Web site, your direct link to a multitude of
  online resources:
www.pineforge.com

Foreword

Sociology for a New Century offers the best of current sociological thinking to today's students. The goal of the series is to prepare students and—in the long run—the informed public for a world that has changed dramatically in the past three decades and one that continues to astonish.

These goals reflect important changes that have taken place in sociology. The discipline has become broader in orientation, with an ever-growing interest in research that is comparative, historical, or transnational in orientation. Sociologists are less focused on "American" society as the pinnacle of human achievement and more sensitive to global processes and trends. They also have become less insulated from surrounding social forces. In the 1970s and 1980s, sociologists were so obsessed with constructing a science of society that they saw impenetrability as a sign of success. Today, there is a greater effort to connect sociology to the ongoing concerns and experiences of the informed public.

Each book in this series offers in some way a comparative, historical, transnational, or global perspective to help broaden students' vision. Students need to comprehend the diversity in today's world and to understand the sources of diversity. This knowledge can challenge the limitations of conventional ways of thinking about social life. At the same time, students need to understand that issues that may seem specifically "American" (e.g., the women's movement, an aging population bringing a strained social security and health care system, racial conflict, national chauvinism, etc.) are shared by many other countries. Awareness of commonalities undercuts the tendency to view social issues and questions in narrowly American terms and encourages students to seek out the experiences of others for the lessons they offer. Finally, students also need to grasp phenomena that transcend national boundaries—trends and processes that are supranational (e.g., environmental degradation). Recognition of global processes stimulates student awareness of causal forces that transcend national boundaries, economies, and politics.

If the goal of Sociology for a New Century is to broaden the students' vision, no book in the series is more ambitious toward attaining that goal than William Roy's *Making Societies*. Roy helps students question the most "natural" of categories: time, space, gender, race, and class. Leading them through examples drawn from around the world, he shows how these categories are social constructions, historically formed, ideologically loaded, and subject to change. This will be a revelation to many readers. Like all revelations, it will be profoundly unsettling, for students will be encouraged to question not only what they know but also the conceptual frameworks they use when they claim to understand anything. It is the series editors' belief that this unsettling, this provocation, will open new ways of thinking about the social world, how it is, and how it might be.

Preface

One of the greatest challenges of teaching sociology is to lift students out of their "natural attitude," the tenacious tendency to identify the familiar with the inevitable. Indeed, one of the deepest changes in sociology over the past decade or so has been the fuller development of social constructionist perspectives on the social world. Conventional sociology, both mainstream functionalism and its emancipatory challengers, has been criticized for its essentialist assumptions about social life, charging that the failure to problematize why social reality exists the way it does misses the opportunity to explain these patterns and the possibility to transcend them. Issues of race and gender have moved from documentation of inequality between races and genders to asking why races and gender exist. Questions of class have shifted from the degree of disparity or the rates of mobility to the historical origins of structured inequality. At the same time, sociologists have joined other social scientists in examining the fundamental parameters of experience such as time and space. Challenging the rationalist perspectives that treat time and space as immanent properties of nature, scholars have problematized how social time and place structure the way people relate to each and underlie institutions.

These issues of social construction can begin to chip away at students' natural attitude by demonstrating that the world they take for granted as natural and inevitable could have, and indeed has, been different. Not all societies divide people into fixed races, assign everyone to only one of two sexes, or accord higher status to those who accumulate wealth. Many societies treat time as a cycle more than a line, and almost none can imagine it as a "thing" that can be sold, saved, wasted, or spent. Few societies think of space in terms of abstract coordinates that can have meaning apart from the activities that happen in particular places. If the things people take for granted as natural are really socially constructed, we must then seek explanations of why particular relations arise. Why does Anglo-European society divide people into races and genders that structure the opportunities they have and the material comforts they are likely to enjoy while pretending that the vast wealth possessed by a few is within the grasp of anyone? Why have complex time systems that barely affect the way people live evolved into standardized systems that permeate social life so pervasively that people feel trapped by time? Why has the conception of space changed from a place where social activities occur to a commodity so basic to the economic system that the language designates areas of land as "real" property?

Presenting social construction as an issue of explanation rather than one of existence can keep the analysis from wandering into the sophistry of postmodern relativism. The understanding that social reality is constructed need not imply that it is any less real than "natural" reality. Rather than dwell on how "real" social patterns are, it is more constructive to discover why the patterns have arisen and explore how they might be transformed. The consequences of distributing resources by race, gender, and class are very real to the members of society, even if those on the losing end are more acutely aware of their importance. The fact that most people must sell their time to live and use some of the payment to buy space is not just an issue for philosophical debate. At the same time, the search for explanation can imprint the contingent nature of realities that students initially assumed to be self-evident.

The search for explanation also goes beyond the more microsociological perspective that originally gave rise to social constructionism. While challenging students to see how reality is constructed in their everyday lives certainly can jolt them out of their natural attitude and help them understand how social life is reproduced by mundane activity, this book is more concerned with showing how things could be different, both how they have been different in other societies and how an understanding of differences in the past can open vistas to differences in the future. The chapters try to show how things that we normally take for granted as natural have been different in other societies and how the patterns of Anglo-European society have arisen historically. Since it would be impossible to authoritatively cover all aspects of either, I have chosen a sample of contrasts in other societies to unharness preexisting assumptions about iron necessity and then give a plausible, though rarely definitive, account of how Anglo-European patterns developed. Though many of these accounts are contested by scholars, I felt that it was pedagogically more important to present solid, coherent accounts of how social construction works than getting students bogged down in debates.

Finally, the macrohistorical emphasis offers an appropriate scaffold for presenting basic concepts of social explanation too often missing from social constructionist perspectives. The issue of why some patterns become adopted rather than others elicits the issue of power. Some people have had a greater hand in developing patterns than others, and some have benefited from the patterns more than others. Eschewing models of history based on either popular consent or elite hegemony, the explanations in this book probe how popular movements have interacted with powerful groups. Much of this interaction has taken place in the context and construction of social institutions. The social relations of time, space, race, gender, and class are not only shaped by dominant institutions but also, to some extent, constitute them. The capitalist economy is based on the commodification of time and space. Chattel slavery, the capitalist form of slavery, helped give rise to the modern concept of race while making possible the industrial revolution that enabled capitalism to spread throughout the world. The modern state has standardized time and space and codified race, gender, and class into law. As discussed in the final chapter, the rise of nations and nationalism reflected and shaped all five issues. Even secondary institutions such as education reflect prevailing time and space conceptions while socializing new generations into them. The role that education plays in reproducing racial, gender, and class inequality is well known.

The book has selected five kinds of socially constructed reality: time, space, race, gender, and class. There is no compelling logic for choosing these; other constructions could have been just as profitably included: nature, science, family, religion, art, and even sociology. I chose time and space because they are so basic and the forms of inequality because they are so consequential for contemporary society and everyday life. The book begins with time and space because they are less controversial than the forms of inequality and because they provide a starker challenge to the natural attitude. If the reader can grasp how time and space are socially constructed, the concepts can be applied in a more sophisticated fashion in exploring the sensitive issues of race, gender, and class.

This book could not have been possible without the support and contributions of many friends and colleagues; any virtues it might possess are much enhanced by their efforts. I have wanted to write a book for Pine Forge Press ever since conversations with Steve Rutter, when he was planning the enterprise, inspired me to imagine what a book written for students could be. His contribution far exceeds the ordinary publisher, helping develop the book's vision, providing feedback and encouragement throughout the process, and tolerantly abiding my missed deadlines. Wendy Griswold was the point person throughout the writing process for the talented and committed series editors, with Larry Griffin and Charles Ragin providing special insight in the early stages. I was blessed with an uncommonly conscientious and talented group of academic reviewers:

Lisa Brush, *University of Pittsburgh*

Joann DeFiore, *University of Washington, Bothell*

Kelly Moore, *Barnard College, Columbia University*

Tracy Ore, *St. Cloud State University*

Teresa Swartz, *University of Minnesota*

Idee Winfield, *College of Charleston*

I am also grateful to developmental editors Kathy Field and Mark LaFleur, who materially improved on my earlieer drafts. Ann Makarias, assistant to the publisher, skillfully helped shepherd the manuscript through the editing process. She was always available with a cheerful and constructive answer to my queries and concerns. Gillian Dickens helped make my often mangled prose readable. Barbara Moroncini far exceeded the expectations of an undergraduate research assistant, reading the manuscript from the perspective of an intelligent student, finding typos and infelicities I missed while correcting the text, tracking down sources I thought were lost, discovering illustrations that not only represented but also enhanced concepts, and cheerfully responding to my panicked call for help when deadlines approached.

Many friends, colleagues, and graduate students enriched the ideas, pointed me to important sources, reined in my wandering from the topic, corrected my errors, and improved my writing. Ron Aminzade, Tyrone Harvey, Cathie Lee, Jennifer Lee, Ruth Milkman, Ruth Stedman, Susan Stockdale, and the members of the UCLA Workshop on Comparative Social Analysis read and made valuable comments on the chapters. Patricia Ahmed was hired to find material for Chapter 3 on space but wrote it up so eloquently that it would have been unjust to not list her as a coauthor. The book has its origins in a course in UCLA's honor's collegium on "Time in Society and History" and was expanded in an undergraduate course, "Comparative-Historical Sociology." It incorporates many ideas I learned from the students in those classes. My wife Alice not only provided the love, support, and tolerance authors typically extol but also made an intellectual contribution. Drawing on the insight that enabled her to do a book on the construction of truth as related to plagiarism and intellectual property, she helped sharpen the central ideas and provided feedback on the entire manuscript.

1

Constructing Historical Reality

Imagine a high school honors student who designs software as a part-time job, plays piano well enough to give private recitals, and is the captain of her debate team. But when her SAT scores turn out to be only average, she is wracked by self-doubt and personal crisis. Is she really intelligent? Are her aspirations to be a surgeon or music professor the silly fantasies of immaturity? Is all the hard work she has invested in making something of herself wasted on a noodlehead? If she were not a noodlehead after all but wise beyond her years, she might ask, "What does the SAT measure anyway?" She might wonder whether it measures only what she has learned in school. Her self-doubt would contend that it must measure "real" intelligence in some way. But her more reasonable side would ask what we mean when we say "intelligence." What if *intelligence* is just a word that refers to whatever the SAT measures? By common sense, intelligence is a quality of the brain, something that some people have more of than others. It is a "thing" that explains why some people get better grades at school, perform better at jobs, learn new skills, understand other people, and operate a VCR.

The idea that intelligence is an inherent, unchanging characteristic that people use to deal with all aspects of life is a relatively recent development. This "internal" conception of intelligence assumed in standardized tests contrasts with "contextual" conceptions. Internal conceptions treat intelligence as an essential quality of the mind—the ability to do abstract problems inside the head. In contrast, contextual conceptions treat intelligence as people's capacity to interact with the world around them. The distinction refers not only to what intelligence is but also how we recognize that some people are more intelligent than others. Internal intelligence can be recognized only by eliminating the influence of everything except the brain itself. Intelligence tests try to measure internal conceptions by reducing all contextual factors to a minimum, putting a subject working on his or her own in a room with paper, pencil, and a proctor. Those who treat intelligence contextually hold that it is impossible to control all contextual factors and that the test-taking situation itself is a social context that affects how people perform. Rather than eliminate contextual factors, they argue that intelligence is a matter of how well a person negotiates the complexity of context such as the presence of other people; the kind of prior experience a person has had in similar situations; the sights, sounds, and texture of the situation; and the ambiguity or clarity of communication received. From the contextualist perspective, intelligence tests do not measure a person's general ability to interact in the real world but only that person's ability to do "abstract problems in one's head while under the surveillance of a stranger draped in great authority, who will later enter one's score into a semi-secret bureaucratic information system which may affect one's future educational and occupation life" (Andersen 1994:128).

What Is Intelligence and Why Does It Matter?

Psychologists have also challenged the notion of intelligence implicit in intelligence testing by questioning whether there is a single quality that people have or whether there are multiple intelligences. People who do well in mathematics may not do well in music; those who learn languages quickly may not understand how to navigate interpersonal relationships.[1] Our imaginary student can take solace in learning that the SAT measures do not predict very well how well she will do in college, on the job, or in life. But she still might have a nagging feeling that the SAT does measure something and that she does not measure up to her expectations.

There is a deeper issue about intelligence than whether it is internal or contextual or whether there is one or many: Why do people think of it as a "thing" at all? Our imaginary student may be surprised to learn that

---

[1]Howard Gardner (1983) identified seven distinct types of intelligence: (1) linguistic (involved in writing, reading, telling stories, and doing crossword puzzles), (2) logical-mathematical (involved in patterns, categories, relationships, math problems, strategy games, and experiments), (3) bodily-kinesthetic (involved in athletics, dancing, and crafts such as sewing and woodworking), (4) spatial (involved in solving mazes and jigsaw puzzles, drawing, and daydreaming), (5) musical (involved in singing and making music; often discriminating listeners), (6) interpersonal (involved in leadership skills, communication, understanding of others' feelings), and (7) intrapersonal (involved in self-motivation).

many societies have no concept of the thing American society calls intelligence. In fact, society has not always had any such concept. There was a very distinct historical process by which all the complex and multifaceted qualities that enable people to perform tasks well or poorly were lumped together as a "thing," an entity that has a name—intelligence.

The concept of intelligence in the English language goes back to the 14th century, when it referred to people's general understanding. In the 16th century, it was first used to distinguish people from each other but described acquired knowledge, as in military intelligence, rather than innate ability. In the centuries that followed, public discourse increasingly cited intelligence as a quality that justified inequality, for example, the argument that intelligent people should govern. Intelligence also took on a more exclusively cognitive meaning in these centuries, creating a distinction between head and heart, mind and body, reason and emotion (Williams 1983).

When a teacher told our imaginary student that perhaps she scored lower than she hoped because she was a member of a minority group, she was not sure whether to take offense. If she delved into the history of intelligence, she would find that people created the concept and then figured out a way to measure it in part to prove that poor and minority people were inferior. Many of the original designers of intelligence testing also were motivated by proving that some men were smarter than women, whites smarter than nonwhites, and higher-class people smarter than lower-class people. Intelligence tests were not designed to identify individual traits and then generalized to gender, racial, and class groups. Intelligence was assumed to be a group trait, and tests were designed to prove it (Andersen 1994; Gould 1981).

In the 19th century, Herbert Spencer's doctrine of "survival of the fittest" gave a scientific luster to the popular belief that it was natural for the poor to suffer. Spencer said of the poor that "the whole effort of nature is to get rid of such, to clear the world of them, and make room for better" (Andersen 1994:121).[2] About the same time, English biologist Francis Galton began searching for a method to distinguish the talented from untalented. Assuming that "eminence" indicated inherent talent, he discovered that people listed in biographical dictionaries of distinguished men of achievement tended to clump in families. Even though

---

[2]Darwin used the term *fitness* to mean the ability to reproduce, not the quality of life that organisms lived. By this definition, the higher fertility rates of the lower classes would qualify them as more fit.

he acknowledged that the children of the upper classes had greater opportunities, he argued that the pattern was explained by innate ability. Because such evidence did not meet the standards of scientific proof, he set about measuring biological variables such as head size, sensory acuity, keenness of sight and hearing, color sense, and judgment in bisecting a line but found that they did not correlate with other measures of intelligence or achievement.

Although Galton failed to find a biological basis for achievement, he inspired the modern science of psychometrics, the science of intelligence testing. For example, a statistician named Charles Spearman created a concept called g, which stood for "general intelligence" when he developed a statistical technique designed to identify a single dimension of data. Once it had a name and a way to measure it, intelligence could be thought of as a real thing. The qualities that are commonly attributed to intelligence—that is, it is distributed along a single, hierarchical continuum from low to high; people are distributed according to a bell-shaped curve, with a lot of people in the middle and a few at each end; and people who score high on one measure of it score high on others—are all qualities of the instruments used to measure it, not necessarily some "it" in nature. People do not naturally fall into a distribution that looks like a bell-shaped curve. The people who designed the first intelligence tests tinkered with the tests, eliminating questions and adding others until results fit the curve. The bell-shaped curve is more a quality of the test than any inherent human quality (Andersen 1994; Gould 1981; Hacking 1999). In other words, the qualities by which people generally characterize intelligence are not natural qualities of humans that science discovered and then measured but were invented by scientists who invented measuring devices that conformed to their preconceptions.

After considering all this, it may be small solace for our student to know that even if the SAT does not really measure her abilities, the admissions office of the college she wants to attend, the people who distribute financial aid, and her parents and friends think it does. Even if intelligence is not "real" in some ultimate sense, it is certainly real in its consequences. People in a position to dramatically affect her life treat intelligence as very real.

Intelligence illustrates the questions addressed in this book: (1) How do the "things" that we experience in social life and study in social science get created? I will argue that these "things" did not exist in nature and then get discovered. Even if people's brains have different capacities, why do some societies treat particular qualities of mind as "things" and distinguish them from other "things" such as emotion, sensory acuity, and ability to make decisions? (2) How do these "things" become understood as explanations of people's place in society? How does intelligence come to be understood as an explanation for why some people have better houses, take nicer vacations, and get more satisfying jobs? (3) How do some "things" become associated with other "things" that are used to lump people into groups? How does intelligence get connected to "things" such as race or gender to characterize groups of people? Why are people with one kind of body—men—assumed to have more of "it" than those with another kind of body—women? Why are groups of people with darker skin sometimes assumed to have less of "it" than groups with lighter skin? (4) Why does the understanding that these "things" are real have such a powerful influence on people's lives and so doggedly resist change? Individuals labeled as lacking intelligence often accept such a designation as a reasonable justification for why they have harder lives than those labeled as having more of it. (5) How have some groups invented and used these "things" to establish and preserve their privileged place in society? How have other groups challenged and affected the outcome of creating such "things"? Why was a concept such as intelligence useful to educated white men in subordinating the social position of minorities, women, and the poor? How have the protests of minorities, women, and the poor against characterizations of themselves as less intelligent affected the prevailing concept of intelligence itself? (6) Can learning that these "things" do not exist in nature but are historically invented help weaken the power that some groups have over others? If the concept of intelligence is used to sustain the dominance of whites over racial minorities, men over women, and the wealthy over the poor, can a challenge to the concept itself facilitate greater social equality? Such a challenge would not change the mental capacities that anyone has but might reconstruct the social processes by which such capacities are assessed and what consequences flow from such assessments.

The Social Construction of Reality

Sociologists call the historical process by which our experiences become put into categories and treated as things the **social construction of reality** (Berger and Luckmann 1966; Hacking 1999; Pollner 1987; Zerubavel 1991). People deal with what they experience in terms of categories, then act on the basis of those categories. Sociologists want to understand how people came to understand intelligence as a category different from other categories such as emotion, knowledge, sensitivity, or character. While much of education teaches students what is real and not real, sociology contributes to education by teaching students to understand how things came to be understood as real.

The "coin" of sociological knowledge has two sides, making familiar what people do not understand and gaining new understanding of the familiar. Most people come to sociology to learn about what they do not understand—such as why people commit crimes or why some acts are defined as criminal; why some people have more wealth, power, and respect than others; why some organizations work more efficiently than others; why racial, class, and gender oppression persists; and why people of different cultures misunderstand each other. But sociology also helps in "peeling back the covers" surrounding the very familiar—how people carry on a conversation; how gestures and motions affect interaction; how racial, class, and gender inequality is acted out and perpetuated interpersonally; how emotions are social as well as psychological; and how the very categories that underlie all social life are created. An important aspect of gaining deeper insight into the world of the familiar is the notion that "reality" itself arose through human activities. Things that people assume "just are"—such as time, space, gender, class, and race—arise through human activities and could be quite different if circumstances were otherwise. Social construction implies that society is not something apart from "reality" and that "reality" is not something outside human interaction; it is constituted from human ideas and interaction.

For sociology, the social construction of reality is less about some ultimate philosophical sense of what is "real" or "not real" than it is about how people explain the world they live in and whether that world can be changed. To say that something is socially constructed means that it cannot be explained in terms of "it's just there" or "it's natural." Sociologists can explain how the concept of intelligence arose historically. It is not just there. Nor was it "out there" waiting to be discovered, even though certain discoveries, such as the fact that behavior is in the brain, not in bodily humors, influenced the process. The sense of what is real does not come just from what is "out there." That is not to say that reality is just "made up" or a figment of the imagination. A rock can hurt you regardless of what it is called, but if people had not constructed the concept of "rock," we would not distinguish the hard, round gray object on the ground from the soft gray round thing in the bird's nest. Its "rockness" is socially constructed. Sociologists can explain why the gray thing on the ground is understood as "rock" or "holy shrine" or "a work of art." For intelligence, the issue is not whether people all have the same abilities to reason mathematically, remember facts, or comprehend what they read. It is why some societies explain those differences in terms of a single, inherent underlying "thing" called intelligence and why the way these differences are constructed has consequences for people's lives.

This book examines how social reality has been constructed in **Anglo-European societies.**[3] These are societies in Europe or former European settler colonies such as the United States, Canada, Australia, and New Zealand. This book explores how the realities that people in those societies usually take for granted have been created—how concepts of time, space, race, gender, and class have been constructed. Time is commonly thought of as something "out there" that clocks and calendars measure, place is assumed to be the "out there" where social activities take place, races and genders are defined as genetic in origin, the differences between men and women or people of different races are often explained as natural, and inequalities in wealth and power are attributed to natural abilities and talents. Insofar as all these things are seen as natural, it is assumed there is no need for a social or historical explanation for why they are the way they are. Both common sense and much social science take for granted what is considered natural and disregard any need to explain such things.

The social origins of these things are often forgotten, allowing people to think that their sense of time and place and their definition of race/ethnicity, gender, and class are the only ways it could be. If the "facts of life" that are most taken for granted have social, not natural, origins, they do not have to be the way they are. People make things the way they are. To be sure, some people have a greater influence on the way they are than others; that is, some people have more power than others. But when members of a society take social reality as a given—something that is just there, not something that is constructed—they participate in its perpetuation. No doubt, there is much of reality that most

---

[3] I use the term *Anglo-European* to refer to societies in Europe and those of former European settler colonies such as the United States, Canada, Australia, and New Zealand. Since the book emphasizes the importance of categories, I avoid using the term *Western* both because it is inexact and implies that there is a coherent obverse category *Eastern*, a concept that makes no sociological sense. When I refer to Europe proper, I will say so explicitly if it is not clear from the context.

people want to perpetuate, but equally certain there are things they want to change. It is hoped that by realizing how much taken-for-granted realities are historically constructed, we can become empowered to change the things we want to change.

Essentialist Views of Reality

Time can be bought and goes forward. Space is something out there independent of us. People are black or white or yellow or red. They are either men or women. They are rich or poor because the most talented and hardest working are appropriately rewarded. In Anglo-European societies, both common sense and much social science take these statements for granted. But each of these statements might seem bizarre to people at certain other times or other cultures. Common sense in Anglo-European societies takes an **essentialist perspective** and assumes that everything that we see and touch is merely a manifestation of a deeper essence. Every chair embodies some essential "chairness"; every woman is but one example of "womanness." One can then establish whether any one concrete object is "really" a chair or not. Is a piece of art that looks like a chair, created by an artist to rest in a museum and never intended to have anyone sit in it, really a chair? Depending on what a person thinks is the essence of "chairness," one could argue that it is or is not really a chair. People generally assume that they can distinguish between a real authentic chair and something that only looks like a chair and that such a distinction is very real.

From the essentialist perspective, things are the way they are by nature (although sometimes "nature" can be defined by humans, as in the nature of a chair).[4] Within essentialist thinking, the essence also serves as an explanation. Why does a particular object in my office have four legs and a seat? The essentialist answers, "Because it is a chair." Why do many women prefer to stay at home and care for children rather than

---

[4]*Nature* is typically used in two ways: (1) to mean not created by human activities, as in "pristine nature." This usually carries a connotation of something living, although geology and astronomy are also considered natural sciences. This is the meaning of nature in the "nature versus nurture" debate over human behavior, for example, whether men are naturally more aggressive than women. (2) "Nature" is also used to describe inherent features of things whether they are made by humans or not, as in "the nature of the game" or "It's only natural to feel that way." Many usages do not distinguish between two senses, such as "human nature." When I mean one sense but not the other, I will state so explicitly.

work in paid jobs? "Because they are women." Why do men commit more crimes than women? An essentialist perspective would assume that it has something to do with the nature of maleness. "Men are naturally more aggressive than women," they might say. Some versions might attribute the differences to an intermediate cause such as genetics, but they still assume that something in the nature of being male creates aggression.

For essentialist thinking, races, genders, and measurements of time and space just "are." People can change how they treat races or what rights and opportunities people of different races have but not the "fact" that races are distinct groups or that each person is a member of one race. Even a superficial examination of other societies reveals that nearly all qualities normally attributed to natural reality are absent in at least some other societies. For Anglo-European society, time is linear, moving from the past to the present to the future, but people in many societies think of time as cyclical; some languages do not even have past or future tense. If time is naturally linear, there is no need to explain why it is linear. But if some societies treat time as primarily cyclical, that is, repeating itself, like the seasons, we not only must understand why that is so but also ask why people treat it as linear. If people from different cultures experience difficulty communicating with each other because they have a different sense of time, or if the linear sense of time affects how people structure their lives or arrange social institutions, the need for explanation becomes even more compelling.

Space and hierarchy also differ so radically among cultures that they cannot be natural nonsocial realities. Like time, people usually think of space in abstract terms, particularly abstract dimensions—length, breadth, and height—within which activities happen. But for most societies, the space in which an activity is set is indistinguishable from the activity itself. People today think of races as people of different physical characteristics, such as skin color, but in 19th-century America, people with white skin and blond hair from Sweden and Ireland were considered different races from Anglo-Saxon Americans. While men and women are distinguished from each other in virtually all societies, the characterization of men or women and the rights, rules, and responsibilities expected of them differ greatly among societies. Anglo-European society before the past few hundred years considered men and women to be biologically one category, not as biological opposites. Some societies have more than two genders, defining a category of people that might share genital characteristics with men or women but who are thought of as fundamentally different. Why Anglo-European society changed to treat men and women as biological opposites and why it does not treat people with ambiguous sexual features as a category in themselves are issues that sociologists need to explain.

The Constructionist View of Reality

In contrast to the essentialist view, the **constructionist perspective** assumes that reality is created by society. Even our sense of what is real does not come just from what is "out there"; we take what our senses register and define what the reality is. There is no "chairness" "out there" outside of society and existing prior to society, but rather people decided to categorize all the things that have four legs (or occasionally three or five), a back, and a seat as chairs. They then decided to distinguish chairs from stools, benches, couches, and pieces of art. In this perspective, it is fruitless to debate whether something is "really" a chair because there is no essence of chair to compare a particular actual object with. If people agree that something is a chair and treat it as a chair, from the constructionist perspective, it is, for all practical purposes, a chair. "Reality" depends on the categories we form and the names we give them.

How Real?

Some constructionist perspectives, especially those called *postmodern*, treat constructed realities as "only" constructed; they hold that nothing is real, that everything is illusion, a fantasy of the imagination. That is not the perspective here. In my view, there is no other essential reality that is "more real" than constructed reality. The difference between an essentialist and a constructionist perspective is not a matter of "how real" things are imputed to be but how we explain that reality. Sociologists William I. Thomas and Dorothy Swaine Thomas articulated what has become known as the **Thomas principle**: "If [people] define situations as real, then they are real in their consequences" (Thomas and Thomas 1928:52). Socially constructed realities are just as real, just as consequential, as if they were determined solely by nature.

The more people act as though something is real, the more consequential that definition of reality becomes. For example, people have long assumed that races are real and that each person is, in fact, really white, African American, Asian, American Indian, or whatever. Most biologists, however, believe that the concept of race has no biological foundation. There are no genetic boundaries between those people that societies define as racially distinct. But to label people as black or white—or yellow or brown—has great social consequences. If a person gets a better job, a different mate, more respect, greater trust, or is killed because of his or her race, the consequences are very real indeed. Saying that race is socially constructed does not make it any less real than if it were natural. But the explanation of why racial differences exist and the prospects for changing racial structures would differ profoundly.

Defining Reality: Categories and Language

When our senses get input, the brain mentally pigeonholes the physical stimulus into learned categories. Depending on the context, you could see the same object as a chair, an art object, or a piece of firewood. When we interact with others, we make sense of whatever we are talking about in terms of those categories. You could categorize the same person as professor, woman, African American, friend, family member, or any combination. Some categories are so taken for granted that people do not think of them as categories but as real "things." Take the week, for example. Although it is merely an aggregation of 7 days, people treat the week as a thing. We have good weeks and bad weeks, busy ones and easy ones. Weeks structure much of our lives. Working on the weekend, going out on a date on Thursday, or having your favorite television show switched to a new night feels unsettling. We do not dismiss such events by saying that the week is just a social construction anyway. It is similar with space categories such as inches, feet, and miles. People are a little more aware that these are constructed because most of world uses a different set of categories based on the meter. But they rarely consider that some societies have no standard measurements that they use to measure most kinds of distance but have many kinds of measurements for different kinds of activities.[5] Racial, gender, and class categories are especially important to understand.

---

[5]Most people use nonstandard measures of distance more than they realize. Some parts of the country measure travel distances in time units rather than distance (for example, when asked how far from work they live, they will say, "Ten minutes"), while other regions might answer in blocks or miles. Most people can probably convert those distances into miles. For specific settings, we often use specific measurements; for example, people in a large office building might think of how many offices they work from someone else. The English language still includes clichés to describe distance such as "a stone's throw."

Language, especially naming things, is one of the most important ways that sociologists have studied how people construct reality in everyday life. Common sense holds that "things" exist in nature and that people name them when they discover or decide to use them. But social scientists who take a constructionist perspective emphasize that the relationship of discovery and naming more often works in the opposite direction—that naming can make things seem real. People ordinarily do not notice things until they have a name. Take colors, for example. The color spectrum in physics is continuous from ultraviolet to infrared. There are no natural divisions distinguishing one color from another. Anglo-European society divides the spectrum into six basic colors: red, orange, yellow, green, blue, and purple—the English-language names given to ranges of color. We can make finer distinctions, either by putting two objects that are similar next to each other or by training the eye to distinguish between finer distinctions that have names such as crimson, scarlet, or cardinal. But most people, when they see what trained eyes would call crimson, scarlet, or cardinal, see red. In contrast, the Shona culture of Zimbabwe has three colors they call *cipsuka, cicena,* and *citema,* while the Bassa culture of Liberia has only two colors, *hui* and *ziza* (Newman 2000). *Hui* includes all the parts of the spectrum English designates as red, orange, and yellow, while *ziza* covers green, blue, and purple. Because English has separate names for red and yellow, people in English-speaking cultures actually see them as distinct colors. For the Bassa, what Anglo-Europeans see as red and yellow would be seen as two variations of the same thing. So names can influence how people perceive something as natural as color. This is not just a matter of mere labels. People from different cultures treat colors in different categories such as red or *cipsuka* or *hui* and, insofar as colors matter, react differently to them.

Do categories dictate *what* we see or only *how* we see things? The answer is really, both. Sometimes it is relatively simple to distinguish between how something is socially constructed and the objects that are constructed (Hacking 1999). Some people have always been able to do mathematics, remember facts, or comprehend what they read better than others even before there was a concept of intelligence. And in some societies, people who were considered gifted in these skills were given privileges, and those found deficient were stigmatized (but there were also cases when the gifted were punished, as were many alleged witches). For these kinds of categories, the way they are socially constructed affects more *how* we see them. Whether we see people who cannot do mathematics, remember facts, or comprehend reading as genetically deficient, a member of a minority group, or the victim of a poor environment has profound effects on how they are treated but does not create the objects that the concepts refer to. Even without the concept of intelligence, some people would be able to do mathematics, remember facts, or comprehend reading better than others. But when the concept exists in a culture, people can use the concept to achieve goals they would have been otherwise unable to attain. The concept of measurable intelligence has been used against those individuals and groups deemed less intelligent. In 1916, Lewis Terman, one of the designers of modern intelligence tests, explained how he hoped they would be used:

> It is safe to predict that in the near future intelligence tests will bring tens of thousands of these high-grade defectives under the surveillance and protection of society. This will ultimately result in curtailing the reproduction and of feeble-mindedness and in the elimination of an enormous amount of crime, pauperism, and industrial inefficiency. (Gould 1981:179)

More recently, Richard Herrnstein and Charles Murray generated considerable controversy by arguing that lower intelligence explains the economic failures of minorities and lower-class people (Herrnstein and Murray 1994). The controversy raged not only over their alleged racism but also over their policy recommendations that educational programs that tried to close the gap between races and classes were fruitless (Fischer et al. 1996).

Other social phenomena have no object other than what is socially constructed. Unlike the ability to remember facts or call the object we sit in a chair, the "things" referred to by concepts such as national states, the week, philosophy, schools, television, cars, and numbers would not be there if they had not been socially constructed. Most social institutions (except perhaps the family), abstract ideas, and technological inventions are constructed in terms of *what* they are, not just *how* people perceive them.

The distinction between *what* we perceive and *how* we perceive can be qualified in two ways. First, many of the things that have objects existing independently of their social constructions might not be noticed if they were not socially constructed. Some of the abilities people associate with intelligence would be less noticed in societies that lack a conception of intelligence or have specific institutions devoted to improving it, as schools do. Urban, industrial societies do not rank people according to their ability to estimate physical distance, although societies where food

is procured by throwing spears or shooting arrows might very well recognize this type of intelligence.

Second, *how* things are constructed can in fact cause the objects that
are constructed to change. If social institutions treat some races as
though they are less intelligent than others, the members of the first race
are likely to perform better in intelligence tests, thereby "proving" that
the races are "really" different. So the "objective" evidence that they are
less intelligent is caused by the assumption that they are different. In
such cases, it is difficult to separate the social construction of intelligence
in racial terms from the object to which the concept of intelligence refers.

Gradients and Bounded Categories

Why do some societies rank people along a continuum from genius to
imbecile? Why do people divide society into distinct racial categories?
Are there really two and only two genders? Because reality is defined by
the categories people use, it is important to understand how categories
are formed and the **logic of how categories are constructed.** By the logic
of how they are constructed, I mean the formal characteristics of how categories relate to each other. Some categories are treated as exclusive from
each other with no overlap (like people usually think of gender—a person is required to be either male or female but not both, although we will
later see it does not have to be that way). Or can categories overlap, as
teacher and student do in large universities where teaching assistants are
typically both?

One especially important aspect in the logic of constructing categories concerns whether categories are gradients or bounded categories.
Gradients can be defined along a continual slope with only fuzzy divisions. Anglo-European societies generally treat intelligence like that. Intelligence tests are designed on that assumption, giving people numerical scores rather than determining whether people can perform specific
skills.

In contrast, other categories are bounded. **Bounded categories** have
distinct, rigid boundaries. Intelligence used to be treated more in
bounded categories than it is now. Early in the 20th century, H. H.
Goddard, director of research at the Vineland School for Feeble-Minded
Girls and Boys in New Jersey, invented the term *moron* (from the Greek
word for *foolish*) to distinguish those children who could learn from "idi-
ots," who could not master spoken language, and "imbeciles," who
could not learn to read and write. These words have lost their technical

FIGURE 1.1

Boundaries and Gradients

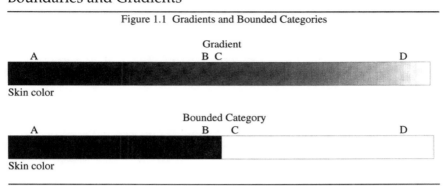

Figure 1.1 Gradients and Bounded Categories

meaning and are now derogatory words in common language (Gould 1981).

In the United States, race is treated as a bounded category, not a gradient. As mentioned earlier, people are generally classified by others as belonging to one race, and they are considered more like other people in that category than people outside of it, even if they are close in skin color.

Figure 1.1 illustrates the difference between gradient and bounded categories. Physically, skin color is like the first rectangle, the gradient. It varies along a continuum from very dark to very light, with people at every point in between. If you think of skin color as gradient, people with skin colors B and C are considered very similar. However, U.S. society has treated skin color as a bounded category. A person is placed on one side of the boundary or the other, as in the second rectangle in Figure 1.1. Although skin colors B and C appear to the senses as in the first rectangle, they are treated as though they match the second one. Because U.S. society has constructed race as a bounded category, people with skin colors A and B are put in one category and thought of as being alike; C and D are similarly put in one category and thought of as being alike, but B and C are put in different categories and thought of as being different. One is "black" and one is "white." There is no gray in this categorization. Conventionally, anyone with one white parent and one African American parent was defined as African American. When American states had overtly discriminatory laws, a person with any African American ancestors was defined black.

Not all societies construct racial categories as bounded categories. In Brazil, for example, although people with dark complexions are sometimes discriminated against, races are conceptualized as a gradient, not a bounded category. A disproportionate number of dark people are poor, but if a person becomes wealthier, he or she is understood by others to become whiter. Race works very differently in the United States and Brazil because of the way that racial categories are constructed. Skin color is just one of the many characteristics that our senses perceive as gradients but that many societies treat as bounded categories. Anglo-European society also treats some characteristics as gradients that others divide into bounded categories. Many cultures have rites of passage that mark the transition from one stage of life to another. Rites of passage, such as Bar Mitzvah or Confirmation, school graduation, marriage, and retirement, mark the entry into specialized roles such as religious membership, school, family, or work rather than comprehensive age-based identities. In contrast, in Anglo-European societies, stages such as childhood, adolescence, adulthood, or old age blend gradually into one another. Similarly, in contrast to many societies with rigid class boundaries between peasants, nobility, and royalty, the dominant American culture defines class as a gradient from impoverished to wealthy. While most Americans "see" the same categories of race and gender, how they "see" the class structure varies greatly. Some people, especially poorer people, would see a family with a police officer and firefighter earning a combined $60,000 annual income as upper middle class; others, especially wealthy people, would see the same family as lower middle class or working class.

The Consequences of Categories: The Case of the Family

One reason to scrutinize categories is to reveal what is omitted from them and to understand the consequences of those omissions. For example, some people argue, in an essentialist manner, that some groups of people who live together are "real" families and other groups are not. Those in "real" families receive economic benefits from employers and governments as well as certain legal rights and social respect that other groupings do not receive.

What groupings of people count as a family, and what groupings do not? For proponents of the "traditional family," the left column of Table 1.1 lists statements that describe what families are supposed to be like or are supposed to do; the right column lists the logical opposite of the statements in the left column. Thus, the traditional family regulates sex-

TABLE 1.1

The Category of Family in Anglo-European Culture

What a Family Is	*What a Family Is Not*
Joined by love rather than material gain	Joined by material gain
Raises children	Does not raise children
Committed to each other for life	Not committed for life
Adults in group recognized by government or religion as married	Adults in group not recognized by government or religion
At least two adults	Less than or more than two adults
Adults are male and female	Adults in some combination other than one male and one female
Adults have sex only with each other	Adults have sex with others outside group
Is the unit within which people live private lives	People live their private lives alone or in some other kind of unit

uality and raises children. All societies have groupings that accomplish these tasks, and biology may even influence these arrangements.

But if we examine other societies, we see that the definition of family summarized in Table 1.1 is not inevitable. Anglo-European society is one of the few societies in human history to emphasize romantic love as the basis for marriage. Arranged marriages are still common in very large societies such as those in India. In 1997, fewer than half of all American families had children under age 18 living at home, and single parents are found in more than a quarter of families that do have children at home (Casper and Bryson 1998). Many societies do not expect mothers and fathers to do most of the child rearing. The Nayar of the Kerala region in India expect the mother's brother, rather than the biological father, to share in raising children; the mother's brother also passes property to his sister's male children. The biological father has no responsibility to his children except to acknowledge paternity (Gough 1974). But on what basis can it be said that some of these families are more "real" families than others? Only by social constructions of what makes a "real" family. The differences in how various societies define families indicate that the family is socially constructed, and a constructionist perspective asks how the family came to be defined in these ways. The definition of the traditional family needs to be explained, not taken as inevitable.

Even if the traditional family is a worthy ideal, the deviations tolerated by its proponents are inconsistent. Why is a legally married heterosexual couple that has no plans of ever having children considered more of a family than a homosexual couple that is raising the biological children of one parent? Why is a single mother with her children less of a family than a married couple with adopted children? Is a couple that marries so one spouse can immigrate to the United States less of a family than a couple that marries because the woman accidentally got pregnant? There is no neat boundary between family and not-family because a family is not a preexisting "thing," and the concept of family has been constructed historically in response to a broad variety of factors. Its construction is continuing today (Holstein and Gubrium 1994).

The Process of Social Construction

How does historical construction of reality take place? How does something that nobody thinks of as a thing become seen as a "real" thing? Let's take a case to illustrate the process: the way that we came to have a week with 7 days, drawing from Zerubavel's (1985) account. The week is a regular sequence of days—in our case, 7 days—in which each day has a name and a social meaning. For example, people generally attach a different meaning to having dinner with someone on Wednesday than Saturday night. Religions define some days of the week as sacred and prohibit or require certain activities. When humans first arose as a species, they probably did not have a regular interval of days like our week. They probably hunted and gathered when they needed to and probably had religious ceremonies on an irregular or seasonal basis. Since they did not know how to count, they probably felt no need for exact rhythms among daily activities. When they started to grow food rather than hunt and gather, it is likely that some people traded extra grain for objects that other people possessed. They may have found that it was easier if they knew in advance when everyone would come together to trade. Depending on what kind of grain most of them grew and how long it could be stored before spoiling, they may have slowly regularized the trading schedule to be every 5 days, 7 days, 8 days, or whatever.

It was probably traders who created "Market Day" to make trading easier and more reliable. About the same time, priests, who were the most powerful leaders in society, began to name and add meaning to the sequence, treating it as a "thing." That is, they reified it—made it a real "thing." **Reification** means that "facts" that were originally merely someone's ideas, speculations, or theories take on a reality of their own. It is the process by which things become real. It is important to remember that reification is a *process,* an activity that specific people do, not just something that happens without intention. The first step that people take is to create a "thing." Following "Market Day," the priests may have proclaimed a day of rest, "Rest Day." In some cases, they began to name not just "Market Day" and "Rest Day" but all the days, using the conventions of their culture, which often meant drawing meaning from nature. So they named days after planets, "Sun Day" and "Moon Day." People began to think of the cluster of 7 days as a thing, a week. Weeks could then be given attributes that we give to things. There could be good weeks and bad weeks, busy weeks and easy weeks, even short weeks and long weeks. As "things," weeks could be talked about as "doing." They could drag on, they could cause conflict, or they could structure people's lives.

What originally was an exact rhythm for market days and holy days every 7 days became a rhythm for other activities. As the names of the days were repeated on a 7-day cycle, people developed a sense of a week. Once created, the week has become a compelling reality around which people organize their lives. When governmental institutions emerged, their meetings were organized by the 7-day cycle. Thousands of years later, when universities were created, their classes were held on that schedule. The week has thus been a social reality for a long time.

Naming is a very important part of reification. It makes the category or activity seem "real" so that people forget that it was created by people. Who thinks any more about why we have 7 days in our week? The category or activity takes on a life of its own as if it were a part of nature. When people forget that somebody created something, they start to treat it as something "out there." They do not think about how anybody created Sunday or Monday but just assume that they are part of reality, external to or outside of them. Not only have the days of the week been disconnected from the people who originally created them, but all social reality has—the discipline of sociology, the categories of professor and student, the institution of the university, and even the concept of society itself.

Like the days of the week, other social constructions feel like "things." Why? We come into this world knowing nothing, just a vague patchwork of drives and urges, but we soon learn what is real. No one tells us that somebody in the past decided that there would be 7 days in a week for Anglo-European society or that other societies have 4, 5, 9, or 19 days. Instead, we learn what day of the week it *is* now. We learn that Monday comes after Sunday as a "fact," not as a social construction. We learn that Friday is a holy day if we are raised Muslim, Saturday if we are Jewish, and Sunday if we are Christian. When we get a little older, we learn that having dinner on Wednesday has a very different connotation than having dinner on Saturday. We learn these things not as "mere" facts but as the way it is. The days of the week become a taken-for-granted part of reality, a piece of knowledge, not a matter of opinion or of human invention.

After an activity or category is created and named, it begins to become a principle by which other activities or categories are structured. Social realities feel real and are treated as though they are real, and for all practical purposes, they *are* real because they have been socially constructed as real through the process of reification. This book is really all about *how* reification takes place and what consequences it has on people's lives.

When reified patterns are bound up in organizational clusters that perform vital social tasks, they become institutionalized. **Institutionalization** goes beyond reification, by which things feel real. Institutionalization integrates reified patterns into activities and categories. The weekly schedule is now institutionalized into every facet of life —from when people wash clothes to when they exercise to when they work or worship. To change the week would require changing the schedules for virtually everything. When activities and events are institutionalized, they become so pervasive and knit together so many aspects of life that they feel part of nature. People have forgotten their human origins and rarely imagine reality being any other way until they discover the human origins of those things they take for granted and gain some appreciation for how they might be different.

History

Although social reality is constructed, it is not created from scratch. People construct new realities from old realities, so whatever is constructed has a continuity with what came before. Institutionalized realities become the taken-for-granted context to which new innovations are adapted. The people who first objectified the days of the week acted in the context of a trading society dominated by religious leaders who used existing knowledge of the cosmos to name the days. Different societies with different configurations of activities, knowledge, and leadership created different kinds of weeks. Universities invented a new division of time, the semester (and later the quarter), but they constructed it on the basis of weeks, which already existed. When radio was invented, they scheduled programs on set days of the week. When television later arose, after some early experimentation, they adopted the same type of scheduling as the radio. In other words, all these organizations changed things as little as possible to achieve what they wanted to achieve.

This sort of continuity means that while society certainly changes dramatically and quickly, there is still stability. The 7-day week has existed for thousands of years and resisted attempts to change it. The double cycle of 12-hour half days has existed since Babylonian times, although anyone designing a system of hours today would probably design it differently. Schools operate on an annual plan designed to make it possible for children to help with summer harvests, even though America has been much more industrial than agrarian for nearly a century. These stable features of social life are examples of **path dependence**, the tendency for innovations once they are institutionalized to reproduce the same pattern over time. Imagine how explorers tramped across a wilderness seeking to get from one place to another, beating down a rough path where resistance was the least. Pioneers followed in wagons, with each group burrowing deeper wheel tracks into the soil and over the rocks. When automobiles became common in the 20th century, the wagon paths were paved. Eventually, some were widened into national highways where the cities had developed along the original explorers' routes. The highways might have followed more efficient routes more suitable for speedy cars and trucks, but by this time, houses, stores, factories, and farms had sprung up along the way. As a result, highways take what seem to be senseless routes sometimes entirely differently from where they would go if they were developed from scratch today. So it is with social life. Each generation travels the social paths of the previous generations.

Path dependence helps us understand some things that otherwise would not make sense today. Many aspects of inequality organized by class, race, and gender were originally developed within very different contexts than those that exist today but became the basis for other kinds of inequality (Tilly 1998). For example, as will be elaborated in Chapter 4, racism was developed to help legitimate North American slavery, but af-

ter slavery was abolished, racism has been used for many other purposes. In the late 19th century, southern farmers and northern manufacturers found that they could use racism to divide agricultural laborers
and industrial workers. Meanwhile, farmers, miners, and industrialists
in the West were creating a racism against Asians, especially Chinese. It
is not coincidental that anti-Chinese stereotypes were similar to those
about African Americans of the same period: They were lazy, ignorant,
promiscuous, violent, and irresponsible. The rhetoric of racism could be
transferred from one group to another. The anti-Chinese racists did not
have to reinvent the wheel.

Dominant Institutions and Power

This last example illustrates another important point: Not everyone
plays the same role in constructing reality. The intensified racism of the
late 19th century resulted from the actions of some groups much more
than others. What becomes socially constructed is disproportionately
the result of dominant institutions in society. **Institutions** are groups of
organizations, categories, and ways of doing things that do something
important in society. Religion, education, the economy, government,
family, mass media, and medicine are all institutions in modern society,
though not all societies have the same set of institutions. Some institutions have more power than others. **Power** is the ability of some actors to
influence the behavior of others and includes all forms of influence, from
persuasion (such as advertising) to authority (such as the professor who
requires students to write papers) to coercion (such as a robber who
forces someone to turn over his or her money). **Dominant institutions**
are those institutions in society that wield the most power, that is, that
most profoundly influence other institutions and affect people's lives. In
American society, economic institutions have more effect on religious institutions than vice versa. Even though religious institutions profoundly
affect the lives of their dedicated adherents, they do not affect the entire
population as pervasively as economic institutions. Different societies in
different eras have different dominant institutions. For a thousand years
or more, the Christian church was the most dominant institution in European society.

One clue as to which institution is dominant in any society is the one
that builds the largest and most monumental buildings. In medieval Eu-

rope, the largest buildings were the majestic and still stunning cathedrals erected by the Catholic Church. In the 18th and 19th centuries, the largest buildings were government buildings, such as the stately U.S. Capitol or the exquisite Chateau de Versailles where the French kings held court. In the 20th century, the grandiose glass and steel skyscrapers that house banking and corporate headquarters etch the skylines of the world's large cities. The changing skyline reveals the history of power. Organized religion, governments, and large corporations have been the dominant institutions in Anglo-European societies over the past several centuries and have disproportionately contributed to the construction of social reality.

The changing roles of these institutions are one key to understanding the social construction and reconstruction of gender during the past several centuries. Organized religion, governments, and corporations have contested (and cooperated) over the meaning of womanhood and manhood. In medieval times, the Catholic Church defined womanhood and manhood primarily in terms of the nuclear family. A woman was defined as wife and mother, a man as husband and father, and these roles were regulated by the sacrament of matrimony. But the rise of large national states created a new meaning for manhood: A man was a soldier and a citizen. Any male who shirked those responsibilities was considered less of a man. Marriage became a civil as well as a religious relationship. In the 20th century, corporations became the dominant force in shaping social relations. Men and women were distinguished by their different relationship to employers. In the first half of the century, men left home and worked as the breadwinners while women stayed at home as wives and mothers. A man who did not provide for his family or a woman who neglected husband and children was considered "not really" masculine or feminine. But in the second half of the century, as real wages fell, more women entered the labor force, provoking a reconsideration of gender roles at home and in public. Men in most industrial societies are not really expected to support a family anymore, but many women expect their husbands or housemates to share in what was once considered women's work. Business institutions are thus indirectly reshaping what is meant by masculine and feminine.

Although some people and groups disproportionately determine what becomes reified and institutionalized, no one has absolute power. The historical construction of society is contested. **Contestation** means that people and groups actively contend against each other over definitions of reality and the consequences of those definitions. Reality is constructed neither by the consensual progress of history nor by the uncontested acts of the powerful. Even if the powerful have greater influence, explaining outcomes requires attention to the social dynamics of the contestation. In recent decades, minorities have protested that standardized tests such as the SAT are culturally biased, forcing colleges and universities to reevaluate what "qualification" for admissions means. The feminist movement has not only won greater career opportunities for women but also challenged whether masculinity is antithetical to housework and child care.

Intersections

Although this book has separate chapters on time, space, race, gender, and class, these topics deeply intersect each other. **Intersection** refers to how the social dynamic of one sphere affects another. Time and space interpenetrate and shape race, gender, and class, and the components of each group cannot be really treated apart from one another. Time and space are interdependent not only in physics but also in society. Race, gender, and class intersect to form highly structured systems of inequality and domination.

Intelligence and Intersections

Intelligence illustrates the principle of intersections. Anglo-European society does not define intelligence only in terms of understanding mathematics, memorizing facts, or reading comprehension. People who can do those things faster than others are considered more intelligent. Virtually all the formal procedures for measuring intelligence have a time component. The English language even labels those with less mental capacity as "slow." Similarly, the ability to reason spatially is an important component of measured intelligence. Virtually all intelligence testing includes items to assess spatial reasoning. As discussed earlier, not only have subordinate racial, gender, and class groups been frequently characterized as less intelligent, but intelligence testing was also designed to demonstrate what scientists believed were differences in intelligence among these groups.

The social construction of intelligence can also illustrate how time, space, race, gender, and class intersect with each other. One of the most common stereotypes about men's and women's different abilities is that men can reason spatially better than women and that they have a better sense of direction and a more fully developed mental map to help them travel around. Related to this stereotype is the common mockery that men refuse to ask for directions when lost. The serious side of this image is that men's sense of direction is tied to their masculinity and that a "real man" does not need to ask for directions.

The relationship of intelligence to race, gender, and class is even more apparent. Intelligence has often been a purported explanation of the subordinate social positions of racial minorities, women, and lower-class people. H. H. Goddard, in 1919, attempted to justify social inequality in terms of intelligence:

> How can there be such a thing as social equality with this wide range of mental capacity? . . . Democracy means that the people rule by selecting the wisest, most intelligent and most human to tell them what to do to be happy. (Gould 1981:161)

This general justification of inequality by reference to intelligence also illustrates another aspect of intersection. Inequalities along each of the dimensions—race, gender, and class—reinforce each other and are dependent on one another. This book will not argue whether race, gender, or class is the most important or the most fundamental but will examine how the different dimensions intersect and affect each other. Lewis Terman illustrated how intelligence has been used to intersect race and class in a 1916 speech at Princeton University:

> Among laboring men and servant girls there are thousands like them. . . . The tests have told the truth. These boys are ineducable beyond the merest rudiments of training. No amount of school instruction will ever make them intelligent voters or capable citizens. . . . They represent the level of intelligence which is very, very common among Spanish-Indian and Mexican families of the Southwest and also among negroes. Their dullness seems to be racial, or at least inherent in the family stocks from which they came. (Gould 1981:221)

He is not just saying that poor people and racial minorities are disadvantaged because they supposedly lack intelligence. He is making a case that poverty is inherited through intelligence, that poor whites are no more capable of self-improvement than blacks and Mexicans. The passage assumes that the audience will already believe that blacks and Mexicans lack basic abilities needed for success and is using his characterization of intelligence to construct class. So in this instance, the construction of class was being built on a preexisting construction of race, linked together through the construction of intelligence.

Intersections are also important because they reveal that the experience of reality is different for different groups. Time and space are experienced differently by people of different races, genders, and classes. Race is experienced differently by men and women, rich and poor. There is sometimes a tendency to assume that generalizations based on the experience of some people apply to everyone. For example, Chapter 2 will discuss how the distinction between work time and leisure time developed. But this is a distinction that makes little sense for middle-class housewives or unemployed people of either gender. Chapter 5 will discuss how Anglo-European societies created a distinction between public life, which was a "man's world," and private life, which was the domain of women. But this applied primarily to white middle-class women. By attending to intersections, the complexity of real life and the penetration of these social constructions into all social relations are affirmed.

Types of Intersections

Time and space interpenetrate with race, gender, and class in three ways. First, race, gender, and class hierarchies can be organized in time and space without any sense that the relationship is inherent. Time and space can be **infrastructures of hierarchy.** Just as phone wires or electromagnetic waves are infrastructures of communication, social infrastructures are the medium through which social relations occur. And just as the infrastructures of communication can be used to plan a crime, express love to a special someone, or order a pizza, social infrastructures do not determine the content of social relations. For example, races and classes are organized residentially across space (race and class segregation), although few would claim that space is inherently racial and class based. The relationship only works in one direction: A neighborhood may be considered white or black, but a person does not become white or black by virtue of living in a neighborhood. A white person who lives in a predominantly black neighborhood would still be considered white, or an upper-class family that lived in a poor area would still be considered rich. But the spatial organization of race relations does have consequences. Many people and institutions respond not just to individuals living within them but to the definition of these spaces as racial or class identified. If a bank treats a neighborhood as a poor risk because many blacks or poor people live there, it damages the credit opportunities of all residents, even if they are not poor. Similarly, property values are determined not only by the size or amenities of particular homes but also by the neighborhood as a whole.

There are analogous relations for time. Just as racial, gender, and class groups control space, so are they organized temporally (although the connection is not as pervasive). Just as some groups are accorded "their" space—women in the home, blacks in the ghetto, or the wealthy in their mansions—so can racial, gender, and class groups be accorded "their" time. Subordinate groups, especially subordinate races, are often seen as "primitive" or "backward"—belonging to the past. If they work hard and play by the (white) rules, they can eventually "catch up." Similarly, the upper classes are seen as "ahead" of the poor. They use the newest technology, wear the newest fashions, and understand the latest trends.

The second type is the **mystification of domination.** Time and space are often surrogates for types of domination that are more fundamentally hierarchies of race, gender, and class. Unlike the infrastructures of hierarchy, in which the race, gender, or class domination is manifest and overt, domination can be mystified as mere time and space relationships. One of the clearest examples is the sale of labor power—someone paying another to do a job. Although a paid job may be conceptualized as an economically equal exchange of time for money, it is the fundamental nexus of hierarchical class relations in capitalism. Depicting it as an exchange of time for money mystifies the social relationship of dominance. What does it mean to "sell" time? It means that the buyer dictates what the seller does. The hamburger chain manager tells the employee exactly how to grill the hamburger, how much special sauce to apply, how long to heat the bun, and what to say to a rude customer. The relationship is hierarchical, even if the employee does not feel especially oppressed. People who sell their labor power—whether fast-food cook or corporate lawyer—are exchanging a certain amount of freedom for money, forgetting that they are submitting to domination because they think of it as selling time. Though corporate lawyers get hundreds of times more money than fast-food cooks, they are both in an analogous social relationship.

The third type is the **construction of hierarchy,** whereby time and space not only affect race, gender, and class relations but also are part of what those categories actually mean to society. Race, gender, and class become defined in terms of time and space. The opposite of mystification, the construction of hierarchy, explicitly enacts the categories of domination and subordination. People in society recognize race, gender, and class by the way that people *do* time and space. For example, in An-glo-European society, to *be* masculine means to control space, so control-ling space helps construct masculinity. By conventional standards, a "real man" controls the couch in front of the television, is better at geom-etry than poetry, knows the directions to anywhere he drives, and owns his own home (the king of his castle). Conversely, to be feminine means to relinquish space, to administer the home for "him," to be the object of public gaze (or protected from public gaze by other men), to be better at poetry than geometry, and to be provided a safe home by "him." Simi-larly, to be masculine means to monopolize time. A "real man" comman-deers the television remote control, initiates dates, values punctuality, and does not "waste time" grooming himself. To be feminine means to have a loose sense of time, to be late, and to spend hours producing one's femininity at the beauty salon or dressing table. To be a worker means to sell your labor power, and to be a capitalist means to buy it. To be upper class means to own land, and to be a commoner means to rent it. Races have not only been characterized as "primitive" or "modern"—temporal concepts—but also alien or native—spatial concepts. The ugly racist in-vective to "go back where you came from" frames racial differences in geographic language.

All three types of intersection allow "taken-for-grantedness" to natu-ralize social relations, numbing people to the effects of inequality. It is not just that people are unaware of inequality but that even when they fathom how deep inequality is, they often fatalistically assume "that's just the way things are." Jolting people out of the natural attitude to ask why things are the way they are can empower people to begin the pro-cess of transformation.

Conclusion

Common sense and most education take an essentialist perspective. Commonsense understandings effectively organize the world around us because they assume that the things we deal with are "real." The week, the mile, whiteness, femininity, and the middle class are rarely ques-tioned by the operation of common sense. Formal education typically adopts essentialist modes of thinking by authoritatively telling students the way things are: 2 + 2 = 4, Columbus discovered the New World, males have an X and Y chromosome, and every society has a distinct cul-ture. People are steeped in essentialist ways of thinking.

A constructionist perspective offers a different understanding. It reveals how social reality—the concepts that people take for granted when they make sense of social life—has been constructed by living people at some particular time and place. Intelligence, the week, the city, the category "Asian," masculinity, universities, and even the "self" did not always exist and do not have to exist. People invented, reified, and institutionalized each of these concepts. Subsequent generations learned to take them for granted as "real" and organized social life around them, very concretely affecting their lives and those they interacted with. But through the course of this book, we will cease to take them for granted, try to understand them in a new way, and learn to comprehend how they could be different.

2

Time

In January 1996, Amy Wu, a 20-year-old student at New York University, wrote a column in *Newsweek* magazine titled, "Stop the Clock: My Generation's Obsession With Saving Time Means Losing Out in the Long Run." She contrasts her aunt, who enjoys a scrupulously clean house and cooking nice meals at a leisurely pace, with her friends, who prefer fast food to home cooking, e-mail to "snail mail," and disposable underwear. What, she asks, are they saving time for? Are they losing any sense of the quality of time because of an obsession with the quantity of time? When the article was passed out in a sociology class, it struck a resonant chord with most of the students. Yes, they said, there is too little time and too much to do. Why can't we have 30 hours a day and 10 days a week? But a moment's thought revealed the folly of that. They readily conceded that even with 30 hours a day and 10 days a week, the demands would quickly fill the time. Yet they persisted in thinking that the source of the problem is "time," not the social relations that put demands on them. In most cultures for most of human history, pressure to get things done has not been conceptualized in terms of time. Why? In few societies has there been so much discussion about time or so many parts of social existence wrapped up in the language of time. If people in Anglo-European societies do conceptualize things in terms of time and do talk more about time than in previous periods or compared to slower, more remote societies, there must be important cultural and historical differences in the way time is conceptualized. This chapter will explore the nature of those differences and suggest some reasons why such differences in the conception of time exist.

Linear and Cyclical Time

Many societies reached a point when various cycles were noticed and when leaders (probably priests) gave names to days within those cycles.

This was an extremely important step in institutionalizing the sense of time because giving names to periods of time conferred reality on them, an existence apart from the people who created them. They would go from "the day we come together in the marketplace," which might happen every 7 days or so but could be postponed or canceled, to "Moon Day," which always came after "Sun Day." Feeling that it is a day for market because the priest said so is very different from feeling that it is "Moon Day."

The first cycles that societies observed were irregular both in length and sequence. Days, as we still experience them today, were not recognized as having equal length. In contrast to our exact sequence of abstract markers such as hours or days that follow one after the other, early societies attributed the definition of time from activities. We party because it is Saturday; they would have called the day "Saturday" whenever they were partying. Social anthropologist Evans-Pritchard (1939) noticed that the Nuer culture of East Africa, which many scholars believe is similar to many premodern societies, had names for 12 "moons" or months that marked the succession from the wet to dry season and back again. But when it was wet, they said that they were in a moon (month) that was known to be wet. As a pastoral society that tended cattle, they were attentive to the succession of activities throughout each day and to changes in season over the year. They had no abstract time concepts at all. Days were unnumbered and unnamed (Rutz 1994). Informally, we speak of seasons much the same way. We know that fall officially begins about September 21, on the autumnal equinox, but for those in northern climates, fall does not *feel* real until the leaves turn to colorful shades, even if they say they *know* it "really" begins September 21. When they say it feels real after the leaves begin to fall, they are treating time as though it is concrete rather than abstract, the way everyone did before calendars. What differs is the feeling and the abstract knowledge of what they think is real.

The relationship between time markers and the activities that are marked is **reflexive**; that is, they explain each other, like the proverbial chicken and egg. The need for coordinating activities has stimulated the development of sophisticated and abstract markers, eventually creating the calendars and clocks that seem to run our life; the existence of these markers has made possible a more complex coordination of activities. Complex time systems that use different kinds of markers for different purposes work only in societies with little division of labor and few activities to coordinate (Sorokin and Merton 1990). Suppose a person can awaken with the sun, hunt when he or she feels like it, eat when the other members of the family gather, and worship when religious leaders call for a service. In this case, a time system that uses the sun, the signal of a gong, and the proclamation of priests is adequate. But when thousands of workers must simultaneously show up at work, when doctors must schedule tens of patients each day, when millions of people need to know when their favorite television show is going to begin, and all these activities have to be coordinated with each other, only a simple, abstract set of time markers will do. Everyone must coordinate these activities with hours and minutes. If some people coordinate by the position of the sun and others by when a village bell rings, coordination is impossible.

The History of Time

The first external markers that people used to synchronize their activities were natural phenomena such as the sun and the seasons or events such as storms. Duration would not be counted in minutes or hours but in concrete activities such as the time it takes to boil rice or fry a locust.

Creating the Week

The construction of the week was a huge breakthrough. As pointed out by sociologist Eviatar Zerubavel, whose book *The Seven Day Circle* is the source of much of the following information, the week is not only a powerful regulator of social life but also the first regular cycle of time that had no basis in nature (Zerubavel 1985). The day is the time for the earth to turn, the year is the time for the earth to orbit the sun, and months originally conformed to the cycle of the moon from full moon to new moon and back to full moon. But the week is entirely arbitrary. Ancient Colombia and New Guinea had 3-day weeks; Meso-America and Indochina had 5-day weeks. There was a 10-day market cycle that worked like a week in ancient Peru, while southern China once had a 12-day week. The Bahai'i religion has a 19-day week, which is set within a 19-week year, which is set within a 19-year *vahid* and 361-year (19 times 19) segments known as *kull-i-shay* (Zerubavel 1985).

Our 7-day week comes to us from the ancient Middle East, where Jewish, Mesopotamian, Babylonian, and other cultures had a 7-day cycle that governed their affairs. Because these cultures knew of seven planets, they treated seven as a divine number. In English, the names for the days of the week come from the sun (Sunday), the moon (Monday), and

Nordic words for some of the planets. Tuesday is from Tyr, the Nordic word for Mars, Wednesday from Woden Olin or Mercury, Thursday from Thor-Donar-Thunar or Jupiter, Friday from Fria-Frigg or Venus, and Saturday from Saturn. Most romance languages (languages derived directly from Latin) still show their Latin roots, such as various words for Monday based on *luna*, the Latin for moon: *Lundi* (French), *Lunedi* (Italian), *Lunes* (Spanish), or *Lunî* (Romanian).

While we can look back and see the origins of our week in the ancient Jewish and Babylonian calendars, there is no straight line of development from then until now, and the inventors could not have foreseen any one system becoming universal or global. Calendars were known only to small segments of society and used only for specific, mostly religious, purposes. Greeks first developed the Anglo-European week into a coherent system in which the days followed a fixed order (Monday always followed Sunday). As the Homeric epic illustrated on an oil flask in Figure 2.1 shows, they conceived of time as a cycle, with a sense of before and after with one day following another. As one god—Helios—rises from the sea, another—Nyx, the night—disappears. Time cyclically pulsates around the flask. The Greeks originally did not think of it as an abstract property of the world at large. Time was a succession of events such as wars or aging, not a universal process in which all reality was set. But as they developed philosophy and mathematics, they increasingly treated time as an abstract, universal property of reality (Fraser 1987, 1990). They integrated their calendar system into a more sophisticated model of mathematics and a scientific understanding of the planets, which they diffused throughout the Mediterranean through Alexander the Great's military successes. The Romans, when they were under Greek influence, adopted the same week. At first, the Jewish 7-day week remained distinct from the Roman week, but the two were joined together by the early Christian church, which over two millennia spread it throughout Europe and around the globe. Over the same period, the 7-day week was spread by astrology to India and then to other parts of Asia and by Islam to much of Africa. European exploration and colonialism eventually introduced the rest of the world to the 7-day week, making this rhythm of time seem natural and universal (Zerubavel 1985).

Controlling and Challenging the Calendar

Our current calendar has more recent origins than the 7-day week. The calendar that we use in Anglo-European societies was achieved only by detaching the month from nature. Originally, months signified the

FIGURE 2.1

Black Figured *Lekythos* (Oil Flask), 500-490 B.C.E.

SOURCE: Metropolitan Museum of Art. Reprinted with permission.

moon's cycle, as the word *month* implies. The months we know go back to Roman times. At the beginning of the fifth century B.C.E., the Romans developed a calendar with 12 months with days of 28, 29, and 31 days, adding up to a year of only 355 days. By the time of the emperor Julius Caesar, the calendar had shifted so much that the spring equinox on the calendar (when the length of the day is equal to the length of the night) was about 8 weeks behind the actual equinox. So Caesar, exercising power that only emperors can wield, created a new calendar based on the old Egyptian system, giving the months 30 and 31 days, except February, which had only 28, and designating a leap year every 4 years. And he used his imperial power to name a month, July, after himself, and another, August, after his successor Caesar Augustus. This system is known as the Julian calendar (Fraser 1994). Because the moon's cycle of 29 days, 12 hours, and 3⅓ seconds cannot align with the sun's cycle of approximately 365 days, our months have from 28 to 31 days, and February has an extra day every 4 years. This goofy system creates problems. For example, people who get paid monthly have to figure that some weekly expenses will cost more in some months than others. Other calendar systems deal with the misalignment in different ways. The Jewish calendar, a lunar calendar, is out of alignment with the solar calendar, so each 12-month year has about 353 days rather than 365 days. Rabbis periodically inserted a 13th month, creating a 383-day year.

The physical layout of the Anglo-European calendar reflects the linear conception of time. The days are arranged to go from left to right in sequence. Each numbered day gets a box of the same size, denoting that all days are the same length. Lines of days are arranged in weeks and weeks get put into months, which usually occupy one page of the calendar. The days and months are named, but the weeks and years are only numbered. As the months pass to one another, the old month is discarded, and at the end of the year, a new calendar, functionally similar to the old one, is adopted. Even when the days of the year fall on the same days of the week, people do not reuse an old calendar because it represents a past year. Contrast the familiar calendar with the Aztec calendar shown in Figure 2.2, a representation of a 12-foot stone now stored in Mexico City. Just as the Anglo-European calendar reflects a sense of time that flows in distinct segments of numbered days, months, and years, the Aztec calendar reflects the Aztec's cyclical view. The various points around the circles, rectangles, and stars represent days. The calendar is read in counterclockwise direction, going from point to point and beginning back again. Three different cycles are the day, a 13-day week, and a solar year. Each particular day, week, or year has a substantive meaning. For example, April 23, 2000, on the Anglo-European calendar is in the year *Tecpatl*, represented by a Stone Knife and associated with the direction north. It was part of the week called *Atl* (Water), associated with instability, unexpected events, accidents, and coincidences. The day was *chicome*, associated with *Centeotl*, the Corn God. Aztecs would find reading the Anglo-European calendar just as confusing as most North Americans would find reading the Aztec calendar.

FIGURE 2.2

The Aztec Calendar

SOURCE: Used with permission of the artist, Fanya Montalvo.

Institutional Conflict Over Time

Although calendars tend to continue indefinitely, a few societies have attempted to intentionally change the calendar, which illustrates the role of dominant institutions and the contestation that can happen over time. After the French Revolution of 1789 and the Russian Revolution of 1917, the new regimes attempted to create a new week—for a while. In both cases, the new regime tried to use the structure of time to reduce the social influence of organized religion, pitting institution against institution to see which one would prevail. If a religion has a holy day based on a 7-day cycle, as Judaism, Christianity, and Islam believe, changing the number of days of the week can make the observation of religion difficult. Since these religions base their holy days on the scriptural passage that God rested on the 7th day when creating the earth, they cannot adopt a regular holy day in any other calendar than one based on 7 days. But that is what the French and Russian revolutionary regimes tried to make them do.

The Catholic Church was one of the dominant institutions supporting the French prerevolutionary social system. It was a major landowner, a major supporter of traditional authority, and an opponent of various subversive Enlightenment ideas, such as "Liberty, Equality, Fraternity," that the new regime was espousing. In late 1793, the new National Convention acted to create an entirely new calendar, based on twelve 30-day months, each broken into 10-day *décades*—there were no weeks as before. The days would be *Primidi, Duodi, Tridi, Quartidi, Quintidi, Sextidi, Septidi, Octidi, Nonidi,* and *Décadi*—words based on the Latin roots for the numbers 1 through 10, plus the suffix "di" from the Latin *dies* for day. They even started to renumber the years—Year I, Year II, Year III, and so on. The plan was promoted as part of a general rationalization project, which included organizing numerical systems around the metric system based on 10, but the motivation was deeper. The chief architect of the new system admitted that the goal of the reform was "to abolish Sunday." *Décadi* was declared the new day of rest. But Christianity cannot operate on a 10-day cycle, so the Catholic Church resisted the change.

The conflict that raged over the new system pitted what pamphlets called "Monsieur Dimanche" ("Mr. Sunday") against "Citoyen Décadi" ("Citizen Décadi"). The government tried to organize all public functions according to the new calendar, but people contested the new order of time, continuing to keep a 7-day calendar for most activities and a 10-day calendar only for official functions. Eventually, the experiment was considered a failure, and France returned to the old system (Fraser 1994; Zerubavel 1985). Two principles about time and historical construction can be gleaned from the experience.

First, time is constructed and changed by dominant institutions. When conflicting time systems vie to organize society, they often pit institutions against each other, and the dominant institution wins. In this case, the state was attempting to replace religion as the dominant institution. The French 10-day calendar was one of the last conflicts in which the state lost to organized religion in a head-to-head contest.

The second principle qualifies the first. Change and continuity of time systems do not depend solely on institutional power. The more a time structure permeates everyday life, the more people will cling to it in the face of change. Contestation can take the form of everyday resistance as well as conflict among the powers that be. Many of the French were not especially religious and did not care very much about the Sabbath, but they organized their daily activities around a 7-day cycle. Their work, leisure, family activities, and household duties were organized and coordinated around it. People resisted the change by trying to maintain their 7-day schedules for their personal lives. It is difficult to say whether the resistance of the Catholic Church or the resistance of people in their everyday lives was more important in the new calendar's failure. Most likely, neither could have resisted the state without the other.

Defining Group Boundaries

The conflict between the French government and the Catholic Church was not the first time that the Christian church had clashed over time. Because Christianity was an offshoot of Judaism, the early Christians sought to distinguish themselves from the Jews. To do so, the Christians made one critical change to the Jewish week: They changed the holy day from the seventh day (*Sabbath* means "seven") to the first day, Sunday. This strategy is known as **calendrical contrast,** which means that a symbolic boundary is created between groups by use of a distinctive calendar (Zerubavel 1985). Since social time is the activity of coordinating activity by means of an external marker, groups can distinguish themselves from other groups and create internal solidarity by adopting their own distinctive markers. Just as having common markers integrates groups, using distinctive markers divides them. In other words, calendars denote social boundaries, linking people within a group and distinguishing them from others.

Holidays are used by many kinds of groups to solidify boundaries —to mark who is in and who is out. Nations, religions, racial groups, gender groups, and ethnic groups have all created holidays to create internal unity and set their members off from others. After the American Revolution, national leaders created Independence Day to celebrate the anniversary of the Declaration of Independence (July 4, 1776) and expanded a New England fall festival into a national Thanksgiving. A century later, newly independent Canada, to distinguish itself from the United States, declared the second Monday of October as its Thanksgiving. The Canadian co-optation of someone else's holiday was an old strategy. When the Christian church expanded throughout Europe, it could not extinguish local holidays, so it redefined them in Christian terms. The celebration of Christ's birth was moved from March to the time of the winter solstice festival. People could keep the evergreen tree (now known as a "Christmas tree"), gift-giving practices, and other trappings of the festival as part of the Christmas celebration. Similarly, the spring fertility rite became redefined as Easter, the celebration of renewed life; the rabbit, a highly fertile animal, and the colored egg became the "Easter bunny" and the "Easter egg," respectively. Instead of creating a boundary between people, through calendrical contrast, the Church brought non-Christians and their holidays into a larger group.

Creating new holidays is difficult, especially if a group lacks power. African American activists in the 1960s attempted to create a new holiday, *Kwanzaa,* in late December as an alternative to Christmas, which they felt neglected African Americans. Although well publicized in many localities and in the mass media, it has attracted a modest following and, when adopted, often is practiced along with Christmas partly because many African Americans are practicing Christians and partly because many felt that *Kwanzaa* is artificial. The new holiday has not only failed to unite African Americans but also has created new tensions within the community.

A more successful attempt to create a holiday is Mother's Day, which was created early in the 20th century when women were seeking the vote. Anna M. Jarvis of West Virginia is credited with originating the U.S. Mother's Day holiday after her mother died in 1905, but it was promoted by antisuffrage activists and greeting card manufacturers. Several states adopted the holiday; Congress made it a national holiday in 1914. Its promoters selected a time between major holidays on a Sunday, a day already set aside by many people, and defined it so that it did not conflict with the activities of other institutions. Florists, candy manufacturers, advertisers, and other industries soon jumped on the bandwagon, and it quickly became a "natural" holiday with forgotten origins (Filene 1998). The different outcomes of equally self-conscious attempts to create *Kwanzaa* and Mother's Day show how a few relatively well-placed organizations commemorating a consensual symbol such as motherhood can create holidays easier than less powerful groups challenging dominant institutions. The more widespread the Anglo-European calendar is, the less conscious we are that it was historically constructed; its origins are forgotten. But many people whose recent ancestors lived in non-Anglo-European societies continue to structure part of their lives around other calendars. They keep more than one calendar in their homes. They use the Anglo-European calendar to keep track of activities at work and at school, but family events, religious life, and holidays might be coordinated with a Chinese, Persian, Jewish, or other calendar. It takes work to manage events from multiple calendars, but because time is a device for giving meaning to group memberships, multiple calendars make multicultural life sustainable. And multicultural social relations remind people that all cultures are socially constructed.

Learning the Clock Time

It is not just the calendar that orders our lives; it is also the clock. The clock is perhaps the most pervasive of all symbols of the modern world (Boorstein 1985; Elias 1992; Landes 1983). To think in a modern fashion means to conceive of reality like the workings of a clock—it is regular, orderly, and predictable. Even the modern image of God in the Anglo-European societies shifted from a pastoral image, God the shepherd or God the father, to a mechanical one, God the watchmaker, who created the world and then let it run.

By the late Middle Ages and Renaissance, Europe had largely agreed on a common calendar. Europeans were beginning the year at the same time, and they consecutively numbered the days in each month. People were beginning to record births by date (though few people had any idea when their birthdays were or any inclination to find out). By the beginning of the 15th century, people were starting to discuss technical inventions in a chronological, progressive way, understanding inventions as successive advances, not just occasional improvements over old technology; that is, they were conceiving of progress. But clocks were barely beginning to organize everyday life. Although the marking of the day into two sequences of 12 hours each, with hours broken into minutes and minutes into seconds, had existed in principle since at least the Babylonian empire, only scholars would have known about it. Even when people knew about hours and minutes, clocks had no more practical value in everyday life than knowledge of quantum mechanics has for people today. Most people coordinated their affairs by using natural markers—especially the movement of the sun—or irregular markers such as a public event or announcement. Much of life was organized by one person taking the initiative to coordinate others, such as a father collecting other members of the family to plow, a military leader commanding his troops to march, or a master telling his apprentices to begin a new task. Life was ruled less by the clock than by identifiable masters or the dull routine of habit.

Monasteries

In Europe, the earliest clocklike regulation of life occurred in monasteries, where Benedictine monks ordered their days according to a strict sequence of devotional rituals, which they marked with bells[6] (Landes 1983; Thrift 1996). Monastic time was meant to set the monastery apart from the secular world, but two of its features spread to secular life. The first was the notion that life is based on a fixed sequence of events, that one kind of event is always followed by another kind. In the monastery, prayers, meals, meditation, and work all followed a strict daily sequence. Similarly, today in high schools, first period always follows homeroom, not because it is announced everyday that it is time for first period but because we know that the time is first period. Even in nursery school, we learn that nap time follows lunchtime whether or not we are sleepy, just because it is nap time.

The second innovation that spread from the monasteries was the use of bells as markers. At first, the bells were probably merely a convenient way to tell the monks when to gather for the ritual, and "third bell" carried a meaning derived from the particular liturgical event it signaled. Over time, however, the bells became general markers for the passage of time and took on meaning in themselves. "Third bell" took on some of the connotations of "three o'clock," that is, an abstract marker that exists apart from the events that are associated with it. With abstract time, the directionality between markers and meaning becomes reversed. But when time becomes abstract, the meaning of the marker is assumed to come first. "Third bell" began to seem the appropriate time for certain activities, much as the "three o'clock slot" became the appropriate time for a television soap opera or talk show but not for a news broadcast.

However, it was not the monasteries that spread these innovations to the rest of the society; it was the city (Rossum 1996). Even though the majority of people lived in rural areas, from the late Middle Ages on, towns and cities became the organizational and cultural centers of society. They

---

[6]Rossum (1996) disputes the conventional wisdom that follows Max Weber and Lewis Mumford in treating monastical time as the prototype for clock time. According to Rossum, monastic time, based on a series of liturgies and prayers, was very much tied to natural rhythms. Monasteries were not organized according to abstract time, which coordinates and synchronizes.

brought many people together in limited areas, and the social life became far more complex than in the countryside. Although there were many things to coordinate, we cannot say that the need to coordinate caused the rise of clock time. Rather, the development of technical innovations and the coordination of events went hand in hand. Innovations enhanced the capacity of city dwellers to coordinate their activities, and the need for coordination motivated innovation. But many innovations were incidental to the need to coordinate complex activities. For example, people in cities began to use the monastic bells to coordinate their own activities—"I'll meet you at the fountain about third bell"—or meetings of a city council would be called to coincide with the monastery bell.

Since not all events could be scheduled to match the church bells, cities began to build their own bells. Soon, cities built bell towers not just for practical reasons but for prestige. A tall and impressive bell tower symbolized an important and progressive city. Clock towers were symbols of communal identity from the 14th century on. Traveling through Europe today, one sees that bell towers remain among the impressive and distinctive symbols of urban life.

The symbolic importance of the bell tower increased when the right to erect one became the equivalent of a city charter. Not just anyone could erect a bell tower. Since the right to have a bell bestowed the right to call public meetings, this power was strictly regulated. However, bells could also be used to challenge authority. Revolts as well as approved public meetings would be signaled by the ringing of bells.

Bells were not the universal marker that the clock has become; they were rung for specific purposes. Cities had a complex variety of particular bells and signals: for curfews, for the opening and closing of city gates, for the changing of guards, for the beginning and end of market, for the beginning and end of the workday, and for religious rituals, funerals, and guild events (Rossum 1996). City life was punctuated by a cacophony of bells of different pitch, volume, and number. As late as the early 14th century, however, nearly all events were still timed by daylight.

Clock Time

To reduce the clamor and confusion of the many bells, cities began to ring the city bell on the hour, even though it created confusion because people did not know how to coordinate activities by a regular marker. For the first two centuries of public clocks, few records noted time in terms of the clock.

From the end of the 14th century, a major change occurred in the construction of time. Contemporaries were not aware of the change; it can be seen primarily in documents that refer to time, especially municipal statutes. Until then, most records continued to refer to markers such as bells, not clock hours. Cologne in 1374 was using the monastic bell to stipulate when workmen were to start and end work. By 1397, however, the city had passed a statute that belt makers were to end work by 10 o'clock in the evening (Rossum 1996).

There were other means of marking time besides bells. Sundials had existed since ancient times, but they depended on the sun to work and were undependable for coordinating activities. Water clocks (*clepsydra*), in which water flows out of a container and marks the passage of time by its level, had developed in many civilizations, including China and Egypt. But in Europe, these were more of a technical curiosity than a means of regular timekeeping. The hourglass, now familiar as an icon used by some computer systems to mark a "wait" state while the computer grinds away at a task, was developed about the same time as church bells and was useful for marking duration but not for telling time. Candles and (in Asia) incense were also used to mark duration (Landes 1983; Rossum 1996; Turner 1994).

The invention of the mechanical clock in the 13th or 14th century was not recorded and seemed to have attracted no interest. But the first *striking clock,* in which a hammer would mechanically strike a bell, as with an alarm clock, was widely hailed. People basically saw the mechanical clock as a way of automating hand-struck bells. Clocks were not "for keeping time" but for *striking* time (Rossum 1996). You could not look at a clock to see the time because they did not have hands to mark hour and minute but only gears and levers that rang a bell.

The use of clocks was constrained by the fact that the length of the hour differed according to the season. Several solutions were tried. In some places, people counted hours according to a 24-hour cycle of equal hours beginning at dawn. In other places, they changed the number of hours during day and night every 3 weeks; winter had 8 hours in the day and 16 at night, whereas summer had 16 hours during the day and 8 at night. Some activities, such as work, were limited by the sun anyway. But others needed fixed duration in all seasons. So some places adopted 12 sequences beginning at midnight and noon, which meant that dawn and dusk each occurred at a different time every day. Eventually, the latter system became the standard.

In the century after 1370, there was a "clock boom" in which mechanical clocks spread throughout Europe. The printing press was the only invention that diffused faster. But cities built clocks and towers to house
them as much for their prestige and symbolic value as for any felt need
for a clock. People do not feel a need for clock time unless they already
run life by the clock (Rossum 1996).

Standardizing Time
Even after the system of two 12-hour segments became widely adopted,
time was still tied closely to nature, especially the sun. Noon was set as
the moment when the sun was at its peak and thus varied from east to
west. Towns 10 or 20 miles apart could set their clocks differently. But not
until the 19th century, when railroads made it possible for people to
travel at "breakneck speeds" of more than 25 miles an hour, did this become a problem. A train might be scheduled to leave Easttown at 10 a.m.,
Easttown time, and to arrive at Centerville at 10:30, Centerville time,
which was 10:45 Easttown time; then it would move on to Westtown at
11:00, Westtown time, which was 11:15, Centerville time, and 11:30,
Easttown time. Stations typically carried several clocks, one for each
company and one for local time (Trachtenberg 1981). Railroad companies and businessmen that frequently shipped goods on railroads began
to promote the idea of standardizing time so that places such as
Easttown, Centerville, and Westtown might all be on the same clock.

For most people today, standardizing time would be an uncontrover-
sial convenience. But back then it threatened prevailing assumptions
about reality. Farmers and religious people vigorously opposed the
change, arguing that it was both inconvenient and sacrilegious. Why
should farmers near Easttown have to wake up with the dawn at 5:00
a.m. with an hour before the children would leave for school at 6, when
those in Westtown would rise with the dawn at 5:30 and have half an
hour before the children left? Linking ideology and practicality, farmers
felt they were defending "God's time" against "railroad time" as they
sought to preserve the rhythms of an agricultural life tied to the sun. The
system of hours they were defending had been institutionalized for only
a few centuries, but many people believed that God had created the day
with noon at the apex of the sun's rotation. To say that noon could occur
at any other time would be like saying a dog is a cat. The Iowa Supreme
Court in 1899 argued that

> we are not quite ready to concede that for the mere convenience of these
> companies, nature's timepiece may be arbitrarily superseded. . . . The ap-

parent daily revolution of the celestial body has from the remotest antiquity been employed as a measure of time. (O'Malley 1990:139)

The proponents of standard time claimed that it represented modernity, rationality, commerce, and prosperity in the face of tradition, superstition, sloth, and squalor. They prevailed. In 1883, a national convention on standard time proclaimed a system of four time zones for the United States—Eastern Standard Time, Central Standard Time, Mountain Standard Time, and Pacific Standard Time. The system has been altered only by the introduction of daylight savings time in the 20th century.

The 1883 agreement created a standard for the United States, but there was still no uniform system internationally. Eleven observatories around the world claimed to be the prime meridian or standard by which the rest of the world could set clocks. A year after the American convention, an international convention proposed to use the Royal Observatory at Greenwich, England, as the standard. France, England's main political rival, refused to agree. The United States and England wanted an English standard, even though any observatory would serve the purpose. Both sides thought that whoever could control the meridian could control time. France finally acquiesced, allowing Greenwich Mean Time to set a standard for the entire world—although some countries held out. Holland, for example, set its clocks 19 minutes and 28 minutes off Greenwich Mean Time until 1937, and Liberia did not conform until 1972 (O'Malley 1990; Whitman 1952).

Time as Quantity and Commodity

The development of the clock as the most common marker for coordinating everyday affairs and the standardization of clock time over territories still miss one of the most significant facets of what we take for granted about time and how it seems to run our lives: the sense of time as an objective quantity, a thing. Many cultures do not think of time as a quantifiable thing but regard it as something that we pass through, like a boat passes through water. Most distinctively, Anglo-European culture, unlike most other cultures, treats time as a commodity, something that can be bought and sold like a bag of rice, a hamburger, or an automobile. As we so often say, "Time is money," a concept that is incomprehensible to people in cultures such as the Nuer, who do not even have a generic word for time. Our language is full of metaphors that link time and money: We save time, spend it, waste it, invest it, and sell it. Americans are sometimes exasperated in other countries when locals repeatedly show up late for appointments or engagements. They feel that this time is wasted and cannot understand that their hosts do not think of time in the same way.

Conclusion

If a fish is the last creature to notice water, time is like water for humans. We swim through it and never notice it. To press the analogy, even if a fish were to notice water, ocean fish would only imagine salt water and lake fish would only imagine fresh water; neither could fathom any water except the kind it knows. So it is with time. When people from Anglo-European cultures do think about time, they primarily think of it as linear, while people from many other societies take it for granted that time is cyclical.

Time is not just a river that flows over us. It is a historical construction that people have made and continue to remake. Understanding how the Anglo-European sense of time developed and why it differs from that of other societies reveals important features of our society and how it differs from other societies. It tells us about large-scale social dynamics such as the rise of capitalism and also about why Monday feels different from Sunday and why so many people never seem to have enough time. In other words, it helps us understand some of the links between the microsociological and macrosociological levels of social life. At each point in history, social power shapes the construction of time. The dominant institutions determine how time is defined. Once invented, the week, the hour, the assumption that time units are equal, and the sale of time became the context within which new institutions were established. The week was established by religious institutions when religion was the dominant institution; governments adopted the structure. We still live by the Gregorian calendar, named after Pope Gregory XIII. Religious influence dominated in Europe until the Enlightenment, when governments became the dominant institution, but even then they could not create a new calendar by fiat, as the French and Russian revolutionaries learned. Governments were especially critical in the development of the hour, although some scholars emphasize the role of religion (Thrift 1996) or business (LeGoff 1980). Capitalist factories instituted time as a commodity that could be sold, giving rise to economic metaphors about time (Biernacki 1995). As other institutions arise, they subordinate their time structures to dominant institutions. All institutions now organize themselves by the 7-day week. For most people in our society today, work is the dominant organizer of time. When schooling became widespread, the calendar adapted to the agricultural cycle, with the school year beginning in the fall after the harvest and ending in the spring before the summer work season. Later on, high schools created an hourly schedule—marked with bells and buzzers—that mirrored the schedule of work. Radio and television, arising in the 20th century, fit their schedules to people's work and school schedule, although now many people try to fit their work and recreation schedules to their favorite shows.

Only when institutions do not have to coordinate their activities with other institutions are they free to organize themselves on their own calendar. Hospitals, for example, generally operate according to their own schedules since patients are relieved of other responsibilities, and doctors have social power to determine—based on their expertise—a patient's needs. But when coordination is necessary, as when supplies must be delivered during business hours, even hospitals adjust their schedules (Zerubavel 1979).

Most of us frequently feel as if we are doing the adapting. That is the feeling that we "have no time." But if we understand that time is a means of coordinating social life and that having time means having control of one's life (or vice versa), we can understand that restructuring time can mean gaining a degree of control over one's life. When we understand how the language of time is a representation of social relations, we can begin to understand how to reorganize those social relations to "give us more time" for what is truly important to us.

3

Space

One of the most challenging problems that college roommates must negotiate is how to allocate and enforce their space. Many agree to divide the room into equal segments, with each person having his or her space, and they try to develop workable rules for the rights and responsibilities they each have. Do they have the right to keep their space sloppy, or must the entire room be presentable for guests? Can they borrow space from each other? How do they allocate cleaning responsibilities for common space such as the bathroom? Does one of them have a tendency to spill out from his or her own space into the others? Do they have objects that they feel must absolutely never be moved, that must always remain in their proper place? To make the issue more perplexing, sometimes when they come from different cultures (or perhaps different genders), they might have very different conceptions about how space should be organized. One of them might feel much more territorial, with much stronger feelings about the privacy of his or her space. Anger can easily escalate, with one person unable to understand why the other has so little respect for his or her space and the other one feeling that the first one is so selfish.

Where do these understandings of space come from? Why is space conceptualized as a category that can be someone's possession? How is it that a person gets the right to control space even when she or he is not present in the space? Why is space specialized so some activities are appropriate in some spaces but not others?

How did space get many of the same qualities of time, that it can be cut into measurable segments, that it can be bought and sold, that it can be wasted or preserved? How did it become understood as existing apart from whatever "occupies" it?

Why do conflicts over space become so intense, from roommate fights to wars between states? Are such conflicts found in all college dormitories or societies?

AUTHOR'S NOTE: This chapter was cowritten with Patricia Ahmed.

Space as a Thing

We cannot see, feel, hear, or taste space. But Anglo-European societies take for granted the concrete reality of space, that it is a "thing" and not just, well, empty space. Indeed, some of the most powerful social and political institutions are premised on the notion that space is a thing. For example, a state—by definition, a territorially based entity—cannot exist independently of space. States are fixed in space, set off by nonoverlapping geographical boundaries that distinguish them from other states. Nor, for that matter, can towns or cities exist without space. Contributing further to the "realness" of space is the fact that it (for example, land) can be owned. In fact, real estate has traditionally been a form of wealth in Anglo-European societies. More recently, it has become commodified, that is, bought and sold for profit. This gives rise to a self-interested attitude toward space. People jealously guard their personal space as though it were a valuable possession. They hope strangers will stay out of "their" space. When people want to be alone, they tell others that they need "their" space. People often refer to their rooms or offices as "their" space.

People often explain their understanding of space, like that of other physical aspects of our world, in terms of scientific and mathematical reasoning. Furthermore, math and science influence Anglo-European understandings of space. Space is expressed in terms of its dimensions, proportions, area, and volume. A house, for example, is said to occupy a certain number of square feet, a city is said to contain a certain number of people, and a state is said to extend over a certain number of square miles. In keeping with this logic, the relative value of space is often determined numerically. The monetary value of land in Anglo-European societies, for example, is often determined in terms of its area or by how much it produces, or how close it is to other valuable areas.

Our conceptions of space are not discoveries of some objective reality "out there" but rather have been culturally constructed by dominant social institutions and contestation operating at historically specific places and times (Foucault 1987; Pred 1990). If the attributes of space were an objective part of reality, then the comprehension of the essential properties of space in all societies should be identical. That is, other people should conceive space as something that exists independently of humans, has mathematical dimensions, and has market value. Instead, perceptions of space vary from one culture to another. The history of spatial conceptions has not been a smooth transition from ignorance to knowledge in which people have gradually discovered the "true" meaning of space. Understandings of space and its qualities have drifted like a feather in the breeze.

The Earliest Known Conceptions of Space

Maps represent the meanings that societies attribute to space. The relative position of places on a map indicate how a society understands the meaning of space. A society that represents places in religious relationships is very different from one that uses physical measurements. Among the earliest known maps are those of the Babylonians, an ancient Middle Eastern people (18th-6th centuries B.C.E.). Basing their numbers on 60, they divided the circle into six segments of 60 degrees each, making 360 degrees, which is now the universal unit for circles and spheres such as the globe. In other ways, however, their understanding and uses of space seem totally foreign to ours. For example, Babylonian priests used spatial units and categories (for example, "mythical worlds") to reinforce local religious beliefs, the Babylonians divided the universe into seven parts, which were presided over by a fusion of seven deities. The Babylonian elders used maps to teach their people about mythic heroes and the lands they had visited (Dilke 1985). The central placement of Babylonia in "world" maps propagated the belief that it was culturally superior to the rest of the known and imagined world (Thrower 1996).

The Babylonian maps show how cultural institutions, such as religion, may shape understandings of space quite differently from Anglo-European societies. In other early civilizations, space was defined by dominant institutions other than religion. Sumer, an even earlier Middle-Eastern civilization understood space in a way that helped the local elite to exercise political authority. Remnants of Sumerian maps (circa 2300 B.C.E.) indicate that the local government treated space as a "thing in and of itself," which could be measured mathematically. Indeed, many maps show urban areas drawn to scale using standardized mathematical units (Dilke 1985). Like "miles" in contemporary American society, these units could be broken down into equivalent lengths and therefore were interchangeable. Often very elaborate, Sumerian maps provided not only the layout of cities but also the dimensions of local plots and buildings; the most complex include the rooms inside buildings. Imagine opening a road map and getting not only the directions to a job interview but also the measurements of the building and office that it was being

held in. Sumerian maps also included intricate illustrations of waterways, which were very important to the economic stability of Sumerian
cities, especially with regard to agricultural development and trade. The
Sumerian obsession with cartographic precision was not just a matter of
high civilization or enhanced technology. Their detailed maps were effective tools of political regulation, allowing the ruling class to efficiently
assess taxes, keep track of who owned what, and settle land disputes.

Non-Anglo-European Conceptions of Space

Although the ancient Sumerians conceptualized space similar to Anglo-European concepts, other societies have exhibited very different understandings of space. A vivid contrast to the Anglo-European notion of
space as a "real" entity, which exists outside of us and possesses mathematical dimensions, comes from the early Bantu tribes of southern Africa. They did not distinguish between humans and the space they occupy. For example, the Bantu did not conceive of towns and cities as a
freestanding collection of buildings, which exist separately from the people who occupy them. Rather, a town was a "people." If the people
moved to a new location, the town would move. They could not conceive
of towns and cities without people (Samson 1974:260). In contrast, Anglo-
European societies readily conceive of cities as being independent of
people. Indeed, people are often absent in representations of particular cities. For example, San Francisco is often portrayed by the Trans-
America Pyramid and the Golden Gate Bridge. If the people of San Francisco were replaced by people from New York, most observers would say
that the culture of the city might have changed but not the city itself. The
Bantu would say it had become an entirely different city because their
conception was tied to the people and the Anglo-European conception to
the space itself, separate from the people.

The traditional Bantu understanding of space has some very interesting cultural consequences. Since space and people coexist, the Bantu did
not believe that land is a form of private property; even the practice of
"renting" was unknown to them. Land was collectively occupied by the
tribe. Although plots may have been allocated to individual families for
farming, the family was not allowed to sell or lease this land (Shaw
1974:91; Willoughby 1923:92). Whereas in Anglo-European societies,
plots tend to be precisely measured regular shapes such as rectangles,
Bantu "farming" plots were usually asymmetrical and were not concep-

tualized in measurable units such as acres. After all, if space does not exist independently of us, how can it be measured? Each person or family would know what land they had a right to farm, and if there were a dispute, it could be settled collectively. Symmetrical, numerically measured plots are needed mainly when land is transferred as a thing.

These understandings of space often conflicted with those of early Dutch and British settlers in South Africa in the 17th and 18th centuries, who found the Bantu relationship to land vexing (Naidis 1970). Since the Bantu did not conceive of private property or how a piece of paper—the deed—could confer rights over land, tribal chiefs would often sign treaties giving British traders and colonists rights to settle in a given area, and later fail to honor them. Nor was it unusual for them to unwittingly "sell" the same land to unsuspecting buyers. The Bantu chiefs often happily signed these documents, feeling that they were getting a one-sided bargain, in which they "received good cheer and gifts and the White man got nothing but a mark on paper" (Willoughby 1923:167). It was not that the Bantu chiefs were dishonest but that they did not conceive of a permanent, noncontextual link between a person and a plot of land. As they and many other societies understood it, people had a right to use land only in particular contexts, for example, when they built a hut or raised cattle on it. They could not conceive that people who lived somewhere else could exclude other people from using it on the basis of an abstract connection between people and land called ownership. Unused land would revert to the society as a whole, and its use was determined by a chief. Not surprisingly, these misunderstandings exacerbated tensions between the Bantu and white colonists. The latter often relied on military force to gain access to their newly acquired "property."

Religious and cultural institutions also shaped Australian Aborigine understandings of space. Aboriginal beliefs are best understood in the context of their creation myths, called the "Dreaming." During the "Dreaming," the Aborigines believe that their ancestors created and populated the earth, later merging with parts of the landscape itself (Standbury 1977). Consequently, these sites are believed to be sacred. For example, the Dieri in southern Australia believe that the spirits of their ancestors—*mura-mura*—often inhabit trees, which thus become sacred (Durkheim 1995). Other geographical features identified with *mura-mura*, such as rocks and springs, are likewise sanctified. In Anglo-European societies, sacred spaces such as temples, churches, synagogues, battlefields, and cemeteries are often designated as sacred by virtue of their functions (for example, a place of worship) or by events that occurred on them (for example, an important battle). A church may be built on a conveniently located lot or on land donated by a rich benefactor; thus, the "space" a church occupies is not necessarily sacred when considered independently of its present function. By contrast, for the Aborigines, the place itself is sacred.

The Aborigines' natural environment becomes so sacred, in fact, that the Aborigines "read" the landscape as a sacred text, which guides their spiritual existence (Cowan 1982; Myers 1986), much in the way that Jews read the Torah and Christians read the Bible. While Anglo-Europeans exercise control over space through manipulating the natural environment in various ways, space or, more specifically, the Aborigines' natural environment, dictates how they lead their lives. Consequently, the Aborigines perceive natural landmarks to be cues provided by their ancestors to help them remember events that occurred during the Dreaming (Cowan 1982). That is, the Aborigines believe that their ancestral gods communicate with them in a visual language expressed in terms of rocks, contours, fauna, and flora.

Collectively, these visual cues are often objectified as totems, animals or natural objects considered to be ancestrally related to a given Aboriginal descent group and taken as its symbol. Each Aborigine has his or her own totem, which has a spatial determinant—the place of his or her conception (Cowan 1982). At the moment of conception, humans are believed to be transformed into ancestral beings waiting to be reborn. The identity of this ancestral being is determined by the child's totem. That is, if a woman conceives a child near the place of the snake, her child's totem will be a snake, and the child will have a dual nature, that of a human and a snake (Cowan 1982). Aborigines become spiritually connected to the land in light of the rebirth cycle. In this manner, the totemic landscape serves to link the Aborigine with the world of his or her superhuman ancestors.

Given this deep spiritual attachment to the land, Aborigines do not make cognitive distinctions between humanity and space. For example, Aborigines believe space, like humans, is male or female, based on its physical characteristics. For instance, they ascribe "phallic" significance to pillars of rock and other vertically orientated landmarks (Basedow 1929). Likewise, Aborigines consider clefts in the earth to have a feminine quality. Furthermore, many clans believe "female" spaces posses curative properties, which they associate with a cultural ideal of the mother-nurturer. If someone suffering from senility or sickness visits a "female" space at the appropriate hour, he or she is thought to be cured.

Aborigine perspectives of space influence their ideas of land as a form of property. Whereas in Anglo-European societies, real estate is legally defined and lots are defined in abstract quantities such as yards or acres, Aborigines define property ownership in terms of Dreamtime sites where sacred rituals are carried out (Standbury 1977). These sites are integral to a person's definition of his or her land, while the precise boundaries remain mathematically indeterminate. Aborigines are culturally prohibited from moving away from their land. Imagine not being able to leave the town or city in which you were born and raised. This reverses the Anglo-European notion of property, in which the land a person owns is connected to him or her no matter where they go; legally, it is still that person's property. For the Australian Aborigines, the link between people and land works in the other direction. The person cannot leave the land; in effect, the people are owned by the land. Given this cultural ideology, it is not surprising that the Aborigines perceived English-sponsored relocation programs to be a form of spiritual murder. British attempts to relocate Aborigines were often met with violent resistance (Standbury 1977).

Meso-American conceptions of space are equally intricate. The Aztecs, who inhabited Mexico and Central America before European conquest, believed that humanity was spiritually united with time and space. This understanding was reflected in Aztec creation myths, which state that humans, space, and time originated from the same cataclysmic event, the destruction of an aquatic goddess called Cipactli (Austin 1997). Prior to the development of time, Cipactli's parts were held in a constant state of inertia, stifling her creative capacity. This state of inertia was destroyed by the motion of time, which jostled fragments of her body, producing the intermediate world between heaven and hell and the various creatures, including humans, who inhabited it. In this manner, humans, time, and space were fused in the Aztec imagination.

These myths reflect many of the Aztec understandings of space. Since they believed that their world was born out of cataclysm, they considered their earthly existence to be precarious (Simon 1997). Owing to the unity of time, space, and humanity, the only way to prevent calamity was to establish spatial/temporal order in Aztec communities (Opperman et al. 1984). Since the earth was a microcosm of the heavens, given their common origin, it was logical to create spatial/temporal order by imitating what was observed in the cosmos. So the placement of ceremonial centers or even entire cities would be guided by astronomy. A temple might be located so that its shadow on the day of the summer solstice falls on a holy spot. Windows might be set so that they allow a view of what we call the Big Dipper. Temporal order was also factored in. Sites were constructed to be directly beneath the sun, moon, or certain stars during prescribed times of the Aztec calendrical cycle (Aveni 1995).

Contrast the sense of space in the Aztec cataclysmic origin myth with the Judaic origin myth of Adam and Eve, which sets humans within pre-existing time and space. God created the world and then people (on the sixth day). Adam and Eve found themselves in a place, the Garden of Eden, from which they were expelled because of their sin. They were then given dominion over the earth and its creatures, emphasizing humanity's separation from nature rather than its unity. Even though the particular meanings of this myth have changed over history, the contrast with unified sensibilities such as the Aztecs' has remained, sometimes with tragic consequences.

When Europeans first came to the New World, the contrast between the beliefs of the Aztec and those of the invading Spaniards often resulted in cultural misunderstandings. For example, when Spanish army officers commissioned native mapmakers for maps of local "towns," their request was often met with bewilderment. In Aztec culture, a "town"—an architectural entity that defined a particular community—had no meaning (Mundy 1996). For the Aztecs, a map was a "portrait" of a community. In keeping with the Aztec ideal of unity between humanity, time, and space, these maps showed not only landmarks but also people, both past and present. In further contrast with Anglo-European cartography, distance was not expressed in standardized numerical coordinates but by the number of rests that the human body required in a route. Thus, for the Aztecs, space was measured by the pace of the human body, reinforcing the idea that humans and space were united. Furthermore, whereas Anglo-European maps have clearly delineated boundaries, borders between neighboring communities were drawn with human footprints, suggesting that for the Aztecs, human activity defined space, both through naming and motion.

Early Anglo-European Conceptions of Space

In classical Greece, there were many understandings of space. For example, in a categorization somewhat analogous to that of the South African Bantu, some politically decentralized societies considered themselves to be an *ethos*—which meant a "people." On the other hand, centralized so-

cieties, such as Athens, were known as *polis*—which meant ruled by people (Mann 1986). To be "ruled by a people" implies a more typically
Anglo-European conception of space—an understanding of space as being "real," existing independently of people. Before a given space could
be ruled, it was necessary to reify it, treating it as an object, a thing in and
of itself. Reifying land was related to its increased political and economi-
cal importance. Economically, private property became a major means of
allocating land among people, while politically, the birthplace of democracy allowed only (male) landowners to vote.

These philosophical battles have profoundly influenced our contemporary perceptions of space. For example, some scholars based their understandings of space on empirically informed geographical studies.
However, rising Athenian cultural dominance presented a challenge to
the empiricists, professing the superiority of "reason" over empirical observation to understanding the world. Deductive logic rather than observation was seen as the key to science. The mathematician Euclid per-
fected a system of logical deduction based on a few postulates, such as
the principle that two parallel lines never meet, the geometry that most
people still learn in school. Euclidean geometry was unfortunately defined as a perfect system with no need for improvement, lasting as the final word on space until the modern era. Besides its rejection of empirical
input, it was limited because it was a system of plane geometry, suitable
only for flat surfaces where straight lines, perfect circles, and precise angles defined space. In the real world, a sphere with mountains, valleys,
and rivers defied Euclidean neatness. Despite its enormous contribution
to the development of rational thought, over the long run, it retarded the
discovery of practical knowledge of space (McLeish 1992).

One enduring construction was the East-West dichotomy, in which
differences between cultures in which one culture was depicted as being
inferior to another were portrayed as spatial differences. Rationally
minded Athenians invented spatial categories that distinguished Greeks
from Persians and other "barbarians" (Gress 1998). Since Greek times,
differences between Christians and Muslims and between capitalism
and communism have been framed on this East-West distinction. In each
case, the "East" symbolized despotism, mystery, hedonism, nepotism,
and irrationality; the "West" symbolized patriotism, civic virtue, freedom, rationality, and meritocracy.

The Greek distinction between East and West underlay another major
contribution to the construction of Anglo-European spatial understanding, the notion of continents. Like an ant whose world exists only as far

as it can crawl in a few hours, the Greeks had little idea of what lay beyond the Mediterranean region. Herodotus, an ancient Greek historian, first developed the division between Europe and Asia to reinforce cultural distinctions between Greeks and Persians in his history of the Greco-Persian Wars. He divided Europe and Asia along the Hellespont —a strait separating Eastern Europe from Asia Minor. The concept referred less to the geographical boundary between major landmasses than to the cultural distinction between societies. If you looked at a globe without political boundaries, you would probably not see the Hellespont as any sort of natural boundary.

The idea of continents caught on, although the geographical boundaries of these landmasses were often decided arbitrarily (Lewis and Wigen 1997). Looking at the globe as a whole, for example, Europe does not appear to be an isolated geographical entity; there is no physical boundary—no body of water, no natural border—dividing it from Asia. In fact, the boundary has changed over the centuries. The current boundaries are essentially the boundaries of Christendom, the area governed by the Catholic Church when it was an organization of political and military power (Mann 1986). But because Europe has been the most powerful region in the world for the past five centuries, it has been able to define the spatial organization in terms of itself. Even the representation of Europe on maps reflects this world. When the spherical globe is projected onto the flat surface of a page, something must be distorted, depending on where the imaginary eye looking at the globe is situated. As seen in Figure 3.1, the standard Mercator projection, the map image found in classrooms and newscasts, distorts physical dimensions by making Europe appear larger in relation to the rest of the world, especially the Southern Hemisphere. The Peters projection gives a more accurate image of the relative size of the continents, faithfully showing Europe as much smaller than Africa or South America. However, the shape of those continents is warped, making them appear longer and skinnier than they appear on a round globe.

Roman constructions of space reflect the importance of political institutions. The Romans adopted some Greek conceptions of space, such as continents and the East-West divide, but adapted them to conform to Roman geopolitical schemas. For example, they shifted the boundary between West and East from the Hellespont to the Roman province of Illyria (20th-century Yugoslavia) (Gress 1998). While the Romans clung to the belief that the East-West divide separated virtue from vice, honesty from dishonesty, and freedom from tyranny, the "rational" Greeks,

FIGURE 3.1

Two Projections of the World

Mercator Projection

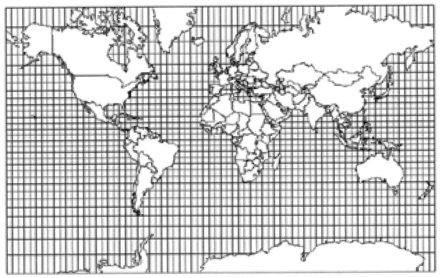

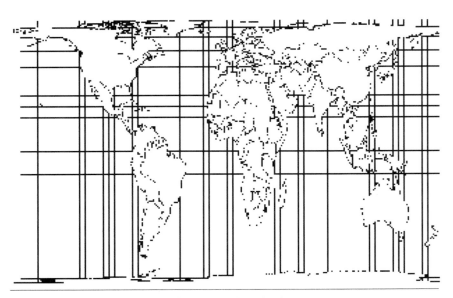

SOURCE: Used by permission of the artist, Robert Crosby.

Figure 3-1 Peters.tif

who invented the distinction, ironically found themselves placed in the "irrational" East.

The Roman understanding of space, however, differed from that of the Greeks in one important way. For the Romans, territory was power, so space was not understood as an abstract concept existing apart from what can be touched and felt. Rather, space was a "real," concrete entity—one that could be exploited economically and politically in the name of the state. Since the Romans perceived space more tangibly than the Greeks, empirical observation informed their understanding more acutely. The Roman state institutionalized this perspective in a variety of ways. For example, the state sponsored large-scale geographical surveys of its territory, employing a large corps of technically trained surveyors to measure and map the reaches of their vast empire (Dilke 1985). They quantified space more thoroughly than the Greeks, measuring distance in terms of abstract mathematical coordinates, the standard unit being the milestone. The maps commissioned by the Roman state helped to further institutionalize imperial understandings of space. These maps were designed to facilitate territorial expansion by organizing and exploiting settled lands brought under imperial jurisdiction (Dilke 1987). The maps were often cast in bronze or carved from semiprecious stones.

The Romans' reification of space was not limited to the military. The state institutionalized land as a form of private property (reinforcing the perception of space as something real and valuable) by making grants of land to Roman citizens from territory it had acquired through conquest. Other developmental policies reinforced the belief that space was exploitable. Land was divided in an orderly and systematic fashion, creating plots that were easy to diagram. For example, grid streets divided urban space into square *insulare*; the cultivated countryside was divided into square *centuraire*. The state commissioned maps of all the plots in an area for assessing property taxes—an important source of revenue for the state (Kain and Baigent 1992).

The decline of the Roman Empire and the diffusion of Christianity throughout Europe provide more evidence that Anglo-European understandings of space have been socially constructed. As the Roman Catholic Church replaced the Roman Empire as the dominant institution, theological belief replaced political need as the basis of the understanding of space. Whereas Athenian understandings of space had been informed by "rational" inquiry and Roman understandings of space informed by empirical observation, medieval perceptions of space were informed by scriptural interpretation. One Church scholar, Cosmas Indicopleustes

FIGURE 3.2

The T-O Map, 7th Century A.D.

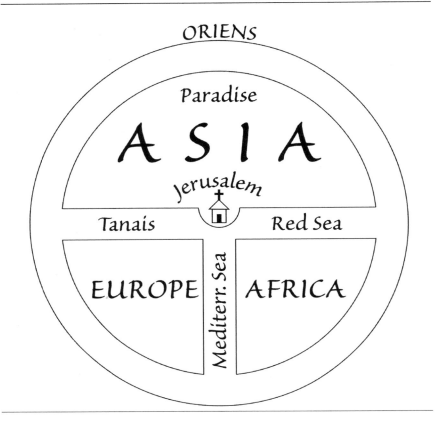

(circa 500 A.D.), placed Jerusalem at the center of his world, in keeping with Ezekiel 5:5, in which God stated, "I have set [Jerusalem] in the midst of the nations and the countries that are around her." Scriptural influences are most salient in the period's T-O maps, as reproduced in Figure 3.2. They portrayed the world as a flat circle, a layout inspired by the prophet Isaiah's admonition to "preserve the circle of the earth" (Wilford 1982:46). The "East"—that is, Asia—occupied the top portion of the map, with Jerusalem placed centrally, underscoring its significance. Asia was separated from Africa by the Nile and from Europe by the Don River—the two waterways forming the top bar of the "T." The Mediterranean Sea was represented by the upright segment of the "T." The world itself was surrounded by an ocean, which formed the "O."

As the Romans used maps to build empire, the Church used them for religious interests. Church elders often used these maps to teach Church doctrine to their most illiterate followers. The most elaborate of these versions depicted heaven and hell and featured various Catholic icons, which priests used to illustrate biblical stories and teach catechism. At the same time, these maps often included rudimentary directions to important pilgrimage spots, such as Bethlehem and Jerusalem.

Greco-Roman constructions of space congruent with Church doctrine were frequently incorporated into medieval thought with scriptural rationale. For example, St. Jerome found justification for the Greek division of the known world into three continents in the Old Testament and wrote, "Noah gave each of his three sons, Shem, Ham and Japeth, one of the three parts of the world for their inheritance, and these were Asia, Africa, and Europe respectively" (Lewis and Wigen 1997).

Although the Church adapted early Greco-Roman conceptions of space when possible, the rise of this new dominant institution changed basic understandings of space. The more abstract Greco-Roman sense of space was replaced by a more concrete sense of place. A hierarchy ranked places from Jerusalem and Rome, the most sacred places, through cathedral cities and holy shrines to parish churches. The relationship of one place to another was conceived less in terms of abstract distances such as miles than in terms of their relationship to this hierarchy of places. Rather than ask how far one place was from another, they would ask how holy it was. The degree of religious commitment was often evaluated by how many pilgrimages to holy places a person had undertaken, with the most devout demonstrating their piety by a pilgrimage to Jerusalem.

Toward a Contemporary Anglo-European Understanding of Space

Anglo-European understanding of space mirrors that of the Romans in many ways. Both have institutionalized private property, measured space in standardized mathematical units, and associated territory with political power. This is no historical coincidence—the Anglo-European perspective, like the Roman perspective, developed within the context of state building.

In early modern France, the connection between state building and the Roman Empire was especially relevant during the reign of Louis XIV (Cronin 1964; Gress 1998). Tracing his legacy to Charlemagne, emperor of the Holy Roman Empire, Louis XIV considered himself to be the legitimate successor to the Roman emperor and consciously used Rome as a model. He had a passion for the Latin language and Roman history, instilled in him during his studies as a child (Cronin 1964). However, Louis XIV's aspirations to the imperial glory did not really fit the France he inherited. Unlike the classical Roman Empire, France at this time was a vague geographical entity, little more than an odd collection of provinces over which the king loosely presided. Local folk culture stressed the region as the unit of cultural and political identity. Most people had no notion of "France." Few spoke the French language, shared little that could be called French culture, and had no idea of a geographical entity called France. Unlike the Roman state, which possessed definite imperial boundaries, no Frenchman, not even Louis XIV himself, could define the country's territorial parameters. Among many of the king's subjects, loyalty was personal, not territorial; they were subjects of Louis, not citizens of France. For them, the king was France—they could not conceive of the state existing as an independent spatial entity. Yet the king was inspired to unite and govern his kingdom in keeping with the Roman model. To this end, he set in motion a series of processes that contributed to the historical construction of the French absolutist state—an important predecessor to the contemporary nation-state.

The king's political aims found support in René Descartes's philosophy of human perceptions. Descartes echoed the Greek idea that we cannot trust sense experience; rather, it is through "reason" that we come to accurately understand our world and our place within it. By this logic, color, taste, sound, and other types of sense perception are "secondary" qualities; they are inferior to "primary" qualities, which are characteristics that can be weighed, measured, and expressed mathematically—that is, understood rationally. Thus, Cartesian theory treats an abstract mental construct such as space as a thing if it can be expressed in terms of numerical coordinates, despite the fact that its reality cannot be confirmed empirically by the senses. This contrasted with the prevailing medieval understandings of space, which were guided largely by scriptural interpretation.

Like most innovations, these ideas were not entirely novel. The existing belief in the dualism between soul and body became formulated as a dualism between mind and body. The dualism of mind and body implies that observers—subjects—are separate from what they observe—objects. This notion of objectivity—treating everything we observe as objects, including time and space—is central to Anglo-European thought. By extension, even though the state of France (an "object") was at best a vague political entity, its existence could be validated mathematically. In other words, it could be represented in the Cartesian sense as a territory defined by numerical parameters that existed independently of the French people. Simply put, an accurate map of France would provide an ideological justification for its existence and command the respect of its citizens. At the same time, such a map could be exploited in the Roman way for military consolidation of the French provinces and for tax assessment.

Strongly influenced by Descartes, as well as by the empirical cartography of the Romans, Louis XIV set out to put together a map of his kingdom. To his dismay, the king discovered that only some of the provinces had been mapped, and not very accurately at that. Determined to improve this situation, he made geography a legitimate area of study at the Royal Academy of Sciences, importing some of Europe's most prominent mathematicians and scientists to work there. Perfecting geographical surveying techniques such as triangulation, they were able to map France for the first time.[7] The king was said to be disappointed with the results—his kingdom lacked the breadth he had imagined. On this note, he complained to his chief mapmaker, "You have taken from me more of my kingdom than I have won in all of my wars" (Cronin 1964:305). However, France had now been defined within mathematical parameters and thus was "real" in both the classical Roman sense and the Cartesian sense. By affirming geography as a scholarly endeavor, the government made space in an absolute Cartesian sense seem more real, which in turn made the territorial basis of the state itself seem more concrete. This was one of the main ways that the rise of the state as a dominant institution shaped Anglo-European understandings of space to conform with scientific and mathematical reasoning.

In the century or so after Louis XIV, the Enlightenment added a new chapter to the modern Anglo-European sense of space. This intellectual

---

[7]Triangulation was used to determine the distance between two points on the earth's surface by dividing a large area of land into a series of connected triangles, the angles of which were measured to determine the distance between three geographical points. This technique was used to measure the height of mountains and other natural landmarks.

movement considered the Church and monarchy to be based in superstition and tradition and called for their replacement by rationally constructed counterparts, such as an elected representative government and civil religion (for example, patriotism) (Smith 1983). The Enlightenment thinkers also had a novel notion of rights. Society had been organized around group rights. Different people had different rights and were subject to different laws, depending on what class, occupation, and religious groups they belonged to. A commoner could be executed for stealing from a nobleman but not vice versa. A priest would be subject to the law of the church, not the law of the state. In contrast, Enlightenment thinkers held that a person's rights would be based less on who they were than where they were. They agreed that people should have rights as individuals, not as members of groups—rights enforced by spatially defined governments.[8] In France, people had French rights and obeyed French laws. Such rhetoric was crucial to contemporary Anglo-European understandings of space—for it contributed to a widespread sense of a "French" nation.

These two ideas—liberal-democratic statehood and nationhood—became intertwined. When applied, they in part gave rise to the 1789 French Revolution and, in its wake, a new spatial entity: the French nation-state and a powerful new ideology, nationalism. With nation-states, people had rights and were subject to law depending on where they were. For example, anybody inside the borders of the United States has the right to free speech and must obey American laws, regardless of their class, occupation, religion, or place of birth. (Chapter 7 will discuss how nations illustrate the intersection of time and space with race, gender, and class.)

This new construction of statehood was institutionalized by the post-Revolutionary government in a variety of ways. The first step was legal recognition of the French nation-state, connecting a group of people, the nation, to a territorial entity, the state. For example, the National Assembly officially declared the existence of the French Republic while declaring the sovereignty of the French nation (Brubaker 1992; Gress 1998). Steps, too, were taken to transfer property from the landed aristocracy to the masses. French leaders believed that the French nation-state could only be fully realized if every family owned its own piece of

---

[8]Although these rights were ideologically "universal" rights, these thinkers assumed that they resided in and were to be recognized and enforced by states. In practice, they were territorially administered.

France. Even more significant was the institutionalization of citizenship, the notion that people were officially recognized as belonging to the nation-state (Brubaker 1992). Before this time, people did not understand themselves to be French, English, or whatever. They might have thought of themselves as being from a village or region, or they may have not had any spatial identity at all, thinking of themselves instead as members of a class (such as noble), clan (such as McGregor), or occupation. Essentially, the idea of membership reinforced the idea of the nation-state by fostering a sense of solidarity and fraternity. The use of passports, the taking of oaths, and the designation of legal identities all contributed to the reality of the French nation-state.

The French revolutionaries employed other methods to lend credence to the myth of the nation-state. For example, in September 1789, Abbe Sieyes called for the establishment of a committee to unify the French nation through radical spatial reorganization (Konvitz 1987). Ironically, the subsequent attempts to reconstruct French geography mirrored those of the old royalist government, in that they were informed by Roman thought, mathematics, and science. They divided the country into standardized administrative units, the boundaries of which were to be based on "rational" criteria as opposed to lingering "irrational" ethnolinguistic distinctions. The new areas were divided according to mathematical principles and physical geography and named for neutral landmarks such as lakes and mountains to accelerate the shift toward a common "national" as opposed to "regional" identity. The symmetrical new departments were reminiscent of the Roman *insulare* and *centurare*, only on a much larger scale. Once geographical units become established as real, subsequent leaders use them for convenience and make them more and more "real."

The Revolutionary regime's use of cartography also reflected Roman and Cartesian influences, treating maps as a political tool to be exploited in the name of the state (Konvitz 1987). Like the Romans, the new regime initiated a national geographical survey of privately owned property plots to aid with taxation. In the interest of cartographic accuracy and in keeping with the rational agenda of the Revolution, the government ordered the development of a standardized system of measurements—the metric system—which was to be derived scientifically, in contrast to earlier measures such as the foot or the yard (the distance from the king's nose to the tip of his finger with an outstretched arm). The Academy of Sciences appointed a commission consisting of famed scientists and mathematicians to develop this new system. The new unit, the meter, would be 1/10,000,000 of the line of longitude between each pole and the equator. While the measurement of the meter was ascertained using rigorous scientific methods, the simple interchange of metric units required only a basic knowledge of arithmetic, so that even the most humble of peasants would be able to use it. Both the "ease" and "practicality" of the metric system, no doubt, contributed to its widespread acceptance among the French population. For unlike conceptions of time, which were widely standardized throughout France prior to the Revolution, systems of weights and measures differed from region to region, if not from village to village, a situation that complicated commercial transactions. Thus, unlike the Revolutionary government's attempts to introduce a new calendar, which were met with violent resistance, the metric system was more easily implemented.

While the creation of the territorially defined nation-state was the most important political development shaping Anglo-European views of space, the rise of capitalism was the primary economic factor. Under feudalism, before the development of capitalism, a small group controlled the land through a personalistic system in which a king nominally owned it all and allowed nobles to use it in exchange for loyalty. People were tied to the land just as much as the land was tied to them because their livelihood and standing in society were based on their control of land. But they could not easily sell it for money and did not think of it as a commodity to sell. The thought of buying and selling land was just as foreign as the concept of buying and selling labor discussed in Chapter 6. Commodities are things that are sold for money. The use of money grew as a way to facilitate barter, making it possible to have indirect trades, with money mediating. For most of human history, markets have existed, in which physical objects such as food, spices, tools, silk, and so on were sold, mediated by many forms of money such as coins, bills of lading, promissory notes, and chits. But only concrete physical objects were generally considered as commodities (Polanyi 1957). Land and labor were not.

Without the taken-for-granted cultural understandings of capitalism, it would seem bizarre to think of land and labor as commodities. What do you buy when you "buy" land? If one thinks of land as something to use rather than something to own, buying it makes no sense. As Karl Polanyi (1957) describes it, "What we call land is an element of nature inextricably interwoven with man's institutions. To isolate and form a market out of it was perhaps the weirdest of all undertakings of our ancestors" (p. 178). How land could be used and who could use it for what purposes were deeply embedded in relationships of kinship, neighbor-hood, religion, and other groups. For example, in feudalism, the relation-ships between lords and peasants were really relationships between families. If your father had a feudal bond with a lord, you had one with the lord's son. It was very difficult for the lord to sell that land for some-one to grow food on it or for you to sell your right to farm it. But what happens when the landlord gets the right to sell it as property?

Property is a set of rights, entitlements, and responsibilities—the right to use it for whatever purpose you want or restrict other people from it, the entitlement to any income that comes from it, and the respon-sibility to keep it and its premises safe. When you buy property, you buy those rights, entitlements, and responsibilities. But there can be no sense of buying land until those rights, entitlements, and responsibilities are recognized and enforced by social institutions such as the state. The spread of the right to treat land as a commodity, which occurred from the 14th to the 19th centuries, swept away feudalism. Under capitalism, land is a commodity bought and sold like a pair of shoes.

The process did not happen gradually or smoothly; it was turbulent and sometimes violent. Across Europe, common lands were privatized and commercialized through the **enclosure movements**, by which gov-ernments removed peasants—often forcibly—and gave land to individ-ual nobles for commercial use. In England, enclosure began in the 1100s. As it continued over the next few centuries, some peasants were able to find jobs, but many were reduced to begging. After landlords gained po-litical power in the 1600s, enclosures again increased; they were further stimulated by the General Enclosures Act of 1801. Peasant resistance and the dwindling availability of common lands ended the system by the be-ginning of the 20th century. In Russia, Hungary, Germany, France, and Denmark, enclosure also was a large-scale process, mainly in the 19th century. One of the biggest single steps in commodifying land was the French Revolution of 1789, which violently swept away all feudal rela-tionships and established modern property relations in that country.

Personal Space

Anglo-European society has personalized many spaces that people do not legally own but that get connected to a person whether they occupy it or not. People then talk of "my" space or "your" space. Early factories in-cluded individual manufacturing spaces. Within these spaces, each indi-vidual was designated his or her own place, and each place was designated its own individual to discourage group associations and collective dispositions, fostering individuality instead (Foucault 1987). Similarly, children are taught at a very young age that they have "their" desks at school and that they are responsible for taking care of their own "space" while respecting that of others. The penalties teachers must apply to enforce such rules indicate that such territoriality is not natural. While children are learning about "their" desks, they are learning about "their" rooms at home and the boundaries around their family homes or apartments.

People are not attached just to objects that are "theirs" but also to the space around their bodies, or personal space: a bubblelike area that surrounds us, beyond which no one may pass. Anthropologist Edward Hall (Hall 1969) has identified four primary "zones" of micro-interactions. The first of these zones is called "intimate distance," which spans from 0 to 18 inches; it is the distance of "lovemaking, wrestling, comforting and protecting." The second of these zones is "personal distance," from 1½ to 4 feet. People engaged in everyday conversation, sitting at a dinner table, or riding in a car are separated by personal space. The third zone is "social distance," which spans from 4 to 12 feet. Relations between clerks and shoppers, students and faculty, or employer and employee are usually at social distance. Finally, there is public space, such as a professor in a lecture room, a politician giving a speech, or a cleric giving a sermon. Hall observed pronounced differences among how these zones are experienced in different cultures. Americans and English, for example, have a much larger sense of intimate space than Italians or Arabs, explaining why conversations between the former and the latter often feel strained, with the Americans or English feeling that the Italians or Arabs are crowding them and the Italians or Arabs wondering why the Americans or English keep backing off from them. English poet W. H. Auden captured this sentiment:[9]

> *Some thirty inches from my nose*
> *The frontier of my Person goes.*
> *Stranger, unless with bedroom eyes*
> *I beckon you to fraternize,*
> *Beware of rudely crossing it;*
> *I have no gun, but I can spit.*

Auden (1966:14)

---

[9]From *W. H. Auden Collected Poems* by W. H. Auden. Copyright © by W. H. Auden. Reprinted by permission of Random House, Inc.

Intersections

Like time, space intersects with virtually all social life. The discipline of geography bears witness to the importance of spatial organization in the physical and social world. Not only is social life set within space, but, as this chapter has emphasized, spatial organization actively shapes and reproduces how we live. This section will briefly review some of the ways that space intersects with time and hierarchy.

Time and Space

The intersection of time and space is more pronounced in Anglo-European society than in many other societies. The abstract time and space of science are inseparable from each other. Time is considered the fourth dimension, differing from the other three primarily in terms of being irreversible—a person can walk back and forth along a line but not go back in time, though it may be possible in theory. Time and space are also measured in terms of each other. We measure time only by the movement of objects through space and measure space by techniques set in time.

The popular press and some academic writers have declared that globalization—the increased connectedness of people throughout the world through technological, economic, and political change—has enfeebled the constraints of time and space on social life. E-mail and the World Wide Web have allowed people to communicate instantaneously from anywhere on the globe. People often do not even know (or care) where the messages are coming from. Corporations assemble computers, automobiles, and shoes from parts produced thousands of miles away and change products constantly. Governments have created regional trade alliances such as the European Union or the North American Free Trade Association, along with global groups such as the World Trade Organization, which now take some of the powers formerly reserved to individual states. Satellite communications make news instantaneously available on 24-hour news channels. This is often trumpeted as a qualitatively new era, the "postmodern" era, in which time and space have been compressed (Harvey 1989).

The literature on new technology, globalization, and time-space convergence is fraught with hyperbole, unsupported generalization, and technobabble. While the effects of new technologies such as the Internet will be profound, it is important to temper these claims with empirical skepticism. Just a few examples: The claim that globalization is rendering the nation-state obsolete is challenged by militant nationalism in places such as Yugoslavia, Rwanda, and Russia. Claims that American English is being linguistically homogenized is contradicted by findings that regional dialects are becoming more pronounced, not disappearing (Labov 1994). And despite the fact that some Americans have become wedded to the World Wide Web, for many it is just a fancy typewriter with faster mail. The computer only made it available to a very large number of people. The number of airplanes packed with business travelers suggests that space has not been conquered, even for those with the latest technology at their disposal. Face-to-face interaction is yet to be replaced with e-mail, faxes, and cell phones. The automobile has not reduced the time that people spend commuting but only increased the distance. Instead of walking a half-hour or so to and from work, people now drive (Burns 1993). Time and space still constrain our lives, even if they do so in new ways.

Moreover, is this time and space compression a new feature of the "postmodern" world or a long-term development of Anglo-European society? Did the qualitative break in how time and space are conceptualized come earlier, with recent developments only accelerating a much longer trend? For example, one of the common themes of the globalization literature is the observation that people can get on an airplane and a few hours later be in an entirely different continent with no sense of having traversed a long distance. While the compression of space from jetliners is important, the transformation in how space is experienced developed with the railroad in the 19th century. Before the railroad, travel from one place to another meant experiencing all the space in between—the landscape, the turning points, the sounds, and even the smells. Travel was something a person lived through and experienced in time as well as space. But the railroad changed that. For the first time, it was possible to enter a closed compartment, cut one's self off from the world, and emerge into a different place. The noise and smell of the railroad itself drowned out any experience of the travel itself. Moreover, in contrast to earlier roads for horses or stagecoaches that were closely contoured to the shape of nature, railroads sliced through space, connecting places like Cartesian lines connecting points (Schivelbusch 1986).

Similarly, the computer did not create instantaneous communication; the telegraph did, invented a century and a half ago (Standage 1998). For the first time, people could communicate instantaneously with others over a long distance. Telegraph lines were erected along railroad lines, wedding the forces that compressed time with those that compressed space. It was the instant communication along the railroad tracks that made local time such a problem for the railroads, motivating the development of standard time. It was not long before underwater cables made ordinary the previously miraculous—communication in a flash between the Old World and the New World.

Intersections of Space and Hierarchy

One of the most important aspects of spatial organization is how various hierarchies such as race, gender, and class are structured in space and how spatial organization reproduces hierarchy over time. The relationship between spatial organization and social hierarchy is reflexive; that is, one does not exclusively cause the other, but they mutually shape each other. The spatial organization of many activities is hierarchical. For example, managerial activities are normally set in offices that are spatially distinct from factories, thereby organizing class along spatial lines. Similarly, the floors of an office symbolically represent the status hierarchy of the firm, with the president on the top, then other top management, middle management, and, depending on what the firm does, various functionaries on the lower floors, with menial jobs such as janitorial, heating supply and plumbing in the basement. Raising children is also done at a different place than making cars, and insofar as women raise children and men make cars, gender becomes organized spatially.

Spatial organization is organized to symbolically represent the values and meanings of what takes place in the space. A courtroom puts the judge higher than anyone else because he or she is to be more exalted, symbolically higher, but the center denotes impartiality to either side (where "side" refers to both parties in conflict and the physical side on which each is placed). Prosecution and defense tables—the two sides—are placed below the judge, equally distant from the center. The jurors are placed off center, representing their role as observers. The courtroom was designed like this to represent the values of a fair trial, and even though it may not actually directly change behavior, it can have an affect. Being above the rest of the courtroom in the center may not make any judges more impartial but reminds others that the judge is supposed to be impartial and could fortify others to compel his or her impartiality. Many of these spatial assignments are only symbolic, with little functional reason for putting activities in one place or another. But whether the assignment of space is purely symbolic, as the vertical organization of the office building, or functional, as the separation of managerial functions in an office building from manufacturing in a factory, the symbolic representation of hierarchy takes on a life seemingly of its own, reinforcing and reproducing inequalities based on gender, race, and class. As will be elaborated in later chapters, one of the clearest examples is racial segregation. Because whites and blacks grow up in different neighborhood environments, they go to different quality schools, have different access to networks that help them find jobs, and have different access to jobs, cultural experiences, recreation, and other activities that they need to get ahead.

Once hierarchical inequality becomes organized spatially, space can symbolize inequality more deeply than the simple fact that activities are set in space. The office becomes a place associated with managerial status, even for the nonmanagers working there. The executive secretary gains status not only because he or she works for a top manager but by virtue of working on the top floor. The janitor in the home office probably has more status than the janitor in the factory. Accountants, secretaries, technicians, and mail clerks often aspire to work in the home office but may be banished to the branch office for poor performance.

Conclusion

Geographers have complained that mainstream social science has privileged the study of time over space, that the big questions that have shaped modern consciousness have been about history rather than geography (Agnew 1996; Soja 1994). "Space still tends to be treated as fixed, dead, undialectical; time as richness, life dialectic, the revealing context for critical social theorization" (Soja 1994:128). They have a point. It is hoped that this chapter will convince the reader that issues of space are just as compelling and just as consequential as those of time. Not only do people live their lives set in space, but how they conceptualize the space they live in also has profound consequences for their lives. The development of abstract notions of space—of space separated from place—facilitated the rise of powerful societies that controlled people by controlling the space they lived in. A small part of the globe defined itself spatially—the West—and treated the rest of the world with contempt. Societies that did not treat space as a thing did not understand how to resist that small part that did, and eventually the "Western" concept spread to the whole planet.

Modern technology has made it possible to physically see the entire globe, a feat imaginable only in modern times and, until recent decades, only achievable by simulation, not direct observation. But now there are photographs of the earth rising over the moon's horizon. But such a view, whether simulated or photographed, tells nothing about what space means to people or how they organize it. Longitude and latitude exist only on the simulated globes, not the photographs, as do boundaries between countries. Photographing the planet does not create the sense of space as a thing, though it may be motivated by such a sense. The essentialist sense of space must be explained by how people have interacted and conflicted with each other and how institutions such as capitalism and states fostered the organization of human activities around "things" that some people owned or some governments controlled.

The essentialist sense of space as a thing feels deeply natural and is thoroughly institutionalized throughout society—from students' division of dormitory rooms to property law to the organization of the globe in nation-states. But it is hoped that this chapter will convince you that such a perception and understanding of space is historically constructed. Whether or not globalization is as far advanced as many pundits proclaim, it, along with challenges from poor people about property rights, minorities about segregated housing and schools, and women to bridge the public-private split, all—to employ spatial metaphors—provide an opening to rethink what space means and how it can be reshaped.

4

Race

Newsweek magazine in 1984 carried a story about a political conflict in a California city where a former councilman representing a predominantly black and Latino district was accused of being white. His successor claimed that he was misrepresenting himself by posing as black. His blue eyes, reddish hair, and light skin made him appear white, and he was raised white but discovered his "real" race only when he was in his early 20s.

What does it mean to say that he would misrepresent who he is by giving a partially false impression about where his ancestors came from? Why do the origins of his ancestors constitute a matter of being rather than just the culture he was raised in? How does having any ancestors from Africa make him a different person from someone with ancestors from Europe? How do the genes that determine his skin color, shape and color of his eyes, shape of his lips and nose, or texture of his hair affect the deep qualities of personhood? What is he allegedly misrepresenting by representing himself as African American?

Even if it does matter where his ancestors are from, why is it necessary to categorize him as either white or nonwhite rather than place him along a continuum of skin color? It would be obvious from his looks that this man had ancestors from Europe. Why does it matter if he had any ancestors from Africa? If the races were reversed and his complexion was dark, would it matter if he had any ancestors from Europe?

Finally, why was this story from a small town in California national news in a leading magazine? The editors must have thought the incident said something important about America. What could that be? In what ways does the printing of this story not only report something about the state of racial relations in America but also help shape them?

The Paradox of Race

Race in the modern world is a perplexing paradox. Virtually everyone agrees that race should not matter. Yet it pervades every aspect of social life: politics, work, education, leisure, sports, mass media, family, religion, and personal relations. Most people agree that society would be improved if we could reduce the impact of race. Yet it persists despite the best efforts of large numbers of people to mollify its force. Why is race such a persistent and pernicious power in modern social life? Like the other topics discussed in this book, the many answers debated by scholars and writers fall into two major perspectives.

The essentialist perspective sees race as a natural phenomenon, a characteristic of people based on genetic traits. Race is seen as an inherent feature of the entire person; an individual is "black" or "white" or "yellow" or "brown."[10] According to the essentialist perspective, race persists because people have a natural and deeply ingrained suspicion of the unfamiliar, of people different from themselves. Thus, well-meaning attempts to eradicate racial differences are bound to fail—racial differences are incorrigible. The best to hope for is that the rule of law contains overtly prejudicial behavior against racial minorities.[11]

In contrast, a constructionist perspective holds that racial categories are not natural but are invented by people. Races are only found in some societies. Where races are found, they vary among societies and change in form over time. The constructionist perspective emphasizes that the physical differences between races are incidental. It makes problematic the issue of why some physical differences are selected to create socially consequential categories (Almaguer 1994; Cornell and Hartmann 1998; Ferrante and Brown 1998; Omi and Winant 1994). Why do people say that people with dark skin and curly black hair are in a fundamentally different category than people with light skin and blond straight hair? The explanation for racial categorization is to be found in history, not in nature. Moreover, racial differences persist less because of primordial

---

[10]The quotation marks here designate that it is not color per se that defines these groups, but colors are only used as labels for socially defined groups. However, it would be grammatically awkward to use quotation marks throughout.

[11]Some essentialist doctrines claim that races are inherently unequal in natural endowments, that some races are smarter, stronger, and more law-abiding than others. Such overtly racist arguments are easily refutable, even within an essentialist perspective.

suspicion of differences than because they are actively and sometimes intentionally reproduced over time, even when the content of racial definitions changes. This implies that racial categories can be radically transformed and perhaps eliminated, although racial categories are so deeply built into many social institutions that change will be very difficult. Finally, the constructionist perspective holds that the pessimism and passivity implied by the essentialist perspective are a barrier to racial progress. Racial progress will require both a vision of racial justice and a commitment to change.

What Is Race?

If the meaning of race is socially constructed, then the meaning of race must be found in history, not in theory or logic. If race is socially constructed, it becomes pointless to say what the *real* or *true* meaning of race is, because there is no "real" meaning apart from what people have made race to be. The meaning of race will vary from one society to another. And the relationship among race and related concepts such as ethnicity or slavery will vary from one society to another. While one society may assume that language differences between people coincide with differences in skin color—everyone who speaks a certain language is assumed to have a certain skin color—other societies may think of language and skin in very different categories—people who speak a certain language could be expected to be any skin color.

The Anglo-European
Meaning of Race

The kinds of human characteristics that Anglo-European societies have bundled together as racial characteristics thus are somewhat arbitrary. This section will briefly review what qualities constitute a race in modern Anglo-European societies. **Races** are defined as groups of people who are assumed to (1) have particular physical characteristics in common, especially skin color; (2) fall into distinct and sharply bounded groups; (3) inherit their racial status; (4) share behavioral characteristics that are imputed to their physical qualities; and (5) are ranked hierarchically. These characteristics create the impression that racial categories are natural.

Selected Physical Distinctions

Easily visible physical differences such as skin color, eye shape, type of hair, and the shape of facial features are the most fundamental component of the construct of race. But there is no inherent reason why some physical characteristics rather than others are selected as the basis for defining groups. Few would group people together into distinct categories on the basis of height, for example. More important, overt racists and antiracist activists agree that the physical characteristics are superficial and arbitrary. Skin color and other characteristics are always seen as merely a way to recognize deeper differences.

The difference between constructionist and essentialist perspectives is how to explain the deeper reality that skin color covers. The essentialist perspective holds that some sorts of physical differences inherently divide people into groups and that it is natural that such groups be suspicious of each other. However, some of the world's greatest violence and strongest hatred occur between groups that are physically very similar. English and Irish, Jews and Arabs, French and Germans, Vietnamese and Cambodians, Serbs and Albanians, and Hutus and Tutsi are all groups that have violently fought each other despite physical similarities to each other. Those inclined to violence toward another group figure out ways to view them as different. In a social constructionist perspective, the analyst must explain why some physical characteristics become the basis of intergroup conflict.

Distinct Rigid Boundaries

When the category of race was fashioned, not only did its builders focus on specific physical characteristics, but they also invented the misrepresentation that people were divided into distinct groups, divided by rigid boundaries, with everyone in one and only one group. In fact, as discussed in Chapter 1, skin color is distributed among the world's people as a gradient, a gradual shading from dark to light. But race has been constructed as a bounded category. Two medium-dark people can be considered as very different from each other if they are defined as "black" and "white." The one defined "black" will be considered more similar to people who are very dark than the person with the nearly identical skin color, and the one defined "white" will be considered more similar to people who are very light. This rigid boundary between races is especially sharp in North America. Brazil, by contrast, does not categorize into rigid groups, even though there is pervasive discrimination based on skin color. Skin color is treated more like a gradient than a

bounded category. When people become richer over their lifetimes, they
are perceived as lighter (Marx 1998).[12]

Inherited

Some "blacks" can be lighter than some "whites" because race is defined
more by ancestry than skin color. African Americans are understood to
be people with ancestors from Africa, while whites are understood to be
people with ancestors from Europe. Asian Americans have ancestors
from Asia. However, most people, at least in the United States, have ancestry from many places. Almost no one can claim to be racially "pure."[13]
When a person has parents of more than one race, he or she is categorized
by the lower-status race. Southern states that had legal segregation defined a black as anyone with 1/16th or 1/32nd African American ancestry. In 1982, Susie Guillory Phipps sued the Louisiana Bureau of Vital Records to change her racial classification from black to white. A 1970 state
law had specified anyone with 1/32nd "Negro blood" to be black. She
had lived her whole life thinking she was white. She lost—not a long
time ago, but in the lifetime of many people reading this book (Omi and
Winant 1994).

The very notion that race is based on blood reflects an essentialist perspective. People from different parts of the world have the same kind of
blood. But the word *blood* is often used as a code to signify that exterior
differences such as skin color or eye shape are superficial markers of
something "deeper," something that is inherited.

Linking of Physical and
Behavioral Characteristics

Defining race in terms of ancestry implies that genetic differences in
physical characteristics such as skin color are inherently linked with cultural differences. If a black is someone with African ancestry, that ancestry "explains" both his or her skin color and preference for certain kinds
of dress, music, and speech. Similarly, an Asian is seen as someone who

---

[12]Similarly, in the United States, dark-skinned African Americans are often more
harshly discriminated against than those who are light skinned, even by other
African Americans. It is more accurate to call this color discrimination than racism, strictly speaking. Just because race is primarily a matter of bounded categories rather than a gradient, the gradient of color can remain socially important.

[13]Notice the connotation that to have ancestry from more than one race implies
that a person is "impure." My computer thesaurus includes among the antonyms
of *pure* the word *vile*.

not only has thin eyes but studies hard and makes good grades. My adopted daughter, who was born in Korea, struggled with great effort to pass arithmetic, but in high school, friends would ask for help in calculus, assuming that because she looked a certain way, she would excel in calculus. That was a painful form of prejudice, even though the assumption about her math ability was positive.

A **stereotype** is an image popularly attributed to members of one group by members of another group.[14] A physical trait such as skin color is treated as a signal of a person's abilities, qualities, or behaviors. Black people's athletic abilities or poverty are stereotypes, as are Asians' intelligence and tenacity.

Permanent

Because races are seen as genetic, they are seen as permanent. Individuals cannot change their race. A race is treated as an inherent part of a person, part of his or her essence. The assumption is, "You are what you are." Just as individuals cannot change race, neither can racial groups. Powerful groups have categorized into races ethnic groups that thought of themselves as different. African ethnic groups, including Assante, Kru, Whi, Ekuono, and Kumasi, were lumped together as "Negro" or "black," while Chinese, Japanese, Korean, Vietnamese, and Thai were lumped together as "Asian." At any one point, people *think* that racial categories are permanent.

Hierarchical

There has never been a society with truly "separate but equal" races. Racial categories always carry a connotation of inferiority and superiority because racial categories were invented as a way of categorizing people

---

[14]It is sometimes difficult to distinguish between stereotypes of groups and empirical cultural differences. For example, members of a social group might characterize another group as "noisy" or "clannish" when in fact the average decibel level of speech or the tendency to socialize with members of one's one group does differ among groups. But a stereotype can be distinguished from genuine cultural differences in two ways: (1) A stereotype is attributed to individual members of a group solely on the characterization of the group as a whole. Each individual of a group whose members on average talk louder than those of another group is assumed to talk loud. (2) Stereotypes are used purposefully by members of one group to gain advantage over another group. It is not that every use of a stereotype is intended to gain advantage, but they typically arise and spread in purposeful ways.

who were already conceived as unequal. As will be elaborated below, the category of race was created by a dominant group, Europeans and their descendants in North America, to make other groups seem something less than human. Subsequent generations have internalized the socially constructed reality of superior and inferior races.

Why the Category of Race Matters

All of these characteristics together create the impression that races are natural rather than social constructions. In fact, as the rest of the chapter will demonstrate, many societies have had no racial distinctions, and there was a time when Anglo-European society did not distinguish people along racial lines. That is not to say that they did not distinguish people by physical or cultural characteristics or did not think in terms of superior or inferior groups. But the characteristics of racial categories—the identification of specific physical qualities, the rigid boundaries among groups, the attribution of cultural differences to inheritance, the linking of physical and cultural differences, the hierarchical ranking of those categories, and the sense that the differences are permanent—together form a distinctive social relationship that is found primarily in modern Anglo-European society. It requires an explanation in history, not biology. Race is a product of human invention, not an objective fact about the world discovered in biology or genetics. It is very real and very material in its consequences, but as a social reality, not a biological one.

Race is, nonetheless, more than an idea; it is a worldview, a way of understanding reality. Why do people act the way they do? Why do Asian American students get higher grades on average? Why do whites score higher on the SAT than African Americans? Why do people tend to marry others of the same skin color or eye shape? If people answer these questions in terms of race, they are adopting a racial worldview. If they do not go any deeper to inquire why race is given as an answer, it is easy to slide into racism. For example, why do African American men commit more "street crimes" than their white counterparts? Statistically they do. But if we ask why and simply answer, "*because* they are black," we are imputing to African American men a criminal nature in being black, a criminal essence. That is a form of racism. A historical understanding of not only whether there is a statistical relationship between race and crime but *why* gives us a more constructive handle on resolving the underlying social problems that create this fact. Such a historical understanding would explain how the construction of race creates social conditions that foster crime and why some behaviors associated with blacks are criminalized.

In addition to asking why people in particular groups act the way they do, examining the category of race also focuses attention on how people are *treated* differently. Why is a particular African American admitted to a university or a particular white person denied admission? Why are more African American murderers executed than whites? Why do African Americans have a more difficult time finding jobs, and why do they get paid less when they do find jobs? Why do Mexican Americans get hired as dishwashers or gardeners? Why are a higher percentage of African Americans poorer than whites? Why is it assumed that Asian Americans are better at math than other groups? Why are American Indians allowed to run public gambling businesses when others are not?

The issue is how the concept of race fits into our understanding of the world in general. The worldview of race is more than just how people perceive skin color or eye shape. When someone says "street crime" or "welfare mother" or "teenage pregnancy" or "illegal immigrant" or "scholarship athlete," what image comes to mind? If people see a white rapist or an African American rapist, do they explain the criminal motives or the social roots of the crime in the same way? Insofar as there are differences in these things, they are thinking with a racialized worldview.

Preracial Categories

What concrete events and specific people forged the category of race? Race was created mainly by Anglo-European, especially English, societies in the 16th to 19th centuries. It was reproduced and transformed over the centuries and throughout most of the inhabited world in the subsequent centuries. To understand the historical specificity of race, we must have a sense of how people conceived of social differences between groups before races were constructed. They did make distinctions among groups, and they did treat some people as inferior, sometimes taking into account some of the features of races, but strictly speaking, they did not understand differences racially. These other constructions were some of the raw materials for the fully-fledged racial concept.

First, many premodern societies distinguished between civilized and uncivilized cultures. As late as 1500, most of the world considered Europe uncivilized. Even Europeans rarely considered themselves more civilized than many other cultures. For several centuries, they had been borrowing civilization from other parts of the world—for example, mathematics, geography, and accounting from the Arab world; spices, tapestry, silk, and gun powder from East Asia; and gold, pottery, and cotton from Africa. When Anglo-Europeans began to colonize the rest of the world, however, they increasingly spoke of themselves as more civilized than the people they were conquering. They began to justify the conquest of non-European regions by contrasting European civilization to non-European barbarism.

Second, Europeans in the centuries prior to the development of race distinguished people on the basis of religion. The Crusades in the 11th to 13th centuries divided the world into "believers" and "heathens." In fact, the concept of "Europe" as a distinct entity, a common bond among diverse people, was forged in the contrast between Christendom and the Muslim world (Mann 1986). Concepts such as freedom, progress, equality, honor, rationality, and individualism that are fundamental to Europeans' self-definition were developed as distinctions between themselves and what they thought Muslims were like. Religion defined a fervent sense of "us" and "them." The word *ethnic* appeared in English around the 15th century to designate a person who was neither Christian nor Jew, that is, a pagan or heathen (Cornell and Hartmann 1998).

Third, people made distinctions among each other in terms of territorial identity. The territory was rarely national, more often regional or local: the people of the Auvergne, the people of the Yucatan, the people of Annam. The meaningful category here is native versus stranger. Think of the dual meaning of *strange*. It can refer to an outsider, someone from a different place, as in "stranger." Or it can refer to the weird, unexplainable, or bizarre. People who live in contact with each other over time develop a sense of "us-ness." They think of strangers as weird and often create labels for "us" and "them" (Simmel 1955). All these categories by which Europeans distinguished groups from each other—civilized or uncivilized, religion, and territoriality—lack essential features of race. First, they are not biological. There was no sense that people were civilized, Christian, or local because of anything in their biology. Nor were these categories seen as immutable; people could change. Indeed, among the world's major religions, Christianity was most oriented toward converting people of other faiths.[15] Similarly, Europeans assumed

---

[15]One important exception was their attitude toward Jews. Before the 15th century, many Jews converted to Christianity, but in the 15th and 16th centuries, Jews and the Christian descendants of Jews, known as *conversos,* were persecuted and even banned from some countries.

that barbarians could become civilized. Pocahontas, the American Indian princess, who in real life would have been considered at best a noble savage, went to England to become an English woman after marrying John Smith. Similarly, there have always been large-scale movements of population from one place to another.

Before the 16th century, Europeans also applied preracial categories to Africans. Europeans went to Africa first as traders, not conquerors. They went first looking for gold and spices, later finding that slaving was profitable in its own right. Early European accounts described Africans as dark, with different religions, but not inherently inferior. Like other slaves at that time, African slaves were seen as the unfortunate victims of circumstances. The first English accounts recognized that they were dealing with sophisticated and intelligent people from well-organized sociopolitical systems.

The overwhelming number of Africans who came to the New World came as slaves, but the categories of African and slave were not equated with each other. In fact, Africans worked in the crews of many early explorers where they were baptized and accepted as part of the Christian community. In 1790, Jean Baptiste Point du Sable, a French-speaking black, erected the first building in what became Chicago. The first Africans in English colonies came as servants in 1619. Many of the early Africans were not slaves but, like many European immigrants, were **indentured servants** who, regardless of skin color, were not free but had some type of binding obligation to someone.[16]

Yet New World Africans were soon reduced to slavery. Why did Africans become the chief source of labor in the New World? First, using Indian or European populations was difficult. The Irish were particularly rebellious. Moreover, European Christians were reluctant to enslave other Christians. Second, there was a ready availability of slaves from highly developed centralized African societies with strong authority that could negotiate with European traders (Wolf 1982). The slave trade further consolidated slaving states, supplying them with arms and other resources to dominate their regions, changing the balance of power within western Africa toward states that were friendly to Europeans. For

---

[16]Indentured servants, who promised to work for a fixed period of time in exchange for passage to America, could be sold like slaves and were often treated like slaves. Most never regained freedom: Only 2 of 10 North American indentured servants became independent farmers or artisans, the rest dying before their contracts expired (Wolf 1982:202).

example, the Assante conquered the Kpembe in 1751 and forced a promise of 1,000 slaves a year as tribute (Wolf 1982).[17] Africans were originally enslaved for the same reasons as Europeans: debts, crimes, conquest, and sale by parents (Patterson 1982). Third, Africans had many features that made them desirable to Europeans colonizing the New World. They were civilized and relatively docile, were knowledgeable about tropical agriculture, had skills such as iron working, and, unlike the inhabitants of the New World, had immunities to Old World diseases, making them a more secure investment for a slave owner. Thus, in the early stages of New World development, Africans were preferred laborers less because they were uncivilized or tribal but because they were more civilized than laborers from other parts of the world.

Fourth, slave traders themselves helped stimulate demand by providing capital and skills to sugar growers in the New World. By the 18th century, slavery was a main commodity with Africa, with the biggest period between 1700 and 1810, when 6 million slaves were transported to New World.

Once Africans were enslaved in the New World, the stage was set for the replacement of preracial categories with the concept of race. The central historical fact is that slavery was absolutely central to the rise of the concept of race. Moreover, it was not just any slavery but **chattel slavery** that defined people as property. African Americans historically are not just a race but *the* race, as the concept is reified in Anglo-European society. It was not that the concept of race existed and people of African ancestry were an example, but the concept was created to fit Europeans' social relationship with people of African ancestry. The social relationship became embodied in the category. Once developed to frame the relation of white to black, the concept of race could be applied to other groups. Chinese, Japanese, and Korean could be defined as "Asian"; Cherokee, Iroquois, and Lakota could be defined as "Indian." And all the characteristics of race could be applied to them.

From Preracial to Racial Categories

How did Europe change from using preracial to racial forms of distinguishing groups? Five factors are especially important: the rise of capi-

---

[17]Colonialism later broke up these strong states and reduced many societies to tribalism. The Kongo had been a West African kingdom with 2.5 million people at the time of European contact but was later colonized until the mid-20th century.

talism, the rise of egalitarian values, the English cultural construct of "the savage," the legitimization of racial concepts by science, and the enforcement of racial dominance by government. Slavery was important to all five factors. Without slavery at the heart of economic, social, and political life in much of the Western Hemisphere, races as we know them would probably not exist today.

The Rise of Capitalism and Egalitarian Values

Before capitalism, people worked for other people because they were forced to, not in exchange for wages and salaries. Some people controlled land because they were given title to it by a king but could not sell it for money. Most food was consumed by the people who grew it, and most products such as clothing were used by the people who made them. The food and manufactured products were sold at prices set by custom even if people were willing to pay more. But, as described in earlier chapters, under capitalism, labor, products, and land became commodities. Even people became commodities, goods that could be bought and sold on the market. Although "free labor" is a fundamental feature of capitalism, slavery, whereby people themselves were commodities, was a central feature of early capitalism.

Before the rise of capitalism, slavery was the most common form of labor throughout the world. Many people conquered other groups and forced the defeated people to work for them. Often, the descendants of the defeated were forced to work as well. Individuals within a society could be forced into slavery as punishment for crime, unpaid debts, or other reasons. But there was considerable variation among the slave societies in the specific rights and obligations that slaves and slave holders had toward each other. Chattel slavery—making slaves a form of property rather than a form of conquest—fostered a more inhuman form of slavery than earlier forms. In many societies, slaves had rights absent in North American chattel slavery: the right to marriage, the right to purchase freedom (manumission), the right to own property, the right to training in some skill, some form of protection for women and children, and some legal redress from cruel punishment (Patterson 1982). When capitalism made slaves into commodities, recognizing a slave's rights contradicted the owner's property rights. Legally, the slave was an object, not a person, and the law supported the owner's right to use his property in any way he wanted to. Before modern states took on the responsibility of guaranteeing other rights, they vigorously enforced property rights. If a person could establish ownership over land, objects, or people, then governments would enforce those claims over other competing claims. Under feudalism, however, when different people had different rights, groups such as clans, guilds, city dwellers, clergymen, nobility, and political leaders each had a different set of rights and responsibilities. With the rise of capitalism, people started to demand equal rights, rights based not on being a member of a group but just by being an individual. Property rights—the right to own, use, and sell commodities, land, and one's own labor—were the most basic of these rights. But other rights such as free speech, religion, and assembly gathered increasing political potency. The language of "rights" became a weapon for the rising capitalist class to commodify and for European people to escape the tyranny of kings. The commodification of humans was historically inseparable from the rise of democracy.

In the 17th and 18th centuries, the contradiction of values became obvious: Negating the doctrine that all people are created equal, there was the stark reality that the economic system, especially in the New World, depended on slavery, in which people were clearly not equal. The contradiction could be reconciled by the concept of race, by defining people who were slaves as inherently, biologically inferior and not fully human. Europeans could sustain the doctrine that men could be treated as individuals rather than members of collectivities and that men were equal before the law at the same time that a major group was enslaved if they could define the difference between free and unfree in terms of natural, biological differences rather than the result of conquest or oppression. It is a profound irony of history that the concept of race was due in part to egalitarian values.

The Concept of "Savage"

The ideology that defined African slaves as racially inferior was strongest in England, where the belief in freedom was strongest, property rights were the most fully institutionalized, and capitalism was the most developed (Smedley 1993). The creation of the modern concept of race did not just come out of the blue. It was not just that someone noticed the contradiction between the ideal of equal rights and economic interests and said, "I have a solution; let's treat slaves as less than human." New developments are rooted in existing conditions. One of the main cultural roots of race concept was the English concept of the savage, which the

English developed to characterize the Irish (Smedley 1993). At a time when the English were beginning to define themselves as civilized, the category of savage denoted the total opposite of everything English; insofar as the English considered themselves the highest form of humanity, savages were considered the lowest. The Irish were defined as incorrigible, unchanging, and, most important, impossible to civilize. Unlike cultural differences by which members of one group could learn to assimilate into other groups, savagery was considered hereditary. The savage was inferior and subhuman. Stereotypes depicted the Irish as lazy, filthy, evil, lying, stealing, murdering, and even cannibalistic. While the category of savagery has obvious similarities to race, it was not fully racial because it was not based on obvious physical characteristics. But as a protoracial category, it played an important role in the rise of race as a category.

The relationship between the concept of freedom and the concept of savage helped distinguish the way that Anglo-Europeans defined American Indians and African Americans. Both became defined as savage. That is, both were seen as categorical "others" who lacked civilization because of their "inherent" inferiority. Neither was accorded basic rights such as property rights. But there was a major difference. American Indians were free, not slaves. Thus, they were defined more often, at least in the first couple of centuries after Anglo-Europeans first came to America, as "noble savages"—as human beings in the state of nature, uncorrupted by civilization (Banton 1998). But this imputed innocence was used against them, justifying the appropriation of their land. As "uncivilized" people, they had no understanding of private property, so their claims to land were dismissed, allowing Anglo-Europeans to settle the "vacant" land. But the English did not enslave them and even recognized their societies as legitimate enough to negotiate treaties, a type of agreement made among sovereign states, even if those treaties were rarely honored. Even after the development of the concept of "savage," there was not a full-fledged concept of race. Many who considered Africans or Native Americans to be uncivilized understood the contrasts to Anglo-Europeans in terms other than inherent biological differences. For example, in the mid-18th century, French philosopher Montesquieu explained differences among cultures in terms of climate. People in northern climates such as Europe were more vigorous and had forms of government appropriate for that kind of people. People from warmer climates such as Africa were slower and more childlike. He felt that people should stay put rather than move, including those forced to move like the enslaved Africans (Banton 1998; Hannaford 1996). Later images of Africa would not bother to "explain" differences among Europeans and Africans by social or environmental factors such as climate but would essentialize differences so that "race" would be the only explanation offered. Africans and their descendants would be stereotyped as lazy, ignorant, vicious, or promiscuous simply because they were "black."

How Science Reinforced and Legitimated the Concept of Race

Although science did not discover or invent race or racial categories, it reinforced and legitimated the concept of race, fostering its reification. Like all the categories examined in this book, race was created for one purpose but has been reproduced and reconstructed for other purposes. The fact that race was constructed to justify and administer chattel slavery does not explain why it has persisted and takes the forms found today. This is where science and law are especially important.

At various times, biology, anthropology, genetics, statistics, sociology, and other sciences have proclaimed not only the essential reality of races but also the superiority of the white race. They defined races as natural, biological groups that are genetically distinguishable from each other and used these differences to explain behavioral differences between people of different races. This biological understanding of race was developed and diffused in the 18th and 19th centuries in a self-conscious and sometimes overtly racist manner (Banton 1998; Hannaford 1996; Smedley 1993). Even before "natural science" constructed the biological sense of race, philosophers imputed race to a state of nature, something rooted in biology and unchangeable. Some scholars such as Hegel, Kant, Hume, and Locke issued "virulently racist opinions" (Omi and Winant 1994:63). The eminent French philosopher Voltaire (1694-1778) wrote that "the negro race is a species of men as different from ours ... as the breed of spaniels is from that of greyhounds.... They are not capable of any great application or association of ideas" (Omi and Winant 1994:63).

Scientific pronouncements on race were not based on the scientific method accepted today. There were no experiments. Rather, scientists' notion of race was based on the attempt to classify different populations. Beginning in the 16th century, they used Latin terms and formal language to convert folk categories such as black and white into supposedly scientific principles. For example, Swedish naturalist Carolus Linnaeus (1707-1778), who invented the system of biological classification, defined species as groups of organisms that have important similarities but do not interbreed. Yet he defined races as different species and attributed behavioral differences to biology. *Homo sapiens afer* (Africans), he wrote, are "ruled by caprice," while *Homo sapiens europaeus* are "ruled by customs" (Gould 1981:35).

Nonetheless, theories of this sort did not have broad social acceptance before the 18th century and did not constitute a fully developed theory of race (Banton 1998; Hannaford 1996), in part because religious understandings still prevailed over scientific thought. The Christian church was still one of the dominant institutions, and its account of the origins of humanity, expressed in the story of Adam and Eve, held that all humans had a common ancestry.[18] Christianity's view of humanity constrained the development of fully developed racism.[19]

In the 18th and especially the 19th centuries, when religious doctrines of a common ancestry were giving way to science, the scientific definition of race increasingly treated races as incompatible with each other. Race became essentialized as a totalistic characteristic of a person, not just a superficial feature such as skin color. More important, science not only tried to "prove" that races were biologically different but also tried to "prove" that blacks were inferior, giving legitimacy to a common folk belief.[20] They compared skulls and studied brains, "discovering" important differences. Charles Lyell, founder of modern geology, wrote in 1812, "The brain of the Bushman [African] . . . leads toward the brain of the simiadae [monkeys]. Each race of Man has its place, like the inferior animals" (Gould 1981:36). Even Charles Darwin, the most influential scientist of the 19th century, wrote that Africans were halfway between Caucasians and apes. Scientists in the second half of the 19th century

---

[18]Some writers claimed a biblical justification for racism based on the passage in which Noah's son Ham was condemned to be a "servant of servants" (in *Genesis* 10:25-26). Although there was no biblical mention of Ham's complexion or any account of his descendants, this was claimed to be the origin of African peoples.

[19]That is not to say that Christians were never racists. Southern slave owners were Christians who had no problem finding a racist justification for slavery, which, they argued, had biblical justification.

[20]The linking of physical difference and inferiority is found even in the thought of Abraham Lincoln: "There is physical difference between the white and the black races which I believe will forever forbid the two races living together on terms of social and political equality" (Gould 1981:35).

continued the quantitative study of humans with the science of "anthropometry," which developed detailed studies of brains to prove that whites were smarter than blacks, males smarter than females, upper class smarter than lower class, and law-abiding people smarter than criminals. In 1906, Robert Bennett Bean found that skulls of blacks were smaller than those of whites and drew behavioral conclusions:

> The Negro is primarily affectionate, immensely emotional, then sensual and under stimulation passionate. There is love of ostentation, and capacity for melodious articulation; there is undeveloped artistic power and taste . . . and there is instability of character incident to lack of self-control, especially in connection with the sexual relation. (Gould 1981:79)

These were the stereotypes of blacks around the turn of the century.

Figure 4.1 illustrates how these scientists distorted their evidence to prove that racial groups were not only different but that blacks were also inferior. These 1868 "scientific" drawings purport to prove that the skull of a "Negro" is more like a chimpanzee than like a white person, represented here by a classic Greek sculpture. A backward sloping face was supposedly a sign of weak mental capacity. The drawing of the "Negro" both misshapes the skull itself and tilts it backwards to emphasize the sloping. Notice also that the drawing of the live "Negro" is drawn to look like the chimpanzee, with dark color, flat nose, and creased brow.

Later researchers remeasured Bean's skulls without knowing which came from blacks and whites and found no differences in skull size. Too easy to falsify, anthropometry eventually died out. The examples cited all share the error of **biological reductionism,** the attempt to explain behavioral differences between groups on the basis of biological differences. The attempt to measure behavioral differences directly can also go awry, as it did with intelligence testing. At the end of the 19th century, Alfred Binet, the director of a psychology laboratory in Paris, set out to find a way to identify children who needed special attention in school. He used pencil-and-paper tests and insisted that intelligence was too complex to capture in one number. Others, however, developed the IQ ("intelligence quotient") score to measure a child's intelligence in relation to his or her mental age.

The IQ test was brought to this country by Lewis Terman, a professor at Stanford University, who revised it into the Stanford-Binet Test, the standard IQ test in this country. While Binet had intended the test only for children, Terman added questions for adults, claiming that the test measured innate (genetic) intelligence. Very soon, the test was used to make comparisons among groups, which Terman explained racially:

FIGURE 4.1

"Scientific" Drawing of Head Shapes

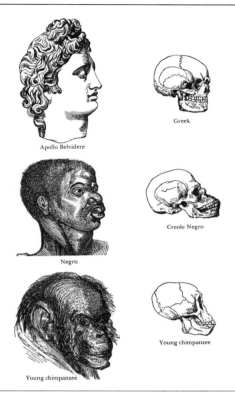

SOURCE: Nott and Gliddon (1868).

They represent the level of intelligence which is very, very common among Spanish-Indian and Mexican families of the Southwest and also among negroes. Their dullness seems to be racial, or at least inherent in the family stocks from which they came. . . . They cannot master abstractions, but they can often be made efficient workers, able to look out for themselves. There is no possibility at present of convincing society that they should not be allowed to reproduce, although from a eugenic point of view they constitute a grave problem because of their unusually prolific breeding. (Gould 1981:190-91)

In retrospect, it is not surprising that testers found large differences between racial and ethnic groups; the tests were blatantly biased. They required knowledge of the culture of the white majority with questions such as the following: "Crisco is: a patent medicine, a disinfectant, tooth-paste, food product. The number of a Kaffir's legs is: 2, 4, 6, 8. Christy Mathewson is famous as a: writer, artist, baseball player, comedian" (Gould 1981:200). When the test was criticized for being biased toward the literate and against recent immigrants, it was replaced by a nonverbal test. Figure 4.2 shows an example. It is easy to see that the nonverbal test is just as culturally biased as the written test. Only people raised in middle- or upper-class white families would know what a phonograph or tennis court should look like.

The problem was that the development of intelligence testing was part of the historical construction of the modern concept of race. The test creators were trying to prove what they assumed, that there was a biological basis to cultural differences. The tests were part of the reflexive relationship between the racial category and science. The existence of folk categories led to attempts to prove differences in races, leading to stronger boundaries between racial groups, reproducing the social "reality" of race, and giving scientific legitimization to popular attitudes about that "reality." Science legitimated the concept of race by naturalizing folk categories and making white dominance seem inherent and unchangeable.

As much as science influenced people's opinions, it can be ignored when people choose. It seems that science was more successful in legitimating the creation of racial categories than in ending them. Contemporary scientists have attempted to correct earlier conceptions. As an account in the *Los Angeles Times* stated,

> Researchers adept at analyzing genetic threads of human diversity said Sunday that the concept of race—the source of abiding cultural and political divisions in American society—simply has no basis in fundamental human biology. Scientists should abandon it, they said. Their controversial conclusion grows out of a more precise understanding of the underlying genetics of the human species and how surface distinctions of skin color, hair and facial features, which may loom large in daily life, have nothing to do with basic biological human differences. ("Scientists Say Race" 1995:A1)

Still, many people consider race a natural and real "thing." The influence of science is also limited by the fact that it only affects how people think; it has no power to enforce its theories. The law is not limited in the same way.

FIGURE 4.2

Nonverbal Army Intelligence Test

SOURCE: Yerkes (1921).

How the Law Fostered and
Enforced Racial Categories

Wherever the fully developed concept of race has appeared, it has been codified into law. "White," "black," "Asian," "Native American," and so on have been legal categories. This has two major consequences: (1) It reinforces the sense that races seem "real." One must have "pure" blood to be white. (2) It creates the conditions that keep races different from each other. Even after the end of slavery, blacks in many parts of the United States were forced to attend black schools, eat in black restaurants, and were prohibited from marrying whites.

When people think of America as "predominantly" white, it is often assumed that this is because more Europeans chose to immigrate here than other groups. But that is not fully the case. American policy has actively recruited European immigrants while discouraging and at times prohibiting nonwhite immigrants. One of the acts of the very first U.S. Congress in 1790 was a law allowing immigrants to become naturalized citizens. But it specifically stated that only "whites" could do so. In the late 19th and early 20th centuries, this led to some interesting court cases in which judges had to decide who was white (Haney Lopez 1996). For example, in 1878, a man of Chinese descent applied for citizenship, resulting in a court case, *in re Ah Yup* (1 F. Cas. 223 [Cir. Ct. D. Cal. 1878]). The court, after considering scientific, legal, and popular knowledge, denied him citizenship, ruling that Chinese are not white. In 1923, the U.S. Supreme Court, in a case involving Syrians and Asian Indians, ruled that common knowledge, not science, was the final arbiter of who is white. The plaintiffs had argued that Syrians and Asian Indians are defined by science as Caucasian, and Caucasians are white. Therefore, they should be considered white. But the Court ruled that it was common knowledge that Syrians and Asian Indians are not white, admitting that race is more a social construction than a scientific concept. It also reflected courts' frustration with science's failure to develop objective boundaries for races, which science could not have done independently of common knowledge because that is where races are constructed (Haney Lopez 1996). Using common knowledge to legally decide who was white, however, only applied to the group, not the individual. If common knowledge held that Asian Indians were socially not white, the Supreme Court validated that legally they were not white. Rejecting common knowledge about particular individuals to legally decide their race, courts used essentialist notions of what race that person really was on the basis of how pure their blood was. In the early 20th century, in *Sunseri v.*

Cassagne (191 La. 209, 185 So. 1), a husband, Sunseri, sued to annul his marriage with Cassagne because he claimed she had a trace of "negro blood"—the allegation that her great-great-grandmother was black. She had been regarded as white in the community, raised as a white, attended white schools, christened in a white church, and had socialized exclusively with whites. Only her birth certificate designated her as nonwhite. The court ruled that she was therefore not white and that the marriage could thus be annulled (Harris 1993:1740). This sort of ruling sustains a hard, uncrossable boundary between the races, protecting the husband from the social stigma of being married to a nonwhite and terminating a marriage that might create "black" children. It also illustrates the principle that whiteness is a status for which purity must be proved. The fact that a person had been always known as white did not constitute her legal standing as a white. "In effect, the courts erected legal 'No Trespassing' signs" into the white race (Harris 1993:1741). In 1857, the U.S. Supreme Court, in *Dred Scott v. Sanford*, ruled that the descendant of a slave could not sue in a public court. The ruling treated races as legally binding categories:

> They [blacks] had for more than a century before been regarded as beings of an inferior order, and altogether unfit to associate with the white race, either in social or political relations; and so far inferior, that they had no rights which the white man was bound to respect; and that the Negro might justly and lawfully be reduced to slavery for his benefit. He was bought and sold, and treated as an ordinary article of merchandise and traffic, whenever a profit could be made by it. ("*Dred Scott v. Sanford*" 1857/1995:323).

The judges stated that the reference to "all men" in the Declaration of Independence referred only to white men.

Before the civil rights movement of the 1960s, segregation was not only permitted but also legally required in southern states. African Americans were required to go to black schools, and whites were legally required to go to white schools. Social institutions from public drinking fountains to marriage were mandated to be racially separate. And anyone with "one drop" of black blood was defined as black. Recent court decisions enforcing employers, universities, and other institutions allocating valued resources to be color-blind require these institutions to be blind to the very real effect of race. For example, in one case, a white person laid off because an employer chose racial diversity over seniority sued to keep his job. The court ruled that seniority had to be honored rather than diversity, despite the fact that older employees were predominantly white because of past discrimination. The effects of race were built into the existing system, and being "color-blind" meant perpetuating that inequality.

Whiteness

These court cases suggest that it is not just minority races that have been constructed. "Whiteness" is just as historically constructed as any other race. In fact, it is impossible to understand how the races in America have been constructed without taking into account how whiteness was being constructed at the same time. One cannot construct minority races without constructing a "majority" race; one cannot attribute negative attributes to one group without attributing positive attributes to another. One cannot have boundaries without groups on both sides. One cannot have "black" without "white." This is not just a logical relationship but also a historical one.

The construction of the white race was neither simple nor uncontested. While it seems relatively clear today which groups are white and which are not, it has not always been so. Jacobson (1998) identifies three periods of whiteness. In the first period, lasting from colonial times to the 1840s, Anglo-Americans defined themselves as white as the obverse side of defining blackness and were fairly inclusive in who was included. In the second period, immigrants from eastern and southern Europe on the Atlantic and China and Japan on the Pacific streamed to the Americas in large numbers. Just as the mere presence of African origins of slaves in North America automatically led to the construction of blackness, groups such as Italians, Irish, Jews, and Poles were considered inferior races, not just different ethnicities. In fact, until the 1940s, it was not clear whether the line between white and nonwhite would be drawn within Europeans or around Europeans. In the third period, after immigration from anywhere except western Europe was blocked by the Immigration Law of 1924, whiteness became inclusive again, as other European groups became redefined as white ethnicities rather than races (Jacobson 1998). The category of race settled into the meaning familiar to most Americans today.

As Anglo-Europeans increasingly lumped slaves together as "black" and indigenous societies as "red," they increasingly lumped themselves together as "white." The first connotation for "white" as a social category was a synonym for *free* (Roediger 1991). Most nonfarming working people were artisans (independent craftspeople who make things such as shoes, silverware, books, etc.). Artisans boldly insisted that they were free and that no matter how bad off they might be, they were better than slaves. Whiteness was an important part of their identity and a matter of pride. This commitment to freedom was important to the development of a revolutionary consciousness. The complaint that the English were treating them like slaves was a powerful stimulus to the unprecedented act of declaring independence from a colonial power. But it was a freedom that was defined in racial terms. They could not stand the feeling that they were being reduced to the level of blacks. And it was a freedom that was reserved for white people. The concepts of freedom and whiteness were developed together and defined in terms of each other. Before Anglo-Europeans enslaved peoples of Africa in the New World, neither freedom nor whiteness meant anything to most people. Although freedom is one of America's most cherished values, many cultures have had little or no sense of freedom as a specific concept. For most people in most societies, material needs, security, and a respected position in a group have been more immediate and compelling aspirations than freedom (Patterson 1982). Freedom developed as the opposite of slavery. Anglo-European society has a negative view of freedom: Freedom means being not enslaved. Without slavery, people could not have conceived of the idea of freedom. While black slaves desired freedom, it was guaranteed for whites—indeed, a privilege of whiteness. Among the freedoms of being white was the right to own blacks.[21] As lawyer Cheryl Harris puts it, "Whiteness was the characteristic, the attribute, the property of free human beings" (Harris 1993:1721). So who is white? The English language still has the term **WASP**—white Anglo-Saxon Protestant—as a synonym for white, and some people lump Catholics and Jews into it. But there was a time when only WASPs were considered white—when the distinction between WASP and other Europeans was constructed as racial. In the United States, what are now considered ethnic groups such as the Irish, Jews, or Italians were once seen as immutable races (Ignatiev 1995; Sacks 1998). In 1891, a New Orleans white supremacist mob lynched 11 Italian immigrants suspected of plotting to murder the chief of police. Lynching made appallingly concrete the rhetoric that Italians were not considered white. The *New York Times* praised the action, characterizing Italians as less than human:

[21]Former slaves were known as *freedmen,* a term that carries the connotation of someone who is "naturally" a slave, freed only by an explicit act. Even blacks born free were called freedmen. *Free man* was a term reserved for whites.

> These sneaking and cowardly Sicilians, who have transplanted to this
> country the lawless passions, the cutthroat practices, and the oathbound
> societies of their native country, are to us a pest without mitigation. Our
> own rattlesnakes are as good citizens as they. (Jacobson 1998:56)

Perhaps someday people will look back on this era and wonder how people in the 20th century considered distinctions among black, white, yellow, brown, and red in the same quaint terms people today look back on those who thought Irish, Italians, or Jews were distinct immutable races. The "whitening" of the Irish illustrates how the meaning of racial categories has changed. Skin color has become a more central feature of racial categories. Most people today find it anomalous to think of people with similar physical features as different races. The largest group excluded from whiteness because of ethnic and religious reasons was the Irish. Earlier, we saw how the English constructed the notion of "savage" to describe their opinions of the Irish. In Britain, the Irish were considered a race with virtually no civil or economic rights. When the Catholic Irish first began to come to the United States in the late 18th and early 19th centuries, they were thrown together with blacks residentially and in the same jobs.[22] In the eyes of the dominant English Protestant elite, and perhaps themselves, they were socially closer to the free blacks of northern cities than to the English. They faced considerable prejudice and discrimination because they were considered "niggers turned inside out," and blacks were sometimes called "smoked Irish." Figure 4.3 illustrates an 1876 cartoon equating the Irish and African Americans. A balancing scale shows the black on the south side of the balance and the Irish, who is not only drawn in dark hues but also with animalistic features, in a pan ironically labeled "white" on the north side. The caption that accompanied this cartoon, "The ignorant vote-honors are easy" implies that both threaten the integrity of the political system. Eventually, the Irish became racially categorized along with Anglo-Saxons and other Europeans by proclaiming themselves as not black. Initially seen in a status comparable to nonwhites, they aspired to define themselves as white. If they became white, they would no longer be restricted to certain occupations and particular industries or excluded from democratic participation. They succeeded in being defined as white by the operation of a dominant institution—politics—and its relationship to slavery.

---

[22]Most of the Irish immigrants before 1830 were Protestant, many of them descendants of the Scottish. When the Catholics began to come in large numbers, the descendants of the earlier Protestants created the term *Scotch-Irish* to distinguish themselves.

FIGURE 4.3

Political Cartoon Equating Blacks and Irish in *Harper's Weekly* (1876)

The truth is not, as some historians would have it, that slavery made it possible to extend to the Irish the privileges of citizenship, by providing another group for them to stand on, but the reverse, that the assimilation of the Irish into the white race made it possible to maintain slavery. (Ignatiev 1995:69)

As with the construction of the black race, it was not racism that made slavery possible, but slavery created racism.

The Democratic Party needed Irish voters to fight the growing antislavery Republican Party. Not only did the Democratic Party ease the inclusion of the Irish into the category of white, but it also rejected attempts to define the Irish as a race halfway between white and black. During the first half of the 19th century, a very active movement called *nativism* expressed vitriolic resentment toward immigrants from everywhere but England and western Europe along with open racism toward blacks and Native Americans. Only native-born white Anglo-Saxon Protestants were acceptable to the nativists. The Democratic Party took a stand against nativism, though not against racism. At a time when only white men of considerable means were allowed to vote, the Democratic Party pressed to expand the franchise for whites while restricting it for blacks. For example, Pennsylvania, which had one of the largest concentrations of Irish immigrants, over the first half of the century gradually broadened white suffrage and restricted black suffrage until 1837 and 1838, when black voters were officially disenfranchised (Ignatiev 1995: 77; Roediger 1991:57, 59). Opposing nativism, the democratic movement drove a wedge between two of the largest dispossessed groups. Instead of the privileged facing off against the lowly, the Irish joined the other fair-skinned Europeans to crystallize the category of whiteness. The conflict of classes was reconfigured into the polarity of race. As part of a proslavery political coalition, Irish radicals were given important offices, allowing them to distribute precious jobs to other Irish Americans. Membership in the coalition was the launching pad to inclusion in political and social life in general.

The construction of whiteness in the political arena was parallel to its construction in the economic institution. Although some historians have emphasized the competition among Irish and blacks for jobs, there was nothing specifically racial about the economic competition (Ignatiev 1995; Allen 1997). The Irish were also competing with Germans, Italians, and other Europeans. The competition did not become racialized until after the Irish began to take over certain occupations, especially in new industries such as textiles and in service jobs such as cooks, stewards, waiters, and house servants. When they competed for these new jobs, they pushed to define these jobs as "white man's work." This meant excluding blacks, refusing to work with blacks, and even going on strike or committing sabotage if blacks were hired. They were inventing a new notion that some jobs "belong" to some racial groups while other jobs "belong" to other groups. For example, a Longshoremen's United Benevolent Society, formed in 1852, declared that "work upon the docks . . . shall be attended solely and absolutely by members of the 'Longshoremen's Association,' and such white laborers as they see fit to permit upon the premises" (Ignatiev 1995:120).

The political coalition against the antislaves Republican Party and the economic exclusion of free blacks from "white" jobs helped crystallize the concept of whiteness as a taken-for-granted category. Whites differ from other races because whiteness is transparent (Hale 1998; Haney Lopez 1996; Harris 1993; Roediger 1991). It is the taken-for-granted or the "unmarked case." That means that people who have it do not notice it until it is somehow challenged. Most whites do not think of being white except when they are in the presence of a predominantly nonwhite group. Their race is thus transparent.

The law reflects this sense of whiteness. Centuries of explicitly racist laws helped create social conditions in which whites had explicit privileges because they were white, leaving a legacy of poverty, crime, and hopelessness among other groups. While those conditions were being created, there was little public discussion about whiteness or white privileges. Yet attempts to change those conditions, to compensate for some of the disadvantages that minorities face, evoke demands that the law become "color-blind." But to be color-blind means to be blind to the conditions that handicap people in slums, those who attend ghetto schools, and those who must cope with street criminals. When people think they are victims of "reverse discrimination," their race becomes very visible, and they may become quite adamant in protecting their privileges. So whiteness becomes reconstructed into a form of victimization that the law must protect against.

Reflexivity

Since the development of the racial worldview in the early modern period, the concept of race has been used to create new forms of inequality; these new forms of inequality reinforce the concept of race as "common sense." Slavery bullied blacks into a docile demeanor and then used the stereotype of childlike servility to justify slavery. Blacks were said to be docile and childlike, to shuffle and mumble, to be lazy. The stereotype implied that they needed slavery because they were not capable of taking care of themselves. Edward Pollard, a proslavery writer, described,

> I love to study his [black person's] affectionate heart; I love to mark that
> peculiarity in him, which beneath all his buffoonery exhibits him as a
> creature of the tenderest sensibilities, mingling his joys and sorrows with
> those of his master's home. (Takaki 1990:117)

After slavery, when blacks began to assert themselves, the stereotype became the exact opposite of the earlier image. Blacks were seen as menac-
ing, threatening, and brutelike. In 1906, the *Atlanta Constitution* editorial-
ized that

> the negro . . . grows more bumptious on the street. . . . When he cannot
> achieve social equality as he wishes, with the instinct of the barbarian to
> destroy what he cannot attain to, he lies in wait, as that dastardly brute did
> yesterday near this city, and assaults the fair young girlhood of the south.
> (Woodward 1969:379)

Such a view implies a need for repressive control. The most extreme reac-
tion was public lynchings, in which white crowds, often with the approval of authorities, would hang blacks accused of sexual misconduct,
disobedience, or public disturbance. During the 1890s alone, more than
1,000 African Americans were lynched, most in the South. This century
repeated the same sequence. Up until the 1950s, African Americans were
widely depicted as docile, incapable of functioning in the white world.
Predominant media images included Stepin Fetchit, an obliging but
cheerful black man usually in a menial job, and Amos 'n Andy, two characters (played by whites), on radio and later on TV, who were usually
shown conniving for money, losing at love, and avoiding work. Then, the
predominant white image of blacks reversed again. Since 1970, the prev-
alent image in white-controlled media has been that African Americans
are demanding and getting more than they deserve. Blacks are depicted
as welfare mothers who shun jobs in favor of handouts and more children, criminals who steal to feed drug habits, and affirmative action beneficiaries who get jobs and other goods that fairness would give to
whites. Instead of paternalism for the docile but inadequate, the image
invites greater discipline and tighter control.

Racial inequality leads to concrete social differences such as residential segregation, educational differences, and language differences that
are then used to "prove" the importance of race as a social category. This
reflexive relationship between race and inequality reinforces the racial
divisions that divide the nation. The causal direction goes both ways between the objective conditions and the images of inferiority, continually
reconstructing and reproducing the categorization of people into races.

Race is also reproduced reflexively on a microsocial basis. The dynamics of everyday life reinforce the visibility and importance of race in the ways that people interact with each other. Less important than the way that people feel about race is what they *know,* because people's behavior is often more powerfully determined by what is "realistic" than what people want the world to be like.

Reproducing Race

People are socialized to learn that races are "real." Children from a very early age are aware of racial differences, long before they are aware of class, religious, political, or other distinctions that are important to adults. Racial differences bombard children from all angles—friends, school, mass media, and family. Even when they are told that racial differences should not matter, they can see that they do. Socialization then continues throughout the life course, as racial categories themselves change over time. Perhaps reading this book is socializing you into thinking of race in a new way.

While the modern concept of race was invented to categorize African Americans, once created, it could be extended to other groups such as Latinos, Asians, and American Indians. The fundamental properties are same: hereditary, rigid boundaries, attribution of behavior from physical characteristics, legal and scientific validation, and so on. But the particulars are adapted. The stereotypes depict Asians as working too hard and being inscrutable and cliquish. Other stereotypes hold that Latinos refuse to learn English, are less capable of abstract reasoning, and that Latino men flaunt the exaggerated masculinity of *machismo* while the women shrink in submissiveness. Reflexivity is at work here too. Every time Asians or Latinos are discussed in racial terms, it reinforces the general category of race. The continuing application of the racial concept allows discussion of Asians and Latinos to "make sense."

Essentialist and constructionist views of race differ less in the degree of difference between the behavior of races than in their explanation of it. Essentialist views treat differences as an essential or genetic characteristic of the race; constructionist views treat differences as cultural or learned. Moreover, behavioral differences apply only as generalities, not to each specific member of a race. While one race may on the average talk louder than another, be more individualistic, be more professionally ambitious, or play some sports better, no single individual in any race necessarily conforms to this. Reflexivity means that some of these differences

reinforce racial distinctions. A poor African American male may learn to talk a particular way, walk a style, and dress a particular fashion. Those behaviors, not just his skin color, signal that he is African American, and those behaviors become reinforced as racial markers. Boys or men who identify and want to appear as African American adopt those behaviors. And racial categories become perpetuated.

Identity

One of the results of socialization is racial identity. **Identity** is the sense that people have of themselves in relationship to others, a sense of "us" and "them," including the attributes that denote some people as "like me" or others "not like me." In the decades since the civil rights movement of the 1960s, minority groups have articulated strong racial and ethnic identities. While self-conscious identity has had many benefits, it does contribute to the reflexive reinforcement of racial categories. Conservative whites have used such sentiments to justify abandoning egalitarian and remedial policies designed to overcome the effects of past discrimination. Self-conscious racial identities have intensified and given new meaning to the kinds of specific behaviors that characterize different races.

Intersections

Given how pervasively race permeates modern society, it is not surprising that basic categories of perception such as time and space structure race relations and help reproduce inequality between races. Residential segregation illustrates the intersection of space and race, while the issue of affirmative action raises important questions about time and race.

Racial Segregation

There is no more compelling example of the way that race intersects with space than racial segregation. It is a social truism that people tend to live in neighborhoods in which most other residents share race or ethnicity. Whites live near mostly whites, blacks live near mostly blacks, and Latinos live near mostly Latinos, and so forth. Many people attribute that to preference, explaining such segregation as choice—people choose to live near other people like themselves. But the American pattern of racial segregation is less than a century old. Before the early 20th century, neighborhoods in most cities were more racially integrated. Whites, blacks, and, in some regions, Latinos or Asians lived close to one another, even if middle-class whites lived in the large homes on the street while poorer blacks, often alongside newly immigrated families, lived in the alleys. Several dominant institutions helped create ghettos in the 1920s. Real estate agents obstructed blacks from middle- and upper-class neighborhoods by refusing to show them houses or apartments. Bankers rejected applications for home loans in minority neighborhoods, a practice known as "redlining" because they used maps with red lines to indicate the boundaries of exclusion. At the same time, in neighborhoods adjacent to where minorities lived, real estate agents would tell white residents that the neighborhood was going downhill because of the influx of minorities and offer to sell their homes quickly. If the homeowners declined, the agents would return after a few homes had sold and make a lower offer. Even people who would have welcomed an integrated neighborhood usually capitulated to avoid losing the value of their homes. So neighborhoods changed very quickly. Once-fashionable neighborhoods such as Harlem in New York, the North Side of Chicago, or Watts in Los Angeles were transformed into racial ghettos, spatializing race. In the 1940s and 1950s, government accelerated the process by promoting the rise of suburbs, regions on the outskirts of cities. The Federal Housing Administration subsidized the construction of millions of suburban homes, while other agencies built the highways and freeways enabling people to live in the suburbs and work in cities. When administered in the context of redlining, the "American Dream" of life in suburbia became available only to whites, leaving cities organized like doughnuts (Massey and Denton 1993).

Once in place, the spatial segregation of races actively reproduces inequality. The ghetto is not only a place where minorities happen to live but also a place of concentrated poverty. When a "declining neighborhood" begins to have abandoned buildings, shabby exteriors, and the visible presence of stigmatized persons such as the homeless or drug dealers, the combination of racial minorities and poverty becomes reified as a ghetto. Landlords refuse to improve apartment buildings; banks, even if they are not racially motivated, refuse to finance building or renovation; crime increases; and people with the means to leave do so. At some point, the process reaches the point when it is nonreversible and self-reproducing (Massey and Denton 1993). People in the ghetto have little access to skills, jobs, contacts, or other resources of the outside world, and those outside have little knowledge of the deprivation, life experience, or lack of opportunities faced by those in it. In other words, the spatial organization of the city becomes an active factor in perpetuating racial inequality.

Space also has a class meaning. Beverly Hills, the Upper East Side of New York, and the Gold Coast of Chicago endow their residents with high class, just as the South Bronx, Watts, and the South Side of Chicago stigmatize their residents in the eyes of many. As the cliché about the three most important factors in real estate says, "Location, location, location." But the meaning of *location* is not coincidental and not just a passing consequence of people of one class living together, especially for the wealthy. Through zoning laws, deed covenants that restrict what owners can do and build on property, and the erection of gates, the well-to-do keep their communities exclusive. One of the most vivid examples is Fisher Island, off the coast of Miami, Florida, which can only be reached by boat or helicopter. Its promoters describe the community of condominiums, villas, tennis courts, and swimming pools designed around a Mediterranean motif as "a unique, exclusive enclave for the elite . . . comfortably insulated from the rest of the world while being only minutes away" (Wyckoff 1989:341). On the other coast, the city of Santa Barbara requires that all construction must be approved by a planning commission that requires conformity to a single architectural style, down to the type of tile that can be used, ensuring that the upscale city maintains an aesthetically uniform image.

Affirmative Action

Although affirmative action to help minorities achieve equality in such social desirables as college admissions, hiring, and promotion illustrates how race intersects with time, opponents of affirmative action believe that past discrimination against minorities does not justify current "preferences" for members of groups who suffered at the hands of earlier generations. They argue that society should be color-blind and avoid "reverse discrimination." Proponents rebut that time does matter, that inequality created in the past perpetuates itself unless there are explicit actions to overcome disadvantages that still exist. Race was historically constructed not only as a concept but also as a set of concrete social relations that people had to major institutions. Inequality is not just a matter of personal prejudice and the attitudes that people have about each other; it also includes institutional racism. **Institutional racism** refers to the practices of institutions that have the effect, whether intended or not, of perpetuating inequality between races. Because of institutional racism, the construction of racism from the past continues over time into the future—unless there is explicit, overt action to reverse the past effects. Races were historically constructed as very "real," not the figment of the imagination and not something well-meaning people can turn off by declaring that it no longer matters. Becoming color-blind to race does not make its effects disappear; it only blinds us to those effects. Time intersects race through the operation of color-blind institutions.

Suppose an employer in an industry with few minority engineers decides she wants a workforce that reflects the population, so she decides to be color-blind, hiring only the most qualified applicants regardless of race. When jobs open up, most applicants will continue to be white because the most common means by which people find out about jobs is through their friends and neighbors (Granovetter 1974). Since friendship groups and neighborhoods are racially homogeneous, most of the current white employees will have white friends and neighbors. But even if applicants from minority groups learn of the job, few of them will be qualified because few of them will have educational qualifications. The legacy of the past is that in fact fewer minorities are as qualified as whites. So the solution is to enroll more minorities in colleges and universities, so that more can become engineers for our color-blind employer. But if colleges and universities are color-blind, they will admit only the top applicants from high schools. A disproportionate number of minorities live in neighborhoods with inferior schools and grow up in homes where parents often lack the skills to help them with homework or the means to buy them books or enroll them in courses to take the SAT. Color-blind colleges and universities will admit fewer minorities. In color-blind elementary schools, teachers will pay more attention to the students who speak Standard English, whose parents help them with homework and come to parent-teacher conferences, and who seem intelligent. Thus, the students who get the teacher's attention will be disproportionately white middle-class students. If more minorities had jobs such as in engineering, they could afford to live in neighborhoods with better schools, buy books, and help their children with homework. Thus, there is a cycle of inequality. Even if all racial prejudice and discrimination ended tomorrow, racial differences would be perpetuated in a color-blind society because of the way that institutions are linked to each other—business to university, university to school, school to family, and family to business. The only way to end racial inequality is to break that cycle.

But doesn't that mean replacing one kind of prejudice with another to substitute reverse discrimination for old-fashioned antiminority discrimination? No, it means defining qualification with a different time orientation. Instead of defining qualification in terms of solely what people have done in the past, qualification can be defined in terms of what people are expected to do in the future. For example, take admissions to higher education, something most of you readers have succeeded at or you would probably not be reading this book. Most colleges and universities base their admissions on grades in high school test scores, such as the SAT, letters of recommendation, and extracurricular activities. When people have identical grades, scores, letters, and activities, they might be considered equally qualified. But if one of those applicants attended an inferior school, had no books at home, grew up speaking non–Standard English, and was treated by teachers as less intelligent because of skin color, that student would be expected to succeed better in college and thereafter, even though the student's current qualifications look comparable. Since 36% of Hispanic children and 43% of black children live in poverty, compared to 12% of white children (Danziger and Gottschalk 1995:90), the minority children are the ones most likely to be deprived of the opportunity to develop the conventional qualifications they need to compete. If one assessed their future and not just their past, their qualifications would be very different. This is what affirmative action does. It considers the effect of past discrimination and institutional discrimination (not just the fact that someone's ancestors were slaves 150 years ago) to redefine that meaning of qualification in the present.

Conclusion

The dilemma is to create potential for change while appreciating how deeply ingrained race is in Anglo-European society. Reflexivity shows that racial inequality is not just a matter of the past. There are alternatives to either a fully racialized society, on one hand, and a homogenized monoculture, on the other. It is possible to imagine a multiculturalism in which boundaries between groups differ from racial boundaries of the past, to have multiculturalism without any assumption that biological differences determine behavioral differences. Boundaries can be continuous or dichotomous. They can be fluid rather than permanent. Most important, multiculturalism can eliminate the domination of "inferior" groups by "superior" groups. This begins by treating all groups as analytically equal; there should never be a "given" and an "other." All groups are racial, including white Anglo-Saxons. If some foods are labeled as ethnic foods, all groups should identify their foods, not just minority groups. But self-conscious white pride can be nonracist only when whites see themselves on the same plane as other groups. In the present historical context, white pride almost necessarily proclaims white superiority. This does not mean anyone should be ashamed of being white, but whites should offer some deference to other groups in how they define themselves culturally. A racially just society is still a long way into the future. It cannot be created by making institutions "color-blind." Paradoxically, a racially just society can only come after a full acknowledgment of how deeply race permeates society, how socially constructed it is, and how fully institutions must be reconstructed to eliminate its inequalities.

5

Gender

When a child is born, one of the first questions asked is, "What is it?" meaning, "Is it a boy or a girl?" On a major network television episode of *ER,* the delivering physician answered, "I don't know." It was impossible to tell from visual examination whether the baby was male or female because its genitals were ambiguous. Testing showed that the child was chromosomally male and that surgery would be necessary to create either fully male or fully female genitals. In either case, it would be unable to reproduce. The father wanted a son, even though the surgery required to make the child a boy would be more extensive than the surgery required for female genitals. If it were given female genitals, she would have to take female hormones to counteract the effects of the male chromosomes. Distraught at the impossibility of having a "normal" child, the parents gave it up for adoption.

Though fictional, the story is not unrealistic and raises critical questions about the nature of sex and society. First, why does the question, "What *is* it?" refer to sex rather than all the many identities each person *is*? Is sex that deeply inscribed into personhood that it can be equated with being itself?

Second, what does it mean to say that to be "normal" one must fit into one sex or the other? "Normal" here is more than statistical; it is a moral imperative that one must conform to entirely. While many parents in real life would welcome such children with love, the television episode suggests that viewers would find the parents' decision to give up the child for adoption understandable even if they disagreed with it. While children with ambiguous sexual characters are almost always surgically altered to appear as male or female in Anglo-European societies, there are other societies, as we shall see, that have institutionalized additional sexual categories. Most third sexes are recognized socially, but some surgically altered male and female bodies, such as the eunuchs, were common in Europe until the 18th century.

Third, why does the physical fact of genitals and hormones loom so large in all the social manifestations of how men are socially different from women? Why is it that the kind of body people have becomes inscribed in their names, the clothes they are given, the toys they play with, the friends they have, and eventually quite likely the jobs they have? Why did the parents of this baby imagine that unless its genitals were surgically altered, it could not live as a social male or female?

Is Anatomy Destiny?

While nearly everyone acknowledges that the physical differences between races are only superficial and that qualities such as skin color or the shape of the eyes should make no difference in how people behave or how they are treated, the physical differences between males and females are commonly believed to have profound effects on how men and women behave. When a writer claims, as does Judith Lorber, that "gender is a human invention, like language, kinship, religion, and technology; like them, gender organizes human social life in culturally patterned ways" (Lorber 1994:6), some readers may be inclined to reply in various degrees of coarseness that genitals and hormones are not a human invention. The question then is, To what extent can social differences between men and women be explained by their physical differences, that is, the extent to which anatomy is destiny? Gender is more difficult to imagine as a historical construction because biological differences between males and females are so obvious. This chapter will make a case that gender is indeed historically constructed.

Not only Anglo-European society but also virtually all societies make social distinctions between men and women. If, as argued earlier, one of the tests of whether something is socially constructed is whether it is found only in some societies but not in others, then must not gender be considered natural? Even if we can imagine societies that recognize no racial distinctions or, as the authors of many utopias demonstrate, societies with no class distinctions, it is difficult for many people to imagine a society without gender distinctions. The differences between men and women feel so natural!

Few deny that on some level, the difference between male and female is natural. It is a biological fact in a way that race is not. But I will argue that the biological differences are socially trivial and that overwhelmingly, the social differences between men and women are historically constructed. The biological differences do not explain social differences. For example, biologically women give birth to babies, but it does not necessarily mean that women should provide most of the child care after the child is born. In some societies, fathers do most of the child rearing, while in others neither parent raises the children. The assignment of child care duties is determined socially, not biologically. Even in America, until the early 19th century, child care manuals giving advice to parents were written more for fathers than for mothers.

If biology cannot explain variations among child rearing and responsibilities among societies, how can it explain social differences between men and women in any particular society? There are vast behavioral differences between men and women in Anglo-European societies. Men, on average, are more aggressive, occupy more leadership positions, do more physical labor, get higher-paying jobs, and do less child care or housework than women. This chapter will explore how such social differences can be explained historically and socially rather than by nature or biology.

Sex and Gender

First, let's get some terminology straight. Most sociologists make the distinction between sex and gender. **Sex** refers to the biological differences between the male and the female of the human species. Except for the narrow issue of procreation, it is irrelevant for most aspects of social life. Humans are much less biologically distinguishable than other species. The male peacock with his splendid plumage is unmistakably different from the bland female, just as a lion's regal mane clearly marks the male of that species. Humans, who routinely cover their genitals, tell men from women more by obvious social inventions such as dress or hairstyle (Lorber 1994). Many people report the disquieting experience of meeting people whose sex is ambiguous from casual appearance. Many have also experienced having their gender misidentified. In social interactions, **gender** refers to the kinds of social relations commonly attributed to differences between males and females. Gender is a social category, not a biological one. For example, if most doctors are men and most nurses are women, it is clearly not because of differences in genitals. How can we explain why these medical professions became **gendered**? When gender is used as a verb, it refers to the process by which certain roles, activities, qualities, traits, emotions, or objects acquire masculine or feminine meanings. In Anglo-European society, doctoring, sports, leadership, aggressiveness, rage, and souped-up cars are considered more "masculine," while nursing, child care, cooperation, nurturing, sentimentality, and flowers are considered more "feminine."

The questions to be answered when discussing the historical construction of gender revolve around the relationship of sex and gender: (1) How are the categorical distinctions between men and women conceptualized? For example, why do some societies conceptualize two genders while some conceptualize three or more? (2) How did Anglo-European gender categories arise? Why are particular kinds of social relations (for example, dominance and subordination) defined in gendered terms? For example, why is doctoring seen as masculine while nursing is seen as feminine? The traits that are defined as masculine or feminine in some societies are the opposite of those in other societies. Even in Anglo-European societies, some traits formerly defined as masculine are now defined as feminine (and vice versa). As with race, the particulars of the category are historically constructed.

The Logic of the Category

Perhaps the most obvious characteristic of the Anglo-European category is that gender is dichotomous. It is assumed that everyone is male or female, that there is nothing in between, and that they are the opposite of each other. Anyone who refuses to define themselves in these terms is stigmatized as deviant. This is the assumption of **dimorphism,** the notion that there are two kinds of bodies, men and women.[23] But many other societies do not share these assumptions. In the first place, many societies identify more than two genders (Herdt 1993a). Many Native American societies have had a gender status known as *berdache*: people who are born with male genitalia but who live as neither men nor women, combining characteristics of both. Because of their high status,

---

[23]This section primarily discusses both gender and sex more or less interchangeably because Anglo-European culture does not really distinguish the two. The relationship between sex and gender varies in different societies. In some societies, such as our own, differences between types of bodies (sex) are seen as very closely matched to differences between the social identities of men and women. In other societies, people with the same types of bodies (male or female) can adopt different gender identities.

parents would rarely discourage the tendency in boys. Berdache educate children, sing and dance at tribal events, tend the ill, carry provisions for war parties, and have special ritual functions. They also met the sexual needs of other men without threatening the institution of marriage. Berdache marry men in many cultures, some of which exact no penalty to the husband. The *Hijras* in northern India are intersexed males who have become social women; some undergo ritualistic castration. As ritual performers or homosexual prostitutes, they are required to wear women's clothes but do not imitate or pass as ordinary women. Rather, they act out an exaggerated caricature of women, burlesques of female behavior using coarse and abusive speech and gestures that would be shocking in ordinary women. They live separately in their own communal households, relating to each other as fictive mothers, daughters, sisters, grandmothers, and aunts (Lorber 1994). Closer to Anglo-European culture, eunuchs—people born as male but whose genitalia were surgically removed—were common as far back as the Byzantine Empire where they were often high palace officials with considerable social status (Herdt 1993a). European *castrati* were talented boy singers who continued to sing soprano as adults because the Christian church would not allow women to sing in public, and later they were used widely in opera until the 18th century.

Cross-Cultural Variation

The relationship between sex and gender is important because people in Anglo-European society use sex as an explanation of gender inequality. While sociologists and feminists make the distinction between sex (a biological category) and gender (a social category), the general culture does not. That is, the distinction between sex and gender is used as a prescriptive distinction, not just a descriptive one, designating what ought to be more than what is. Many people believe that women ought to be more nurturing, more deferential, more involved in child care, and more responsible for the home environment than men because they think women are "naturally" that way. And they know men and women are "naturally" different because they have different genitalia. Not all cultures make this link. Oyèwùmí (1997) argues that equating sex and gender is a specifically Anglo-European trait. Her study of the Yoruba society of southwestern Nigeria showed that

> the fundamental category "woman"—which is foundational in Western gender discourses—simply did not exist in Yorubaland prior to its sus-

tained contact with the West. There was no such preexisting group characterized by shared interests, desires, or social position. The cultural logic of
Western social categories is based on an ideology of biological determin-
ism: the conception that biology provides the rationale for the organization
of the social world. Thus this cultural logic is actually a "biologic."
(Oyèwùmí 1997:ix)

That is, in the Anglo-European culture, but not in Yoruba society, the
presence or absence of certain organs determines a person's social position. Before European contact, a person's body in Yoruba society was not
the basis of social roles, of inclusions or exclusions, and was not the foundation of social thought and identity. Age was the major category and
determinant of social position. Just as nearly every social relationship in
Anglo-European societies revolves around whether men interact with
men, women with women, or men and women with each other, in that
society, all social relations revolved around people's relative age.

Cross-Cultural Variation in Gender

Even in societies that define dimorphic genders, the behaviors that are
treated as masculine or feminine vary greatly. The Tahitians, for example, are dimorphic in that they have two sex-gender statuses, men and
women, but there are few social differences between them. The Tahitian
language does not express gender in its grammar. Pronouns do not indicate the sex of the person being referred to, so it is possible to talk with
someone about a third party without a listener knowing his or her gender. Most proper names apply to people of either sex. One of the first Europeans to write about Tahitian culture, John Forster, remarked in 1778
on the high status of Tahitian women, noting that they could do almost
anything men did, including government and sports. American writer
Henry Adams wrote home about the Tahitians in 1930: "The Polynesian
women seem to be too much like the Polynesian man; the difference is
not great enough to admit of sentiment, only of physical divergence"
(Gilmore 1990:202). An anthropologist who did fieldwork in the 1960s
observed that the men were no more aggressive than women and the
women no more soft or maternal than the men. Men shared the cooking,
and the women did most of the jobs men did outside the home. The culture placed no stress on proving manhood, and men expressed no fear of
being effeminate. The Semai of central Malaysia also defy conventional
images of aggressive men and passive women. As a culture, both men
and women are so retiring and submissive that an extensive scholarly lit-

erature has debated whether they have any aggressive impulses at all. They call resistance to advances from other people *punan,* which can be translated as *taboo,* a term applied to any act, no matter how mild, that frustrates another person. If one person makes a sexual request of another, the other is supposed to submit, even if married. Nor do they express jealousy, so adultery is rampant. "It's just a loan," they say (Gilmore 1990:211). As a result, outsiders have sometimes taken sexual advantage of them. The rules of conciliatory behavior also apply to making demands on others. In difficult situations, especially with a potential for conflict, they withdraw, so there are no sporting contests in which one person would lose and feel bad. Unlike the Tahitians, their language does distinguish male and female, and gender is an important feature of the kinship terminology. But they make little difference of gender in social interaction, treating few traits as masculine or feminine.

The History of Bodies

If the way that Anglo-European society conceptualizes the relationship between biological differences (sex) and social differences (gender) is not natural, how did this conception arise historically? Where did the sense of biological destiny or the meaning of femininity and masculinity come from? Exploring the history of sex and gender can help unchain the iron-clad bonds of biology and culture that have demeaned women and emotionally handicapped men.

Prehistoric Societies

There is no evidence of gender differences in the earliest hominids, so gender division probably happened after development of tools, when settlements became more permanent. They distinguished between child caregivers and nonchild caregivers, which was roughly women versus men, although this was not explained by biological necessity or instincts; it was a convenient division because someone had to care for the children. Women probably hunted and gathered; some men probably still cared for children. "The gendered division of labor grew out of the exigencies of expanded food production and child minding; it was a cultural solution to a technological problem that resulted in changed social organization" (Lorber 1994:129). When these differences were later legitimated through ritual, women would become obliged to do what was expected of women, and men did what was expected of men. Rather than taking on jobs because of preference or immediate need, people were assigned to jobs on the basis of permanent statuses, including gender. This created dimorphic categories of people, notably men versus women.

When humans began to use stone tools (the Paleolithic period) and later when they began farming (the Neolithic era), the social importance of childbearing probably gave women high status, symbolized in the female meaning of *earth*—mother earth—and the linking of maternity and fertility. As social institutions began to develop, gender began to be a principle by which resources were distributed. The **mode of production**—how basic needs such as food, shelter, and clothing are organized—and **kinship rules** that govern who gets what kinds of resources are the keys to the status of men and women.[24] Lorber (1994) cites the type of goods buried with male and female corpses and evidence from age at death, indicating that women had better nutrition than men.

When societies shifted to agricultural production, women's economic roles were reduced. The control of resources became tied to the control of land, in which men had an advantage because of their physical strength. At the same time, women's lives became centered more on childbearing, resulting in **patriarchy**—society dominated by men. Wealth was distributed by families, so a person's wealth depended on the wealth of his or her family. People had few alternative ways to meet their needs other than families, which were dominated by men. "These agrarian feudal societies were the true patriarchies: the landowning fathers ruled, and sons inherited everything" (Lorber 1994:143). But this does not mean that all societies since then have been patriarchies. Societies have differed not only in terms of the relative power of men and women but also in the way that sexes have been categorized and the relationship between what we now call sex and gender.

The One-Sex and Two-Sex Model of the Human Body

Until the modern era, the most common conceptualization in the Anglo-European society was a *one-sex model*. Rather than two distinct and opposite sexes, humans were ranked into a single hierarchy of perfection, an image derived from Greek culture. God was the symbol of per-

---

[24]The mode of production is broader than the modern economic institution, and kinship relations are broader than the modern family. Modern institutions are organizationally distinct from each other, unlike earlier societies in which economic, family, and other institutions are often indistinguishable.

fection, then going down the chain were men, "created in God's image," and then "inferior" categories such as women, eunuchs, dwarfs, and others (Laqueur 1990). These lower types were seen as biologically similar to men, but imperfect, rather than the opposite of men. Scientists followed the eminent Greek physician Galen (third century B.C.), who believed that men and women had similar genital organs, except that men's were on the outside and women's were on the inside and that women's genitals were inverted versions of men's. Until the early 19th century, the ovary, arguably the most fundamentally female organ, did not even have its own name but was called by the same name as the male testes, *orcheis*. About 1800, Anglo-Europeans reconceptualized how they imagined sex differences, treating men and women not as superior and inferior versions of the same creature but as polar opposites. They reified two sexes rather than one. As Laqueur (1990) describes it, "Not only are the sexes [now conceptualized as] different, but they are different in every conceivable aspect of body and soul, in every physical and moral aspect" (p. 5). In other words, the conceptualization became dimorphic, a matter of two kinds of bodies. A one-sex model was replaced by a two-sex model. Earlier, the social differences between men and women had been understood in sociological rather than biological terms. When women were reconceptualized as having an opposite kind of body, people increasingly explained social differences between women and men biologically. Instead of seeing women as subordinate because men were more powerful, analogous to how some races dominated other races, women's subordination became seen in biological terms. Laqueur emphasizes that this new conception did not arise from biological discoveries showing that women's genitals are not inverted forms of men's genitals; most of those discoveries came after the two-sex model was widely accepted. He concludes that historically, gender explains sex. Like Oyèwùmí's (1997) study of the Yoruba, Laqueur's work shows not that inherent biological differences give rise to social differences but that social conceptions of biological difference are themselves socially constructed. They are not denying that there are two biological types—humans with one set of genitals and humans with another set. Some authors even question whether there are inherently two types of bodies (two sexes) (Herdt 1993a). There are hundreds of **true hermaphrodites** in America—individuals born with both ovary and testicular tissue who are genetically neither fully male nor female. Many more are so-called **pseudo-hermaphrodites,** whose sex at birth is ambiguous, for example, with both penis and vagina. Most are surgically altered to either male or female anatomy. But many children are born with the sexual traits of either male or female and start to develop the characteristics of the other in adolescence, for example, people who are born with a penis but grow breasts as teenagers. Some respond by switching their gender; others have surgery to maintain their original sex. **Transgenders** are people who make a decision to change their sex and gender. Some report that they always felt like a man in a woman's body or a woman in a man's body, but some say that they made a decision to change (Polanyi 1997). The presence of hermaphrodites and transgenders in society raises the issue of how different societies conceive of the relationship of sex and gender—how people with different kinds of bodies become defined as men or women and how people identified as men and women take on masculine or feminine identities.

Changing Gender in Anglo-European Society

If the modern Anglo-European gender definitions are not natural but are historically constructed, how did they arise? Why do we associate certain traits, behaviors, attitudes, emotions, and roles as "feminine" and others as "masculine"? Why have some gender meanings become the opposite of what they once were? A historical examination seriously challenges the notion that men act "masculine" and women act "feminine" because nature dictates it.

Anglo-European Women Before Femininity

While most people believe that social life has become less gendered over time, with men and women becoming more alike as they become more equal, if you look at Europe over the long term, that is not necessarily the case. In premodern times, there were ways in which men and women were more alike. Gender differences were smaller than today. The modern sense of women being "feminine"—as being weak, soft, emotional, and in need of male protection—was not common. Women plowed fields, chopped wood, and toted water. In medieval Europe, while men and women were hardly equal, most institutions permitted women, on occasion, to fill most social roles, including property ownership, the monarchy, and even military leadership, such as Joan of Arc. Indeed, Elizabeth I of England, Catherine de' Medici in France, and the Russian

Catherine the Great were among their nations' historic rulers. Medieval laws were written to keep property in the family, which meant that widows and daughters had rights to property. In other words, class could trump gender: It was more important to have someone of the "appropriate" class than the "appropriate" sex fill important positions. Even at the outset of the Industrial Revolution, which transformed agrarian society into industrial society, women workers not only were common but also predominated in many industries. Figure 5.1 shows mostly women working at a Connecticut munitions factory in the 19th century. Any assumptions that they were too weak or the work too dangerous wilted before the desire for cheap, dependable labor, regardless of sex.

However, dominant institutions increasingly subordinated women and gave power to men. In the late 12th century, a new professional class of celibate men gained control of the Catholic Church and educational institutions. The early Christians had defined celibate women as "manly" and had given them many of the same rights as monastic men. Some nuns became very learned, and others became leaders. It did not threaten the larger social order because the celibate were considered dead from the world and excluded from the social structure. But after celibate men extended their influence beyond monasteries and sought power in the entire Church, the presence of women in leadership positions became more threatening. Citing the ancient Greek doctrines on women's biological inferiority, they excluded women as well as married men from both the priesthood and educational institutions. But with more men remaining unmarried, the increased number of unmarried women aspired to positions of importance. The male-controlled Church then defined women as a moral threat to men's virtue. Married men were warned of the dangers of unattached women lustfully tempting them into sinfulness. Conrad of Marchtal wrote that

> we and our whole community of canons, recognizing the wickedness of the world, and that there is no danger like that of women, and that the poison of asps and dragons is more curable and less dangerous to men than the familiarity of women, have unanimously decreed for the safety of our souls, no less than for that of our bodies and goods, that we will on no account receive any more sisters to the increase of our perdition, but will avoid them like poisonous animals. (McNamara 1994:18)

The movement took extreme measures to exclude women from all aspects of public life and from all religious roles except the lowest ones.

Celibacy was imposed on secular clergy (nonmonastic priests), and monks were ordained into the priesthood. But the issue remained of how

FIGURE 5.1
Munitions Factory, Bridgeport, Connecticut, in *Harper's Weekly* (about 1880)

priests could be celibate without sacrificing their manhood. Although priests were required to remain unmarried, they generally did not have to be sexually chaste and could enjoy the companionship of concubines or affairs with nuns. "In effect, clerical men could affirm their masculinity only by committing sin" (McNamara 1994:8). Church leaders resolved this contradiction by blaming women, who were condemned in sermons, pastoral letters, and public statements as dangerous, aggressive, poisonous, and polluting. The celibate clerics instructed laymen to enforce their dominance over women through sexuality. Marriage, which had formerly been a private agreement, became the institutional control of the Church, which made consummation the measure of whether a marriage was formalized, symbolizing male ownership of women through sexual subordination. Men who did not enforce sexuality within marriage were defined irresponsible and effeminate. At the same time, chastity for unmarried men became increasingly seen as a virtue, as literature glorified unmarried heroes such as Galahad and Percival. In fact, most heroes from Ivanhoe to the Lone Ranger have been portrayed as single men. Only in the late 20th century have heroes become depicted as sexually active.

Public and Private Spheres

Modern Anglo-European notions of femininity and masculinity arose with the separation of private life and public life.[25] Life in modern society has become organized into separate public and private institutional spheres that have different kinds of social relations and different modes of thought. In the **private sphere,** social relations are holistic and emotional. People are supposed to reveal their authentic selves—who they really are—not just play a role. Private life is intimate and subjective. People share private thoughts and feelings and expect others to do the same. Private life is the world of friends and family where people take off the masks of public life and have the freedom to be "natural." Private life is the world of family, of home, of friendship, of "true selves."

In contrast, public life is the world of the economy and politics and other nonfamily major institutions. Rather than being holistic, it is specialized: People reveal only part of themselves. Whether going through the checkout stand at a store, talking in class, or meeting someone at a party, people act differently than when they are with close friends or family, revealing only what is appropriate for that particular interaction. Rather than being emotional, the **public sphere** is rational and imper-

---

[25]The distinction between public and private is defined in many different ways. Some divide between government and nongovernment. In economics, companies that openly sell their stocks are public, and those that do not are private. The usage here is commonly found in gender studies.

sonal; it is objective. When you buy a hamburger, you want to know how much it costs, not how the salesperson feels about eating meat or whether he or she likes you. Rather than acting in terms of their authentic selves, people act in terms of roles: citizen, employer, customer, or student. Most people generally think it is best to keep the public and private spheres separate. In the private sphere, it is considered inappropriate to think in terms of achievement, competition, and rational calculation. But in the public sphere, people are not supposed to react emotionally, joyfully, and sorrowfully, except within restrictive bounds.

This separation of public and private spheres is one of the foundations of gender relations in Anglo-European culture. Women and femininity are associated with the private; men and masculinity are associated with the public. An old cliché puts it succinctly: "A woman's place is in the home." To be feminine means to be emotional, understanding, expressive, and "natural"—the qualities of the private sphere. An 18th-century English poem by Hannah More captures this sensibility:

> *The sober comfort, all the peace which springs*
> *From the large aggregate of little things;*
> *On these small cares of daughter, wife, or friend,*
> *The almost sacred joys of home depend.*
> *There, SENSIBILITY, thou best may'st reign,*
> *HOME is thy true legitimate domain.*

> Hannah More (1745-1833),
> *Sensibility,* in More (1787)

Another cliché captures the men's side: "It's a man's world." Masculinity means being objective, rational, nonemotional, and able to play a specific role without getting too wrapped up personally, the characteristics associated with the public sphere. This separation did not always exist. Before the modern era, life had the qualities that we associate with the public sphere. What was it like for Europeans to live life without any inkling that there could be a private life, that all life was public? Shakespeare's adage that "all the world is a stage" was taken quite literally. People had little sense of an "authentic self" different from the roles they played but felt that all of life was like acting on a stage. Today, dramatic roles are treated as separate from the true self. "Acting" is inconsistent with authenticity. But before the modern era, life was lived in public (Sennett 1974). As Poggi described Louis XIV King of France,

The king of France was thoroughly, without residue a "public"
personage. His mother gave birth to him in public, and from that
moment his existence, down to its most trivial moments, was acted out
before the eyes of attendants who were holders of dignified offices. He
ate in public, went to bed in public, woke up and was clothed and
groomed in public, urinated and defecated in public. He did not
much bathe in public; but then neither did he do so in private. I know
of no evidence that he copulated in public; but he came near enough,
considering the circumstances under which he was expected to deflower
his August bride. When he died (in public), his body was promptly and
messily chopped up in public, and its severed parts ceremoniously
handed out to the more exalted among the personages who had been
attending him throughout his mortal existence. (Poggi 1978:68-69)

Even in intimacy, people would express feelings without having to
reveal selves to each other. Love poems were read without any pretense
of representing one's true feelings because courting was just a role that
people played. Effective courting meant playing the role well, not sharing one's true self. This relationship is captured in the play *Cyrano de
Bergerac* in which one character—dashing, handsome, but uncomfort-
able with words—persuades another, who has a very long nose but an
exquisite way with words, to supply the rhetoric by which the first one
tries to woo a lovely lady. But the play takes a modern turn when she falls
in love with the eloquent, ugly man. What is important here is that the
play does not condemn the handsome man's deceptions in getting
Cyrano to speak for him because people did not feel there was any authentic "real" self to misrepresent.[26]

Over a period of several centuries, people developed a notion that
there were two different spheres of life, a public and a private. One of the
most important causes was the rise of capitalism, during which people
who had worked at home, either on a farm or in a shop, were increasingly working outside the home, on someone else's farm or in a factory.
As discussed in Chapter 3, capitalism spatially reorganized life as work
and family became physically separated and the enclosure of common
fields pushed people off their land and into paid employment.

It was not that capitalism somehow dictated that the separation of
work from home would be gendered. Rather, it was the way that capitalism developed that explains the separation of public and private

[26]And the "true love" relationship is never "consummated"—Cyrano survives
the war and (maybe) reveals himself to Roxanna, who winds up as his lifetime
friend but retreats to a nunnery when her "physical" suitor is killed in battle.

spheres. The notion of public and private spheres became a conscious doctrine that prescribed new meanings of gender, not just described them. In 1859, Rev. Philemon Fowler preached to his New York congregation that the male is to "go into the world an engage in business or laborious occupation for the maintenance of the family," while the wife is to stay at home and

> advise and counsel her husband in his doubts and perplexities, and by her presence, her affection, and her smiles to make home an elysium to which he can flee and find rest from the storm and strife of the selfish world. . . . Each [gender] has a distinct sphere of duty—the husband to go out into the world—the wife to superintend the domestic affairs of the household. (Ryan 1981:189-90)

The fact that he is preaching this indicates that his congregation did not take it for granted; they had to be convinced. The separate spheres were being constructed. There did not have to be two separate public and private spheres. As noted above, many women, especially those who were not wealthy, continued to work. The majority of workers in many early factories were women. And though biology dictates that women bear children, it is not necessary that women raise them.

When people left home and went to work on other people's farms or factories, the nature of home life was redefined as a new private sphere where women were to be sheltered from the tough realities of the "man's world." Although there was little consideration of the tough realities of home life or the many women who worked outside the home, the home became seen as a woman's space. And with it, the meaning of femininity was changed. As the relationship between men and women was redefined in biological terms, women's social roles were reduced to biologically defined roles—motherhood and wife. For the first time, women were imputed with a maternal instinct, even though parenting had earlier been defined as the responsibility of men. Other aspects of this new femininity were explained in biological terms: Even though women had plowed, hewed, and carried, femininity was becoming characterized by physical weakness and a tendency toward passivity.

Why Voting Was So Important

The biological understanding of women, the way that gender was structured by the separation of public and private life, and the rights that women would enjoy in society all intersected on the issue of women's vote in the late 19th and early 20th centuries. Many people today are puzzled by opposition to women voting in public elections. Voting is one the fundamental rights that all citizens now enjoy, yet women were not guaranteed the right to vote in the United States until the 19th Amendment was ratified in 1920, more than half a century after all races were given a constitutional right to vote (although widely violated in practice). The bitter, decades-long resistance against women's suffrage was more than the simple reluctance of men to share power. Most Americans would have affirmed the abstract principle of universal suffrage by which all people have the right to vote. But universal suffrage was understood within a conception of society that embraced the split of public and private life. Electoral politics was in the public realm, which was very much "a man's world." Women were understood to be situated, by "nature," in the private sector, in the family, not government or business. The notion of the "universal citizen," the foundation of democracy, was originally constructed as a male. Citizenship was shaped as part of the public sphere, in opposition to the private sphere or home, the place where women were situated. Because men were the unmarked case (the gender that is assumed when no gender is specified) and because it was assumed that men would be active in politics and economic life while women remained in the home, when people talked about rights of citizenship, they meant the rights that men (primarily white men) had—to vote, hold property, and speak publicly (Pateman 1989). Indeed, the qualities of citizenship—independence, rationality, and courage—were defined as masculine in explicit contrast to women's dependence and sexual subordination. For proponents and opponents alike, suffrage represented a woman's independence from the family and her entry into the public sphere, where she could vote as an individual, not as a wife or mother. Opponents saw such aspirations as selfish, placing her own self-interest above her family. Allowing women to vote for their own interests rather than allowing men to vote on behalf of the entire family's interest would weaken the family. And presaging current debates on family values, insofar as the family was seen as the foundation of society, allowing women to vote would threaten social cohesion as a whole. As minister and editor Lyman Abbott put it, "Because their [women's] functions are different, all talk of equality or non-equality is but idle words, without a meaning" (Filene 1998:38). Or as Edward Cope, professor of zoology at University of Pennsylvania and author of more than 500 publications, stated more sensationally,

> In woman we find that the deficiency of endurance of the rational faculty
> is associated with a general incapacity for mental strain, and, as her emo-

tional nature is stronger, that strain is more severe than it is in man under similar circumstances. Hence the easy breakdown under stress, which is probably the most distinctive feature of the female mind. This peculiarity, when pronounced, becomes the hysterical temperament. (Cope 1888/1985: 211)

Even many women agreed with this perspective. Susan F. Cooper wrote in *Harper's Magazine* in 1870,

There must, of necessity, in such a state of things, be certain duties inalienably connected with the position of man, others inalienably connected with the position of woman. For the one to assume the duties of the other becomes, first an act of desertion, next an act of usurpation. . . . To be noble the man must be manly. To be noble the woman must be womanly. . . . In woman we look more especially for greater purity, modesty, patience, grace, sweetness, tenderness, refinement, as the consequences of finer organization, in a protected and sheltered position. (p. 439)

It is ironic that Mother's Day, which seems so nonpolitical today, was proclaimed as part of this controversy. In 1914, when there was much concern about the declining family, rising divorce, and the weakening of the genetic stock, Congress passed a resolution honoring the place of women in the family.

Whereas the service rendered the United States by the American mother is the greatest source of the country's strength and inspiration, and Whereas we honor ourselves and the mothers of America when we do any thing to give emphasis to the home as the fountain head of the State; and Whereas the American mother is doing so much for the home, for moral uplift, and religion, hence so much for good government and humanity. (Filene 1998:43)

They declared the second Sunday in May to be Mother's Day. In the context of the era, this was widely interpreted as hostility toward the women's suffrage movement. The members of Congress—all men— were proclaiming that women, as mothers, were "the greatest source of the country's strength" and that mothers did "so much good for govern- ment and humanity," implicitly rejecting the demand that women be rec- ognized as citizens, invoking instead language with transparent affinity to antisuffrage arguments.

Faced with the choice of trying to overthrow the entire conception of gender and the best tactical means for attaining the vote, the suffrage movement opted for the practical rather than visionary, recognizing the constraints of political power. Women reframed their case for voting to emphasize the humanizing, softening effects that women voters would offer the polity, reinforcing the doctrine of separate spheres rather than challenging it. After 1910, the movement took off and even became fashionable because the rhetoric changed from one of independence and equality to one of separate spheres: Women's vote would be more moral than men's, bringing compassion into politics. Suffragist Ida H. Harper put it this way: "To extravagance they [women voters] will oppose economy, radicalism they will temper with conservatism; to physical they will add moral courage; masculine brain they will supplement with feminine heart" (Filene 1998:39). They won the vote by embracing feminine virtues.

As it turned out, granting women the right to vote had sparked neither the revolution that was hoped for by earlier suffragists nor the calamity feared by the opponents. Women did gain the right to play a larger role in the public sphere, but real progress has been won more through decades of social activism than statutory fiat. Like the limited gains from the civil rights movement of the 1960s, the right to vote did not achieve as much equality as many women had hoped. But like the civil rights movement, a social movement did transform a major social institution, politics. The half of the population that had been denied one of the fundamental rights of citizenship because of an "accident" of birth now have the right to participate. And a government that calls itself the most democratic government in the world is closer to living up to its claim. However, the conflict also demonstrates the power of a major institution to help shape taken-for-granted gender definitions, even when those definitions are contested. Women got the right to vote but under the terms set by government.

Masculinity

This analysis is important and helps understand women's roles but still takes masculinity as the given.[27] As with whiteness, time, and space, si-

---

[27]Recent writing on masculinity has emphasized that it is not a single quality but that there are many masculinities for different people and different contexts (Connell 1995). For purposes of simplicity, the discussion here focuses on what is sometimes called *hegemonic* masculinity, which is the meaning that most people would understand in terms of manhood. Other types of masculinity such as gay masculinity, hypermasculinity, and so on are beyond the scope of this volume.

lence on masculinity's historical origins makes it seem natural. Masculinity and femininity must both be problematized if they are to claim analytical equality. Even if we understand that the place of women in society is socially constructed, unless we equally understand that men's place is socially constructed too, we implicitly treat manhood as natural. When men are the unmarked case, they forget that they have gender, no less than women do. Just as femininity has become reified and framed as natural, so has masculinity. The difference is that men have used dominant institutions to their advantage.

Although Anglo-European men have socially dominated women since Greek times, masculinity and manhood have had many meanings, some in opposition to others. At some times and places, masculinity has been associated with physical strength, at others with restraint and civility. Manhood has been associated with homosocial—men only—gangs and friendship groups or, alternatively, with strong family ties. "Real men" have been those whose independence chafes at all conformity to authority or, alternatively, those who respectfully accept their station in life. This historical variation further attests to the socially constructed (rather than naturally given) character of masculinity.

Earlier European Notion of Masculinity

Just as today women's social position, legal standing, and identity revolve around the institution of marriage, so too has men's place in society been shaped by marriage. Before the 12th century, when people could create a family by privately agreeing to do so, marriage merely marked a passage in life; it did not define a man's identity relative to his wife. People did not even have surnames. Men were named descriptively on the basis of an occupation (John Carpenter), physical characteristic (Harold Strong), place (William Glen), or behavior (Robert the Crafty). Marriage did not provide a common name for husband, wife, and children. Surnames became adopted across England and Europe from the 11th to the 15th centuries, when two dominant institutions, church and law, took control of marriage. The powerful aristocracy wanted a more reliable way of identifying who owned what, and the practice spread throughout the rest of society. Surnames meant that the husband and father defined the identity of the entire family. They all became known by their relationship with him. During the same period, the husband's and wife's roles were reciprocally changing, with the husband assuming greater responsibility for the wife (and her dowry) and the wife being further subordinated to his authority. Men were increasingly seen as strong, responsible, and authoritative, and women were seen as weak, passive, and dependent. But men's freedom to leave the marriage was also restricted. Before the late Middle Ages, men had been free to leave a marriage, without the wife's permission, often to join a monastery. As the church and law increasingly compelled men to stay with their wives, they also enlarged the scope of gender identity, treating people according to their gender. Marriage came to denote the transition to adulthood with all the rights and responsibilities entailed. Men's rights became less distinguishable from husbands' rights, and women had fewer rights apart from wives' rights. Both the rights and responsibilities of adulthood were defined in gendered terms (Stuard 1994).

Masculinity and the State

One of the main institutions that solidified modern Anglo-European notions of manhood has been the state. Before about 1500, Europe was governed by all sorts of entities, including city-states, theocracies (government by church), trading federations, and various petty principalities. But in the centuries leading up to 1800, Europe was consolidated into a few very large, territorially organized centralized states, each of which exercised supreme authority within its borders. England, France, Germany, Spain, and the others became the chief powers. Two activities were especially important for constructing manhood.

The first has already been mentioned—the legal control of marriage. Governments increasingly linked male privileges, especially control of property, to the family. For example, in the first half of the 15th century, Venice (then a strong city-state with considerable authority outside the city) passed new legislation defining the rights and duties of patricians (wealthy heads of families), reinforcing formal dominance of the father in public and private life. Fathers were explicitly required to introduce their sons into public life and were responsible for their sons' behavior in public. They were also given explicit responsibility for daughters' dowries and could be held liable if the daughters or wives spent too much. Thus, fathers had a legal basis to exert increased authority in the family, and their authority in the family was tied to their place in the community.

> Nearly every aspect of patrician status celebrated masculinity, starting with its essential entitlement, that of participating in government, an activity reserved to men. Membership in the political class thus entirely depended legally upon one's birth to a father who possessed the same privilege, inherited in turn from his father. (Chojnacki 1994:75)

The second way that the rise of the state helped to construct modern masculinity was through the military. While wars have nearly always been fought by men, all societies have not equated military prowess with masculinity. Only the nobility was permitted to engage in war. The medieval notion of chivalry, a set of norms that required knights to be brave, virtuous, and loyal, defined the values of a class more than of a gender. As the Middle Ages waned in the 14th century, English armies spread beyond the nobility when they found that the armies with bows and arrows could defeat armies of knights in armor. But truly mass warfare, in which all able-bodied men were expected to fight, did not arise until the Napoleonic wars of the early 19th century. As warfare evolved from knights in armor to mass war, the honor of war became increasingly defined in gender rather than class terms. It became manly to be a soldier and unmanly to avoid military service.

Manhood in America

If gender is historically constructed, it must change during different historical periods. Masculinity in America does indeed show such change, with late 20th-century masculinity embodying some of the opposite qualities of earlier masculinities.[28] In early America, masculinity was defined in social and spiritual qualities, especially in terms of service performed for others. Then in the 19th century, the "self-made man"—masculinity based on how men improved themselves—became the new ideal. In the late 19th and early 20th centuries, masculinity was reconstructed as physical prowess and raw energy, contradicting the altruistic manliness of the first period and the self-control of the second. In our own period, mostly in response to the feminist movement, masculinity is once again being explored and renegotiated.

The Useful Man

In the first period, when the nation was just beginning, manhood was defined in terms of social and spiritual qualities, especially the concept of *usefulness*. To be a "real man" meant giving service to the community, serving others. Here is a father giving advice to his son in 1788: "The more knowledge you acquire . . . the more useful you may be to yourself, your friends, and your country." A later letter that the same father

---

[28]The three periods and much of the evidence in the foregoing text are based on Rotundo (1993).

thought might be his last closed with, "May God preserve you, my child, and make you eminently useful" (Rotundo 1983:24). A New England clergyman eulogized a late colleague: "He led a useful life. . . . Upon the whole was the most useful man of his age" (Rotundo 1983:24). Historical analysis of magazines in the late 18th century has found that "publick usefulness" was the standard of success for heroes. Other virtues such as courage were defined in terms of usefulness. Even during revolutionary times, courage implied service more than daring. Washington and Lafayette were admired as heroes who risked their lives for political principle, not just for killing people or being tough. Devotion to the community and willingness to defend it were the hallmarks of courage.

In a similar vein, gentleness and Godliness were considered masculine virtues. Men were praised for their acquiescence to "the will and pleasure of the Sovereign of the Universe." According to one writer,

> When a man is found, who does not profess much, nor despise all, who is pure from guile, peaceable in his life, easily dissuaded from revenge, with a heart to pity and relieve the miserable, impartial in his judgment and without dissimulation—this is the man of religion. This is an apostolic description of a good man. (Rotundo 1983:24)

How different from descriptions of manliness in our times! Manliness was the opposite of pride or self-aggrandizement. Instead, humility was a virtue. Because society was based on a hierarchy of authority and community dominance over the individual, compliance was a respected attitude. Humility was also important for those exercising authority because authority was based less on personal qualities than on social position. Men of rank did not have to prove their right to exercise authority but could exercise authority without having to assert it for the sake of asserting it. They could be humble but stern because they were exercising the authority of the community. A contemporary praised George Washington for his reluctance to assert himself:

> This is the seventh year that he has commanded the army, and that he has obeyed the Congress; more need not be said, especially in America, where they know how to appreciate all the merit contained in this simple fact. (Schwartz 1983:27)

One of the structural features that made it possible to combine authority and humility was the lack of separation of public and private life. Although the family is often considered the symbolic center of society today, institutionally, the present-day family is much more separated from politics, economics, and other centers of power than in colonial times. Just because a family member may have a position of economic or political power, his or her family members do not necessarily enjoy the same influence. Presidents Clinton, Reagan, and Carter all had brothers who were—to use a bygone but apt phrase—ne'er-do-wells. These presidents brought their brothers notoriety but not respect or influence.[29] When the family was the main unit of society and when society was organized hierarchically, as in the 18th century, men ruled over families but were subordinate to men above them. So it made sense that manhood could be defined in terms of usefulness, whether a man was in a subordinate position, a dominant position, or frequently both at the same time.

The Self-Made Man

In the 19th century, the meaning of masculinity and manhood changed dramatically. For the first time, masculine discourse included the word *self*. The new sense of manhood was the "self-made man," someone who rose from modest circumstances to make himself into a commercial success, the myth of "rags to riches." People started to talk about "self-improvement" rather than service to the community. Rather than emphasizing service to God and others, ministers, lawyers, and businessmen were urged that it was "no less our privilege than our duty to cultivate the talent with which we were endowed" (Rotundo 1983:25). In 1818, a New York merchant wrote to his son at West Point,

> It only requires a young man possessing the talents which God has given you, to improve those talents, to make you conspicuous in the American World—There is a wide field, Henry, for young men of talents, and exemplary character, in this fine Country, to place themselves in pre-eminent situations—The Presidency itself is open to all—cultivate the talents which God has endowed you with, and you need not despair, of promotion in this fair land of Independence. (Rotundo 1983:25)

The young man did not become president, but one man who did, Rutherford B. Hayes, kept a diary while at Kenyon College, fortifying himself with similar sentiments:

> By keeping a diary in which to record my thoughts, desires, and resolves, I expect to promote stability of character . . . if I commit to writing all of my

---

[29]Today, only religion has an institutional relationship to the family that government and economics once did. Today, the religious institution intersects with the family as other institutions did in the past. Typically, people belong to churches, synagogues, and mosques as families and clergy minister to families, not just individuals. But unlike the past, people work, vote, and get most public services as individuals.

resolves. I shall be more careful not to make them hastily, and when they are made I shall be more anxious to keep them. (Rotundo 1983:24)

By the 1830s, economic achievement was embodied culturally as the "self-made man" had replaced the "useful man" as the measure of manhood (Kimmel 1993; 1996; Rotundo 1993).

The self-made man was the male side of the separation of public and private spheres (Ryan 1981). The man who went out into the world to become a breadwinner, who used only the resources of his own character to meet the challenges of a merciless and dangerous marketplace, complemented the sedate and subservient wife who remained at home. Both images depicted the household less as the site of production than as a haven from it. John Mather Austin (1838) wrote in *A Voice to Youth* that the male is to "go into the world and engage in business or laborious occupation for the maintenance of the family" (Ryan 1981:189-90). While men were advised to prove their manhood by vigorously grappling with the marketplace, they were to find sustenance, devotion, and reinvigoration at home. A Utica, New York, publication prescribed what the home should be for middle-class men: "That hope which aims at a beloved partner—a family—a fireside—will lead its possessor to activity in all his conduct. It will elicit his talents, and urge him to his full energy and probably call in the aid of economy" (Ryan 1981:180). Books and magazines promised to help ambitious young men become successful, thus launching the self-help industry that continues to thrive. Orison Swett Marden, author of 30 books and editor of the successful *Success* magazine, emerged as the preeminent self-advancement publicist. But Marden still considered manhood the greatest distinction, writing, "Manhood is greater than wealth, grander than fame" (Kimmel 1996:102). The most remembered advocate of success was Horatio Alger, Jr., a Unitarian minister who published 120 novels, all about poor, ragged, but confident and respectful boys, often street urchins orphaned in the big city, finding a lucky break through acts of kindness, industry, and pluck to achieve wealth and propriety.[30]

Masculinity Gets Physical

One of the most significant changes of the 19th century was the cultural connection of the human body and character. The previous chapter de-

---

[30]A Horatio Alger Association of Distinguished Americans continues to honor the author and induct members who have realized the rags-to-riches dream.

scribed how the cultural connection of body and character shaped the constitution of race. So too did it shape gender. While a person's character had been seen to reflect his or her nature since the ancient Greeks, in the 19th century, "nature" was increasingly seen in terms of the physical body, not just God's plan or the order of the universe. Anglo-European society takes it for granted that manhood and womanhood are matters of the human body, associating masculinity with physical strength and femininity with beauty. In the 19th century, the bodily dimension of manhood was expressed more in terms of morality than physical strength. In contrast to today's culture, when "real men" might display masculinity by binge drinking and sexual conquest—at least in the eyes of other self-described "real men"—a real man in the early 19th century was one who could control his sexual impulses and his drink. "Manhood" was primarily a middle-class concern, achieving respectability by making sobriety a class and gender distinction. The man who could control his impulses was contrasted against the allegedly promiscuous, primitive, and intoxicated lower classes and the new immigrant groups. "True men" of the middle class were more civilized and restrained. They also distinguished themselves from upper-class men, whom they considered effete and hedonistic.

The qualities of gentlemanly restraint, bodily masculinity, and self-improvement converged on the rise of formal sports (Bederman 1995; Dubbert 1980; Filene 1998; Lorber 1994; Messner 1987). Today, it is difficult for boys to become accepted by other "masculine" boys—and often by their fathers—unless they show some inclination to sports.[31] While people have played games in nearly all societies, the idea of sports—physical games with teams, official rules, winners and losers, requiring skill and strategy—did not catch the Anglo-European imagination until the second half of the 19th century. There were no football, basketball, baseball, hockey, or any of the other competitive team sports that are so popular today. While some kinds of competition were widespread—schoolchildren still learn that Abraham Lincoln gained renown by his wood-splitting prowess—few men would have sought to affirm their

---

[31]But there is a contradiction. Michael Messner describes how sport, one of the common routes by which boys seek friendship and companionship, simultaneously makes deep connections among boys difficult: "Contemporary males often feel empty, alienated, isolated, and as failures because the socially learned means through which they seek validation and identity (achievement in the public worlds of sports and work) do not deliver what is actually craved and needed: intimate connection and unity with other human beings" (Messner 1987:208).

masculinity on the playing field. Over the late 19th century, winning became defined not just as a matter of physical skill but one of character.
And manhood was closely connected to character. In this new conception, the "real man" was a winner because he worked hard, maintained
sobriety, controlled his passions, focused his energies, and maintained
discipline. Athletic skill was seen not just as a matter of talent but as a
quality found in a well-rounded self-made man. Popular opinion continues to demand that famous athletes be role models for children, an idea
that goes back to the 19th-century assumption that the body is a reposi-
tory of both physical skill and moral character.[32]

Masculinity Today: Men Get Tough

Organized team sports spanned their "self-made men" image of masculinity with today's tough masculinity. A young woman at the turn of this
century expressed sentiments about virility that would be quite recog-
nizable today but novel at that time: A virile man is "very strong; and
mistrustful; and relentless; and makes you feel as if somebody had taken
you by the throat; and shakes you up, awfully and seems to throw you in
the air, and trample you underfoot" (Rotundo 1983:26). President Theodore Roosevelt thought it a good thing to "make the wolf rise in a man's
heart." He went to Africa in the summer and to Montana in the winter to
prove his manliness by discovering a "nearly animal existence"
(Rotundo 1983:27).

The Crisis of Masculinity

Roosevelt was president at a time of general crisis of masculinity. As
more men worked in offices, the opportunities for independence and individual achievement that had been so central to the ideal of the
self-made man were slipping away. Novelist Henry James worried in *The
Bostonians* that "the whole generation is womanized; the masculine tone
is passing out of the world; it's a feminine, nervous, hysterical, chatter-
ing catting age, an age of hollow phrases and false delicacy and exaggerated solicitudes and coddled sensibilities" (Bederman 1995:16).

---

[32]We also idolize the excesses of masculinity—unconstricted sexuality, violence,
competition—in some particularly "masculine" sports and stigmatize men (such
as basketball player Dennis Rodman) who seem feminine despite their athletic
powers. Boxer Mike Tyson presents a very different template of masculinity from
golfer Tiger Woods.

Working-class men who had earlier hoped to become master artisans were increasingly trapped in factory jobs, often subordinate to domineering foremen. Middle-class men who had anticipated owning their own businesses took office jobs that doubly threatened their manhood, depriving them of both independence and physical virility. An 1873 description of a government worker was explicit: He "has no independence while in office, no manhood . . . he must openly avow his implicit faith in all his superiors, on pain of dismissal, and must cringe and fawn upon them" (Kimmel 1996:103). The theme was still alive at the turn of the century, when a writer describes how men were being emasculated by working in an office:

> A change in the bearing of these men was noticeable even to young people. They no longer had either the responsibilities or the dignity of their former position. . . . They were no longer business men, in the old sense. They were servants, in their powers were obedient to the decisions of another; and they were removed from the stimulus, intellectual and moral, which the necessities of meeting the conditions of independent business require. . . . Such a man came into the employ of the firm for which I worked, and his struggle to maintain his self-respect, and his little repressed exultation in being a member of a social club to which his ambitious employer could not obtain election, were to his fellow clerks both intelligible and pathetic. (Stimson 1904:338)

Middle-class men responded to this crisis of masculinity in several ways, including organized sports, both as participants and spectators. Prior to the end of the 19th century, organized sports had been unimportant in college life. But things changed quickly. The newly invented sports of basketball and football became focal activities that attracted large crowds and elicited generous financial contributions from alumni. The Harvard/Yale football game soon emerged as the biggest sporting event of the year. Outside of college, the modern Olympics was established in 1896 but for men only. The Olympics expressed the ideal of the amateur athlete, proclaiming that sport for money was bad because it revealed a lack of character. Until the 1940s, professional athletes were not respected, and sports heroes such as Babe Ruth were known as drunkards and philanderers. But the newly developing sports offered a way for office workers and others whose masculinity was being threatened by rapidly diminishing opportunities to express their virility. For youth, Boy Scouts and similar organizations dedicated to developing physical and moral character were created to protect boys from effeminacy (Bederman 1995; Filene 1998; Gilmore 1990; Hantover 1998; Kimmel

1987). Ernest Thompson Seton, founder of Boy Scouts of America, explained the goal of scouting:

> Realizing that manhood, not scholarship, is the first aim of education, we have sought out those pursuits which develop the finest character, the finest physique, and which may be followed out of doors, which, in a word, make for manhood. (Filene 1998:101)

Like Teddy Roosevelt hunting for wild game in Africa, boys could discover manhood in an emasculated culture by contending with raw nature. By 1920, 1 out of 10 American boys had been Scouts. These quasi-military organizations combined old-fashioned manly virtues (trustworthy, loyal, helpful, courteous, kind, cheerful, brave, obedient, etc.) with the new sense of outdoor adventure, training boys in camping, Indian lore, and other escapes from civilization. In an image that evoked similar drawings of soldiers protecting the motherland, a 1909 drawing in the English journal *Punch* depicted a Scout leading a grateful matron over the caption "Our Youngest Line of Defence," as seen in Figure 5.2. Scouting is an activity in which boys, under the close supervision of men, learn to master nature, both in their inherent masculinity and the raw elements they conquer in hiking and camping.

Before the rise of sports and camping, manhood had been contrasted primarily against boyhood and secondarily against womanhood. The emphasis on service to the community in early America, the notion of the self-made man, the control of one's emotions, and the contrast between civilized man and raw nature all distinguished boys from men. But manhood in the 20th century has been contrasted with femininity, while boyhood is seen as fully masculine. Unmasculine boys are chastised for being sissies, while "real men" are now supposed to keep their boyish sense of adventure. In sports, men play like boys, and boys imagine themselves to be men.

Manhood as service to the community distinguished men from boys by holding out manhood as an aspiration that boys could reach when they proved their manhood by demonstrating their character, maturity, and responsibility. Manhood as the self-made man also set men off from boys more than women. Like service, it was a goal that boys could only aspire to, not participate in. The seriousness, sobriety, and propriety to which the self-made man attributed his success were shared by women but not by boys. Men who failed to live up to both these standards were considered more boyish than feminine. In fact, the term *boy* had as much of a class connotation as an age one. *Boy* was used to refer to any male in a

FIGURE 5.2

Boy Scouts to the Rescue (in *Punch* 1909)

PUNCH, OR THE LONDON CHARIVARI.—September 1, 1909.

OUR YOUNGEST LINE OF DEFENCE.

Boy Scout (*to* Mrs. Britannia). "FEAR NOT, GRAN'MA; NO DANGER CAN BEFALL YOU NOW. REMEMBER, *I* AM WITH YOU!"

subservient position such as servant, waiter, or farm helper.[33] Other languages carry the same connotation—the French valet or *garçon* and the Italian *servire*. However, the masculine qualities that replaced these virtues distinguished manhood from femininity more than boyhood.

Homosexual and Homosocial Relations

When femininity replaced boyhood as the main antithesis of masculinity, many people became increasingly troubled about differences among men. Another binary opposition emerged—homosexual men versus "real" men. A new cultural construct, the male homosexual, was reified as a type of person, not just a type of activity. The creation of this new category both reflected and contributed to the crisis of masculinity. Homosexuality became something someone *was*, not just something that person *did*. There have always been people who have engaged in sex with people of the same sex. But until the end of the 19th century, Americans did not have a special term for a homosexual personhood. Mainstream society had condemned *sodomy* as an unnatural sexual *act*, using the term to refer equally to sex that men had with men, sex with animals, heterosexual oral and anal sex, and even prostitution. Treating homosexuality as a type of person, distinguishing the masculinity among different men, increased the concern over what sort of childhood experience causes someone to become that type of person. If homosexuality were a matter of what a person was rather than what he or she did, the roots had to be found in childhood, not their experience as adults. For boys, the prevailing answer was "too much mothering." A 1926 book giving advice to parents vividly contrasted masculinity to feminine men, describing a homosexual as "a man of broad hips and mincing gait, who vocalizes like a lady and articulates like a chatter box, who likes to sew and knit, to ornament his clothing and decorate his face" (Kimmel 1996:203). The message to parents was to protect their sons from expressing femininity. The fear of homosexuality had not always suppressed the "soft" side of manhood. When manhood was defined in terms of service to the community or the self-made man, relationships among men were often close and intimate. Because the extreme separation of spheres discouraged men and women from social relations except in the home, virtually all social life for both men and women was homosocial—man to man or woman to

---

[33]Whites used the term racially to refer to any African American male, which was widely interpreted as a device to emasculate them.

woman. Since gender was less a matter of the body than of character, homosocial behavior was not equated with homosexual behavior as it often is today. Many 19th-century young men had affectionate, even loving, relationships with other men. Letters between men sound remarkably like letters between lovers. Alexander Hamilton, a framer of the U.S. Constitution and the first Secretary of the Treasury, wrote to John Laurens, a friend and fellow soldier in 1779,

> Cold in my professions, warm in [my] friendships, I wish, my Dear Laurens, it m[ight] be in my power, by action rather than words, [to] convince you that I love you. I shall only tell you that 'till you bade us Adieu. I hardly knew the value you had taught my heart to set upon you. (Hansen 1991:95)

Daniel Webster, one of the most prominent U.S. senators of the 19th century, wrote to his friend, James Bingham, as "the only friend of my heart, the partner of my joys, griefs, and affections, the only participator of my most secret thoughts." After graduating from college, he pined, "I knew not how closely our feelings were interwoven; had no idea how hard it would be to live apart" (Filene 1998:83). These letters were written before the word *homosexual* entered the American vocabulary in the 1880s—words such as *sissy, she-man,* and *fairy* became popular in the masculinity crisis of the 1890s. These close relations between men could be physical, without necessarily being sexual. Boys commonly grew up sleeping in the same bed with brothers and would not find it embarrassing to share a bed with other young men. Abraham Lincoln shared a bed with his best friend as late as age 30. It is not that these men were necessarily more tolerant about homosexuality as much as they did not recognize homosexuality as a specific type of person with an encompassing identity.

Similar to the close friendship of young men, middle-class women of the 18th and 19th centuries shared what historians have called "romantic friendship" in which they expressed intense affection and physical feelings, although it is not known how many ever engaged in full sexual relations. For example, Rose Elizabeth Cleveland, sister of President Grover Cleveland and chief hostess for the bachelor master of the White House, shared a long correspondence with her devoted friend Evangeline Simpson Whipple. Wrote Cleveland to Whipple in 1890, "Ah, how I love you, it paralyzes me—it makes me heavy with emotion. . . . I tremble at the thought of you—all my whole being leans out to you. . . . I dare not think of your arms" (Faderman 1991:11). Cleveland later became the editor of the magazine *Literary Life,* and Whipple married a 74-year-old Episcopalian bishop who died 5 years later, after which the two women settled together in Italy. After the turn of the century, such romantic friendships became more difficult as mainstream society increasingly constructed a boundary between homosocial and homosexual behavior. Public consciousness became more aware of lesbianism, which had been invisible during the sexually repressed Victorian era, discouraging women from openly affectionate friendships.

Cross-Cultural Variation in Gender and Homosexuality

Different cultures variously conceptualized the relationship between gender and homosexuality. Romans did not distinguish between heterosexual and homosexual but between sexual penetration, which indicated power, and submission to penetration, which represented subordination. Powerless people, regardless of sex, would be expected to submit to penetration. Men who engaged in homosexual activity were not considered less manly (Laqueur 1990; Lorber 1994). Up to the 13th and 14th centuries, the early Christian church recognized same-sex unions in rituals that solemnized a marriage-type union of brotherhood, *adelphopoiesis*, literally, the making of a brother. Although it is not clear that these unions were sexual, the men committed themselves to a permanent, exclusive, and voluntary bond (Boswell 1994).

In contrast to Anglo-European culture, in which homosexuality is associated with people assuming the "wrong" gender identity—male homosexuals are (erroneously) assumed to be effeminate and female homosexuals are (erroneously) assumed to be manly—some cultures associate masculinity and homosexuality. For the Sambia of Africa, men generally adopt a style of masculinity that we would find very familiar, emphasizing warfare, hunting, and the approval of women. But in contrast to Anglo-European notions of masculinity, the key to manliness is ingesting other men's semen since in that culture semen embodies masculinity. The more semen you ingest, the more masculine you become (Herdt 1993b). Other cultures have treated homosexuality as a life stage. The transition from boyhood to manhood is achieved by entering the society of men through a homosexual rite of passage, symbolizing separation from the mother and independence from women. In ancient Greece, when homosexuality was a life stage, it was acceptable for men, including married men, to have sexual relations with boys they took on as protégés, as long as they did not exploit them (Martin 1996). The presence or absence of a category of bisexuality also varies among societies.

Bisexuality refers to the practice of having sexual relations with both men and women. Anglo-European societies have no clear category for bisexuality but instead rigidly enforce binary categorization into homosexuality or heterosexuality. People are forced to choose between heterosexual and homosexual identities despite evidence that many people who consider themselves heterosexual have had some homosexual events at some point in their lives, and many who identify themselves as homosexual have had sexual relations with people of the opposite sex. Ever since the famous Kinsey surveys of the 1940s documented that people's behavior ranges along a continuum from exclusively homosexual to exclusively heterosexual, scholars have questioned the binary homosexual-heterosexual classification, but the mainstream culture has changed little. Even though many now adopt an explicit bisexual orientation and identity, in many places redefining the gay movement as "GLBT"—Gay, Lesbian, Bisexual, Transgender—the binary classification scheme remains strong.

Intersections

The intersection of gender with time and space differs from the intersections of race because gender has been historically constructed somewhat differently than race. Women and men are in each other's presence for more time than people of different races. Such temporal and spatial proximity of men and women have allowed the intersection of time and space with gender—compared with race—to more typically take the form of constructing hierarchy. For example, while living in a ghetto does not make a person more black or less white, working at home as a housewife or house husband, in the eyes of many, would make a woman more feminine or a man less masculine.

Paid and Unpaid Work

Time and gender intersect in the distinction between unpaid and paid labor (Paolucci 1996). In Anglo-European society, paid work outside the home in the public sphere is considered "real work," while unpaid work that is done at home in the private sphere such as housework, child care, or cooking is often called "not working." Labor in private life, such as child care, household chores, or cooking, tends to be task oriented. A person does them when they need to be done rather than beginning or ending them by the clock. Imagine trying to raise a small child by the clock. It is impossible to set diaper changing, napping, or crying to a schedule. People typically do other household chores such as vacuuming or raking leaves when they "have time" and stop working when they are finished, not when a particular time is reached. Women working in the home are probably more likely to measure time by other events in the home, beginning housework after the husband leaves, doing the crossword as long as the pie is in the oven, and planning to be finished with shopping by the time the kids return from school, but even those events might happen at different clock times on different days. That is not to say that clock time is irrelevant to life in the private sphere, but the structure of time is more fluid. The markers used to coordinate activities are more diverse than the clock that dictates the schedule of work in most paid jobs. When doing paid work, a person goes to work and returns home at a certain time. Only professional occupations such as doctors, professors, lawyers, or clergy, in which there is a high investment of the person's identity in the job, operate like housework. For most people, starting and stopping a paid job are set by the clock, not the task. Factories were the main institution that instilled time discipline, the consciousness of doing tasks by clock time rather than the task itself. At first, factories allowed workers to come and go as they pleased, but gradually owners required workers to come and leave by clock time and to work continuously while at work. Figure 5.3 shows an 1853 timetable for a factory in Lowell, Massachusetts. Notice that the schedule varies depending on the number of daylight hours in the day, beginning at 4:30 a.m. in the summer months and 5:00 in the winter. Most days, they worked 12 hours, except on Saturday. The schedule was kept by a series of bells, not a visible clock. Workers in many factories complained that the bells were inaccurate. Notice also that there is not an assumed time standard but that the sign specifies the source of the time standard by the name of the regulator of the clock in Lowell.

When women are housewives, their contribution to society is devalued because "women's work" is not "real" work, while essential tasks such as housework, child care, and cooking are devalued because women do them. Common language describes housewives as "not working." But when they work in paid employment, time use looms larger in gender relations, especially in the home. Most women who work in paid employment continue to do most of the work inside the home, taking on a "second shift," essentially working two jobs, one of which they get paid for and is "real" and the other unpaid and not a

FIGURE 5.3

Timetable of the Lowell Mills

TIME TABLE OF THE LOWELL MILLS,

Arranged to make the working time throughout the year average 11 hours per day.

TO TAKE EFFECT SEPTEMBER 21st., 1853.

The Standard time being that of the meridian of Lowell, as shown by the Regulator Clock of AMOS SANBORN, Post Office Corner, Central Street.

From March 20th to September 19th, inclusive.

COMMENCE WORK, at 6.30 A. M.   LEAVE OFF WORK, at 6.30 P. M., except on Saturday Evenings.
BREAKFAST at 6 A. M.   DINNER, at 12 M.   Commence Work, after dinner, 12.45 P. M.

From September 20th to March 19th, inclusive.

COMMENCE WORK at 7.00 A. M.   LEAVE OFF WORK, at 7.00 P. M., except on Saturday Evenings.
BREAKFAST at 6.30 A. M.   DINNER, at 12.30 P.M.   Commence Work, after dinner, 1.15 P. M.

BELLS.

From March 20th to September 19th, inclusive.

Morning Bells.	Dinner Bells.	Evening Bells.
First bell,............4.30 A. M.	Ring out,.............12.00 M.	Ring out,.............6.30 P. M.
Second, 5.30 A. M. ; Third, 6.20.	Ring in,.............12.35 P. M.	Except on Saturday Evenings.

From September 20th to March 19th, inclusive.

Morning Bells.	Dinner Bells.	Evening Bells.
First bell,............5.00 A. M.	Ring out,.............12.30 P. M.	Ring out at.............7.00 P. M.
Second, 6.00 A. M. ; Third, 6.50.	Ring in,.............1.05 P. M.	Except on Saturday Evenings.

SATURDAY EVENING BELLS.

During APRIL, MAY, JUNE, JULY, and AUGUST, Ring Out, at 6.00 P. M.
The remaining Saturday Evenings in the year, ring out as follows :

SEPTEMBER.	NOVEMBER.	JANUARY.
First Saturday, ring out 6.00 P. M.	Third Saturday ring out 4.00 P. M.	Third Saturday, ring out 4.25 P. M.
Second " " 5.45 "	Fourth " " 3.55 "	Fourth " " 4.35 "
Third " " 5.30 "		
Fourth " " 5.20 "	DECEMBER.	FEBRUARY.
OCTOBER.	First Saturday, ring out 3.50 P. M.	First Saturday, ring out 4.45 P. M.
First Saturday, ring out 5.05 P. M.	Second " " 3.55 "	Second " " 4.55 "
Second " " 4.55 "	Third " " 3.55 "	Third " " 5.00 "
Third " " 4.45 "	Fourth " " 4.00 "	Fourth " " 5.10 "
Fourth " " 4.35 "	Fifth " " 4.00 "	
Fifth " " 4.25 "		MARCH.
	JANUARY.	First Saturday, ring out 5.25 P. M.
NOVEMBER.	First Saturday, ring out 4.10 P. M.	Second " " 5.30 "
First Saturday, ring out 4.15 P. M.	Second " " 4.15 "	Third " " 5.35 "
Second " " 4.05 "		Fourth " " 5.45 "

YARD GATES will be opened at the first stroke of the bells for entering or leaving the Mills.

SPEED GATES commence hoisting three minutes before commencing work.

Penhallow, Printer, Wyman's Exchange, 28 Merrimack St.

SOURCE: Baker Library, Graduate School of Business Administration, Harvard University.

"real" job (Hochschild 1989). The definitions of time around these two jobs are often quite different because of the power wielded by employers. The paid job is considered nonnegotiable, inflexible time. Women themselves and other members of their families take that time as a given and would rarely think of asking an employed woman to skip work unless necessary (although if it is necessary for one person in a married couple to skip work, such as caring for a sick child, it is usually the woman who does so).

However, when dominant institutions need women's labor, they accommodate gender images to fit their needs. Within the long-term trend from the melding of home and work to the separation of public and private spheres to the recent reintroduction of women into the labor force, there have been shorter-term deviations in response to economic and political crises. Times of depression have tended to evoke images of nurturing women who should stay at home, while war time has stimulated propaganda campaigns to get women into the factories. The most explicit campaign was during World War II, when the U.S. government mobilized a formidable publicity effort based on an imaginary character named "Rosie the Riveter," who would take a job on the assembly line helping the war effort. Millions of women, many with husbands and boyfriends away at war, took jobs that had previously been defined as suitable only for men. The imperious expression on the face of Rosie in Figure 5.4 comes with a muscular body that would have little trouble handling the riveter sitting in her lap while she enjoys her lunch with her foot resting on a copy of Hitler's *Mein Kampf.* After the men came home from the war, most of the women working in factories were cleared out and expected to return to their domestic chores.

Unlike time in work and politics, private time is negotiable and flexible. Many women are expected to do the housework, care for the children, find time for relationships, and make time for themselves from the same limited pool of time. Children, husbands, friends, and other relatives all make demands on private time, often expecting that pool of time to expand to fit their needs (Jurczyk 1998). Although people talk about time as a quantity—"having time"—the social relationship between husband and wife is one of power. A husband might say he "has no time" for child care or housework, even though he has the same 24 hours a day as a wife. To the extent that husbands have more power over their wives, couples can be expected to have different attitudes about the private time available for husbands and wives. While women take on the second shift, men treat their private time as an opportunity to recover from the stressful demands of their jobs. They can fit their household chores into

FIGURE 5.4

Rosie the Riveter

SOURCE: Printed by permission of the Norman Rockwell Family Trust.
© 1943, the Norman Rockwell Family Trust.

their "free time" and can use the "lack of time" to postpone or omit chores.

The result is that many men have a different sense of time than many women. All people live by clock time, but many women—especially those who do housework and care for children—live and organize their lives by other sorts of time. Women working at home probably feel more variance in the length of the day, for example, with some days seeming to fly by while others drag on forever (although, of course, everyone feels that to some extent). Housework is less segmented into particular activities than other kinds of work. And women have been found to pay more attention to their "internal clock," deciding when to do things and how long to continue them in accord with their own feelings, than the external clocks. It should be emphasized that many men and women do not fit this pattern. It is not that gender in an essentialist sense explains differences in the experience of time, but gender has been historically constructed so that men and women tend to have different social experiences of time. As more women work in paid work and self-consciously challenge male, dominant forms of time, the differences between men's and women's experiences of time will diminish. However, as long as the public-private split is structured along gender lines, time will be gendered (Leccardi 1996).

Public and Private Space

In contrast to how space is racialized, space is gendered less by place of residence than by the designation of private space and public space. The earlier discussion of how public and private spheres became separate said little about the spatial setting. Men's neighborhoods and women's neighborhoods are not analogous to white neighborhoods and black neighborhoods. Space and gender intersect at a much smaller scale. Homes are considered private spaces, where women have some degree of jurisdiction, while places of work or governance are dominated by men. Women have much more relative power in the home than in the public sphere because it is "their" place. Women at home may not have more power in interpersonal interaction with men. Many men dominate their wives or partners; some abuse and batter them. But most allow women to administer the home itself, remaining indifferent to domestic matters. When men orient their lives too much around the private sphere, they become labeled as nonmasculine "house husbands" and are depicted wearing women's aprons.

FIGURE 5.5a

Public Life in 1890 (*Harper's New Monthly Magazine*)

FIGURE 5.5b

Private Life in 1890 (*Harper's New Monthly Magazine*)

Moreover, space within the home is gendered. The more public spaces, such as the living room, are more the preserve of the husband. Our stereotypical image of the couple at home is the man sitting in the easy chair reading the paper or monopolizing the television remote control while the woman works in the more private part of the house, the kitchen. The most private part, the bathroom, while used by both for biological functions, is also the site where the woman fabricates her feminine persona at the makeup table.[34] Women typically clean the bathroom so it is available for men to use.

Conversely, public space "belongs" to men. To inhabit public space, especially open areas where people can congregate, women typically must choose between behaving as the objects of men's attention or adopting a nonfeminine style (Gardner 1994). The qualities used to characterize public space are typically considered more masculine than feminine. Public space, at least in the Anglo-European culture, is brawny compared to the elegance that homes are expected to be. Public space

---

[34]The other private part of the home, the bedroom, does not fit this pattern neatly. While very private, it is not a woman's domain but is, at best, contested.

shows off concrete, glass, and steel, while home interiors camouflage the stark walls with mementos and ornamentation. And public space occupies large dimensions—plazas, skyscrapers, rotundas, boulevards, assembly halls, and factories—where men regulate, trade, deliberate, orate, officiate, and fabricate. Figure 5.5 illustrates how space became divided into gendered public and private spheres. Woman in the 19th century were typically visually depicted in small-scale settings, usually the home, interacting with other women or other children, as in this 1890 drawing from *Harper's New Monthly Magazine.* Another drawing in the same issue displays the public world, an expansive breadth of Wall Street with towering edifices, very much a man's world.

Gender and Race

The mutual recognition of race in gender studies and gender in racial studies has been one of the more vibrant areas of scholarship in the past decade or so. Racial minorities protested that too many studies about gender described primarily white women and men. Likewise, women claimed that race studies have focused more on men than women. Scholars of many disciplines have been energetically working to show that these silences have distorted both fields. It is not just that women have been omitted from race studies and racial minorities from gender studies; it is that looking in new places will add to existing knowledge. Many scholars have argued that the omissions distorted earlier understandings of race and gender.

One of the clearest examples of how race would require a rethinking of how gender has been constructed is the relationship between public and private life. Many women objected to the confinement of women to the private sphere, especially when they attempted to enter public life. As noted above, the movement for the women's vote challenged the division. However, many middle- and upper-class white women eagerly embraced the cult of domesticity. Sarah Josepha Hale, editor of the Boston *Ladies' Magazine*, advised her readers that "our men are sufficiently money-making. Let us keep our women and children from contagion as long as possible. To do good and to communicate, should be the motto of Christians and republicans" (Cott 1977:68). But as men withdrew from child care and rising middle-class standards of cleanliness and hospitality crystallized into a "cult of domesticity," the demands of womanhood became more difficult to achieve. The solution was hiring lower-class women, usually of minority races and ethnic groups. The

"Irish washerwoman" became a fixture in New York. Ninety percent of nonagriculturally employed black women in the South were servants or laundresses. In the Southwest, about half of all Mexican American women were domestic or laundry workers, and in the far West, white middle-class families hired Japanese and Chinese women (Glenn 1999). Thus, the ideal of white womanhood would have been virtually impossible without racial inequality.

This relationship of poor minority and white middle-class women also made it impossible for the poor minority women to live up to their responsibilities as women. Working in other women's homes, they could not care for their own children (few of whom were permitted in white schools), cook very many meals for their families, or regularly clean their houses (before vacuum cleaners or washing machines). The dominant ideology then defined them as irresponsible and inferior because they could not live up to the white standards (Glenn 1999).

The number of domestic servants and child caregivers declined in the first half of the 20th century but rose again in the past several decades as more middle-class women (of all races) have taken full-time jobs. Once again, most are minority women. At the same time, racial minorities perform a disproportionate share of the labor to reproduce families outside the home. As working women buy more and more food from restaurants or the growing deli sections of supermarkets, it is generally low-paid minority women doing the preparation. As more middle-class children are put in day care, it is disproportionately minority women who care for them. Just as minority women made it possible for white middle-class women of the 19th century to live up to the standards of "true womanhood," lower-class minority women today make it possible for middle-class women of all races to combine career and family, the ideal of today's "new woman."

Conclusion

Gender is the archetypal "natural" category. Not only does it have a physically obvious biological representation—sex differences—but it inscribes a deeply felt identity, an identity felt so pervasively that it "must" be natural. As natural as gender identity feels to many people, nature cannot explain the content and force of gender. The comparative and historical approach demonstrates that different societies treat very different characteristics as male or female. There are societies such as the Yoruba that barely distinguish between men and women except for procreation, and there are societies in which basically all social distinctions revolve around sex and gender. There are societies in Tahiti where manhood is marked by passivity and others where it is marked by aggression. Even in Anglo-European society, the meanings of sex and gender have changed dramatically. Whereas women were once seen as biologically similar but inferior to men—the one-sex model—women are now seen as biologically opposite of men—the two-sex model. This was a change in biological understanding that derived from cultural understandings, even though many people generally assume that culture is determined by biology. While women have always been subordinate to men in Anglo-European societies, the character of the relationship has changed. When the family and church were the dominant institution, some women could occupy positions of power as monarchs, merchants, or landlords but were subjugated to male patriarchs in the family and church. The separation of the family from the public sphere raised women to a symbolic pedestal while excluding them from institutional authority. Women became defined by their bodies, that is, as sex objects, mothers, and nurturers. Men reversed their gender roles even more dramatically than women. Masculinity, once defined in terms of modesty and selfless contribution to the community, was turned on its head and defined as triumphant toughness. Men were defined by both body and mind—athletic and capable of thought or leadership.

As natural as those gender definitions feel to people who grew up with them, it is not easy to socialize boys and girls into masculine men and feminine women. Rigid and incessant indoctrination enforced by rewards and punishments meted out by dominant institutions betray how unnatural gender definitions are. Parents, teachers, Boy Scout leaders, and peers emphatically cry "sissy," "wimp," "wuss," or "nerd" to boys who fail to assert sufficient fortitude—or anxiously give Barbie dolls, pink dresses, and invectives to "act like a lady" to recalcitrant "tomboys." The family system, schools, mass media, religion, and other dominant institutions succeed less at creating fully "masculine men" or "feminine women" than at enforcing a pervasive and powerful gender system in which many who do not conform feel either like they have failed or that they are fighting the system. The gender system is part of a complex configuration of domination and subordination. While women in general are subordinated by it, white women have been able to gain privileges at the expense of African Americans, both male and female. While white men have been the chief beneficiaries, white working-class men have too often turned their class frustrations against working-class women, and white middle-class men have endured the insecurity of reaching for an ideal few could achieve.

Despite impressive progress toward equality between men and women, women remain a subordinate group. Men and women still have very different relationships with dominant institutions. American women working full-time earn on the average only 71 cents for every dollar that men earn. When race and ethnicity intersect, the gap is greater, 65 cents for African American women and 55 cents for Hispanic women. Part of the reason is that women are employed inordinately in occupations that are gendered as women's jobs. Nearly half of all women work in occupations that are at least 80% women—librarians, nurses, elementary school teachers, secretaries, and so on—reaching into nearly every major institution. At the same time, most women are still expected to run the household and do housework. Women who work full-time outside the home still spend about 33 hours a week on housework, compared with 18 hours for men. And in most households, it is still the woman who is expected to take time off work to care for sick children or meet with teachers, while they are less free to work overtime or take out-of-town trips than men (Newman 2000).

These facts only beg the main issue of this chapter—how the differences between men and women are explained. Are differences between men and women explained in terms of essential qualities of men and women or because of the way gender has been constructed and continues to be reconstructed? Even when women move into jobs conventionally dominated by men, very often the qualities considered necessary for success or promotion are conventional "male" qualities. In working-class jobs, this means physical toughness, while in managerial jobs, it means aggressiveness, the ability to set aside emotions, and open ambition. If women act in ways that are conventionally considered female, they are considered less capable and less likely to be promoted. If they act in ways that make them effective on the job, they are vulnerable to being considered masculine.

Perhaps the most innovative feature of gender in 20th-century Anglo-European culture is how self-conscious people have become about it. Although feminist movements existed before the 20th century, gender has become a politicized and contested identity alongside race, nationality, religion, and class. Not only have women increasingly demanded and partially achieved access to social positions previously monopolized by men, but they have also increasingly asserted their place in society as women. Not only have men begrudgingly begun to yield a few of their privileges, but manhood is also less unambiguously the "unmarked case," as public interest in gender has expanded to include both masculinity and femininity. Despite a backlash against feminism in the mass media over the past few decades (Faludi 1991), television, film, and the print media continue to debate the rights, responsibilities, and appropriate behavior for men and women, sustaining the cultural self-consciousness about gender. Parents and teachers socialize gender behaviors, whether with traditional or innovative designs, more intentionally and less habitually. This chapter itself, as well as the literature on which it is based, is a signal that we have become more self-conscious about gender in recent years.

While this chapter has argued that the gender system has inordinately burdened women, the concept of social construction implies that the system can be changed. If gender inequality is the destiny of biological difference, little can be changed. As deeply as gender is woven into the fabric of society, including all its institutions, culture, and language—so deeply it feels natural—fundamentally the system is still social and can be changed by social action. Changing it confronts both the resistance of entrenched interests and the inertia of tradition, not the least of which is the feeling that it is natural. And as the history of gender relations shows, change can be sluggish, reversible, and unintended.

6

Class

A story in the *New York Times* tells of the daily life of a 33-year-old Chicago woman named Mary Ann Moore (DeParle 1994). Each morning at 3:30 a.m., she rises from the couch she uses as a bed and wakes and feeds breakfast to her three small children, whom she then drives to her mother's place where they wait an hour before going to school. Mary Ann drives on to her job as a cook at the Salvation Army homeless shelter. Before working there for more than a year, she had worked driving trucks, peddling nuts, bathing invalids, skating the aisles of a warehouse, and carrying a revolver as a security guard at the public housing project where she was raised. Her $8 an hour pay is among the highest where she works, a result of a junior college course that earned her a food and sanitation license, her diligence in maintaining a 52-hour week schedule (including 13-hour shifts on Saturday and Sunday), and her supervisor's evaluation that she is "a self-starter." Working every week of the year would still not generate enough income to raise her above the official federal poverty level but exceeds the eligibility level for welfare, food stamps, or subsidized housing. Returning to the welfare system she has escaped would improve her standard of living, but she says, "It's a big self-esteem thing for me to be working." When the reporter was working on this story, her used car with 100,000 miles (still not paid for) broke down, costing more than $500 to repair. Losing transportation would jeopardize her job, as would the illness of herself, her children, or her aging mother.

If hard work is the route to a comfortable middle-class life, why does Mary Ann Moore's life remain so difficult? Does she work any less hard than millions of people in much more comfortable circumstances? What is it about society that gives some people a much higher return on their work, their talent, and their effort than other people?

Is Mary Ann Moore's life different from those of the middle and upper class only because she has less money? To what extent are the differences a matter of degree (along a continuum), and to what extent are there categorical inequalities such as race or gender? Is part of the explanation for her getting less return on her effort a result of her being put into social categories such as welfare mother, poor person, failure, or loser?

Besides Mary Ann Moore having less material comfort and security, how is her life different from those with higher incomes? How are the social attitudes, worldviews, cultural tastes, and leisure activities different from rich and poor? To what extent are such differences merely a result of different resources, and to what extent do these differences help explain why some people have more resources than others?

To what extent are Mary Ann Moore's difficulties a matter of her own personal qualities versus the result of how various institutions have treated her? How have teachers, employers, social workers, doctors, and law enforcement officers treated her differently from the way they treat people who dress better, speak Standard English more correctly, have more respectable parents, and grow up in better neighborhoods? To what extent are her dress, speech, family, and neighborhood a cause of her material circumstance rather than a result of it?

When about one in seven Americans—including a fifth of all children and nearly a third of Latinos and African Americans—live below the poverty line, and when the top 20% of American households have incomes nearly 14 times as high as the lowest 20% ($122,764 compared to $8,872), why does the image persist that nearly all Americans are middle class?

The Meaning of Class

While time may be the most difficult topic in the course to understand as a historical construction, class may be the easiest. Many idealists have imagined a classless society. Scholars and activists have passionately debated whether class inequality is inevitable, but both sides of the debate are readily plausible to the imagination. Even if they think it is unrealistic, most people can conjure up an image of how class developed historically more readily than they can imagine a society without a week, without races, or without gender. While it is easy to imagine society without social classes,[35] many are inclined to explain why some people dominate others or have more wealth and prestige than others in terms of their natural aptitudes such as intelligence, character, or fortitude. Like race and gender, this chapter addresses the question of how to explain inequalities of class. Can the class differences among people be more fully explained by people's natural differences or by how powerful institutions have shaped the class structure? This chapter will describe how the overall class structure of societies is historically constructed much the same way time, space, race, and gender are, and we can best understand why individuals end up at one place in the class structure or another by their social relationships with other people, not their inborn qualities.

What does *class* mean anyway? Different sociologists use the term *class* in very different ways. Rather than asserting that the approach to class taken here is the only correct way or even the best way, I will take a serviceable definition that helps us understand differences among societies and gives some leverage on understanding how people get along in any society. **Class** will be treated as social relationships that are understood by participants to be hierarchical on the basis of socioeconomic group membership, reinforced by major institutions and recurrent over time. Let's look at each of the parts of this definition.

The Components of the Definition

Hierarchical: The meaning of *hierarchical* may be the most straightforward but also the most elusive because, in fact, hierarchy is a metaphor, not a literal description of social relations. Although society can be depicted on a vertical scale from high to low, people are not physically higher or lower. Sociologists treat "upper class," "middle class," "lower class," or "underclass" as very real and use many descriptive terms of physical height to describe class position: *stature, position, level, ascent, mobility, climbing up the ladder,* and so on. Even the word *position* is a spatial metaphor. The metaphorical language for higher class generally re-

---

[35]There is a biological explanation of classes based on evolutionary thinking. Some have argued that classes are natural because of the survival of the fittest: Those who are stronger or fitter dominate the weaker. Others argue that societies organized on hierarchical lines are more efficient and more likely to survive than egalitarian societies. Because neither of the arguments is grounded in historical evidence, they will not be seriously considered here.

fers to a person having more of something that the society values.[36] In Anglo-European society, that can be more money, but in some societies, status is gained by how much a person gives away at a ritual called a pot-latch. The great sociologist Max Weber suggested three kinds of things that many societies treat as higher class when people have more of them: **economic class,** by which people are distinguished by material posses-sions such as income or wealth; **social status,** by which people are distin-guished by prestige or cultural honor; and **political power,** by which people are distinguished by how much influence they have over govern-ment.

Bounded categories: Americans tend to think of the class structure as a fluid continuum from top to low, using metaphors such as "the ladder of opportunity." In contrast to race, in which the social construction of cate-gories is more bounded than the actual distribution of skin color, class is constructed as more continuous and less bounded than the actual distri-bution of resources in society. Class is bounded in three ways. The first is that there are bumps that make the class structure less of a continuum. For example, while education is a major determinant of how well people do on the job market, it is not entirely continuous. Having 11 years of schooling is much different from having a high school degree, just as $3\frac{1}{2}$ years of college is much different from having a college degree. These bumps in the continuum come when there are categories of people. These can be formal class statuses such as nobility or peasantry found in Europe for many centuries or the caste system of India, where a person is born into a caste that brands him or her for life. In American society, "high school dropout," "college graduate," and "Ph.D." are categories that can follow a person for life. So one of the things to explain about class and the way that class is historically constructed is how class cate-gories get created.

The second way classes are bounded is that classes can become de-fined as us-them distinctions. While class categories are often seen as groupings that join people in a larger category of "us-ness," many class categories become ways of dividing "us" from "them." Rich soldiers and poor civilians can fight shoulder to shoulder against a national enemy but can be divided at home, the richer claiming that more police is a

---

[36]Some things gain higher status by being less of something—a quality of exclu-sivity. Joining a high-status club that restricts members; owning a rare coin, stamp, or work of art; or having a high-status job with few occupants, such as be-ing a Supreme Court justice, all gain higher status because they are exclusive.

better solution to urban decay than assistance to the poor and the poor resenting the bloated salaries given to corporate executives. Compared to many societies, American society has fewer boundaries in the class structure, provoking the important issue of how class boundaries are defined and put into practice.

The third and most important way that class is a bounded category is the distinct ways that people in different categories have different relations with institutions. The most fundamental class division is people's different relations to the economic institution, especially whether they primarily get their income from wages and salaries, from assets they own such as stocks and bonds or rental property, or from noneconomic institutions such as government or charity. While many people get income from more than one of these sources—the employee who owns stock, the corporate president who gets a salary, or the welfare recipient with a part-time job—most people fall into one category or another. Class differences also involve different relationships that people have with other institutions. For example, whether a person gets medical care through insurance connected to his or her job, a private physician paid out of pocket, or a public hospital paid by Medicare has momentous consequences for that person's health. Whether a person drops out of high school, has only a high school diploma, or has a degree from a prestigious university strongly affects many aspects of life from marriage partners to income.

Groups: While some inequality is based on individual attributes, class inequality is between socioeconomic groups. **Socioeconomic group** means a category of people defined by their social and economic attributes. Doctors, poor people, yuppies, welfare recipients, and middle-class people are examples. Such groups not only describe differences but also explain them. Class means that people have more income, prestige, or power *because* they are members of a group. Take a child from a wealthy family that has books in the home, whose parents help with homework each night and consult regularly with teachers, who wears nice clothes so teachers think she is responsible, and who speaks confidently and grammatically correct so the teacher thinks she is smart. Compare her with a student from a poor family without books, whose parents lack the education to help her with homework and work during the day at jobs that do not allow them to consult with teachers, who wears shabby clothing so teachers think she is slovenly, and who speaks timidly and perhaps with a foreign accent or the dialect of Black English. Not only are teachers likely to give the first student better grades, but they are also likely to spend more time and give more attention to the first student, helping her to learn more. So the first student's better grades must be explained less in terms of her personal characteristics than her membership in the middle or upper class. She will get better grades than the second student for the same effort. The doctor who works 60 hours a week will get paid much more than the janitor who works 60 hours a week, perhaps just as hard as the doctor. The difference is due to the fact that they are members of different occupational groups. So class differences are differences of the return a person gets by virtue of being a member of a socioeconomic group.

Relations to institutions: But classes are not just any groups; they are groups whose common relationships to institutions result in the unequal distribution of resources. A person's **relationship to an institution** is the title he or she occupies in organizations, the connections to other people, and the rights, privileges, and responsibilities that come from his or her position. Doctors get paid more than orderlies because they have different relationships to the medical institution. Investors may get higher profits when workers get paid less because of their different relationships with the economic institution. In capitalism, classes most fundamentally have different relationships to economic institutions, although they also have different relationships to other institutions such as education, religion, family, government, and the health care system. But classes in different societies can have different institutional relationships, that is, a different way that scarce resources are distributed. Virtually all institutions are structured along class lines.

Family

A person is born into a family that is situated in the class structure. You cannot have an upper-class husband and a lower-class wife, even though the husband may have come from an upper-class family and the wife from a lower-class one. In kinship-based societies, resources are distributed based on a person's relationship to clan or kinship organizations. People are grouped through families to the broader kinship structure and get land, cattle or sheep, food, and prestige depending on what family they belong to and what position they hold within their family. Some societies have a royal family, noble families, and common families. The English royal family is still one of the wealthiest families in the world, distinctive by more than their monarchical titles. In the traditional Islamic world of North Africa or the Middle East, it was not people's relationship to specific economic or political organizations that determined their wealth or poverty as much as their place in the kinship structure, a departure so far removed from Anglo-European patterns that some scholars have questioned whether the arrangement should even be called class relations (Charrad 1999).

It is not just that an individual has more of something such as money, prestige, or power that constitutes class. It is that the person has more of these things because of his or her relationship to social institutions.

Occupation

In Anglo-European society, people's occupations are a major determinant of their economic class. Another is whether they get their income from the work they do, as in wages or salaries, or from what they own, as in dividends or selling stocks and bonds. Most people think of the job a person gets as a reward for personal qualities; talented, hardworking, and ambitious people get good jobs, and incompetent, lazy, and shiftless people get bad jobs or no jobs. To some extent, that is true. But the job a person gets is also determined by the relationship he or she has with other institutions such as family, school, or previous employers. Let's take schools. Most jobs except the most menial ones require a minimum level of education. Low-wage jobs such as salespeople in department stores require high school education, managerial jobs require college education, and professional jobs generally require professional degrees. Such requirements are typically justified by the demands of the job itself. But in practice, the certificate—the degree—is more important than an applicant's skills. Many people without college degrees have educated themselves enough to competently perform managerial jobs that require a college degree, but no one will hire them. The degree itself is used as a proxy for qualification and comes to represent qualification. So in practical terms, it is the person's relationship to the educational institution, certified through the degree, that determines a person's economic class.

Education

Schools are organized along class lines in another way. The schools that lower-class children attend differ radically from those attended by middle- and upper-class children. Schools attended by lower-class children are generally poorly funded, understaffed, and underachieving. Upper-class children attend elite private schools with smaller classes, better teachers, more resources, and a much higher percentage of graduates going on to college. Colleges are also stratified from junior and community colleges, attended primarily by lower-class students, to state universities to elite private colleges. The kind of college a person attends strongly influences the kind of job he or she will get.

Medicine

The medical institution is also stratified, with lower-class people getting care at impersonal, poorly funded public hospitals and upper-class people going to private doctors or plush, private hospitals.

Religion

Religions tend to be organized along class lines, with upper-class people more likely to belong to Episcopal or Presbyterian churches, middle-class people to mainline denominations such as Methodist or Lutheran, and lower-class people to Evangelical or Pentecostal churches, although this has changed in the past few decades. Jewish and Catholic churches tend to include a broad class spectrum, although individual congregations can be primarily members of one class.

Leisure

Even sports and leisure are organized along class lines, with upper-class people more likely to be involved in golf, tennis, and watching football and lower-class people more likely to participate in bowling and watch baseball. Please remember that all of these generalizations have many exceptions and that no individuals should be typecast because they contradict these tendencies.

Recurrent over time: The final characteristic of class is that it is recurrent over time. People who have more of life's valued resources will use those resources to influence how institutions reinforce their class position and that of their children. Wealthy parents will enroll their children in good schools either by moving to nice neighborhoods or paying high tuition in private schools. They will use the best medical facilities when they are sick so they miss less work time and return without penalties (and they probably have jobs that allow more paid sick leave). They will use the status of respectable jobs to get better jobs and climb up the occupational ladder. They will belong to religious organizations where people of their own class not only affirm their faith but also can be valuable business and job contacts. So it is not surprising that even though the opportunities for people to create their own future are better in Anglo-European societies than in many other times and places, people born into lower classes tend to end up in lower classes, and people born into upper classes tend to end up in the upper classes.

The Origins of Class-Based Societies

While there is inequality in all societies, even animal societies, where some members have more goods or dominate others, human societies have not always been organized around inequality that is structured through its institutions. If there were a perfect **meritocracy,** where people's livelihood depended solely on achievements, there would be no classes, just inequality. People who were smarter, worked more, and contributed more to the society would be rewarded more than those who were not. A garbage man could earn just as much, be just as respected, and exercise just as much political influence as a doctor. In nonclass societies, inequality was based mainly on gender, age, or individual characteristics, not on class. People got more food, better housing, and more honor and influence because they were male, older, or better hunters. But when there are classes, some people are assigned better hunting grounds or sharper spears, get more land, or get better jobs because of their clan or their position in a clan, and everyone must often share their bounty with a chieftain. If religious organizations, family systems, or governance structures all work together to systematically benefit some people at the expense of others, there is a class society. The question, then, is how such societies have arisen. The social process by which classes are created and become a major means of distributing valued resources is **class formation.** Like race and gender, class relations must be explained historically.

The human species *homo sapiens* has been on the planet for about 200,000 to 300,000 years. First civilizations appeared in about 3000 B.C.E., so the era of civilization is less than 4% of human history. If we think of all human history as a day with 24 hours, humans have been civilized for about half an hour. And since social classes have existed only in civilized societies, for 23½ "hours" of that day, there have been no social classes. They clearly are not natural.

Perhaps the most compelling piece of evidence that classes are not natural is that most changes in the past 5,000 years have been cultural, not biological. In the blink of an eye in evolutionary terms, a period in which there were no major mutations in the human species, there has been phenomenal social transformation from simple communal sharing of hunting and gathering societies to the complex, lopsided class structures of today. While biology sets certain limits on human behavior, the variation among human societies is cultural, not biological.

Nonclass Societies

Understanding how class is historically constructed requires a sense of what nonclass societies are like. Given the enormous variety of human societies, there is no single type of nonclass society. Because class-based societies have spread throughout the world, most of the examples are anthropological. In hunting and gathering societies, the most common form of society throughout human history, people did not grow food or manufacture merchandise but ate animals they hunted and plants they gathered. Rather than prizing what people accumulated, they valued cooperation and sharing. Very often, skilled hunters would be honored less because they amassed wealth than because they provided for the whole community. But they rarely had permanent hierarchies of status and privilege. Only when hunting and gathering societies developed a surplus and capacity to store it did they create permanent hierarchies (Sanderson 1999).

A more hierarchical type of society, but still not fully a class society, is a **rank society,** in which some positions had higher status and authority but not any material advantages, usually with strong norms against using privilege for material gain. Rank societies in general had no organized structures that enabled people to use power for themselves. Authority was typically used on behalf of the whole group. For example, central authority helped build the huge structures at Stonehenge in England and on the Pacific Easter Island. The ceremonial stones at Stonehenge were developed over a 1,000-year period from 3000 B.C.E. to 1800 B.C.E., but the society that erected the giant stone monoliths disappeared. It was a remarkable achievement in a society with no evidence of an organized social class system.

The Siuai of Bougainville in the Solomon Islands also illustrate a rank society. They recognized some members as *mumi* or "big men"—people with leadership qualities and enough valuable possessions to share. Generous men were well liked and celebrated when they gave large feasts for the entire community. But they strongly resented anyone considered selfish and condemned anyone who did not share. Selfishness was even a basis for divorce. People showed deference to the "big men" by fetching water for them, lowering their voices when they arrived, or lowering their eyes (Sanderson 1999). While Anglo-European societies still honor those who share wealth, usually in the form of charity or philanthropy, they also accord great prestige to those who amass great wealth such as Bill Gates or Ted Turner.

The Earliest Class Societies

Before a class structure organizes human life, two conditions must exist. First, the opportunities for easy escape from the society must be eliminated. If people can easily move to somewhere else without sacrificing their quality of life, it is difficult for some people to heavily exploit others. But if they cannot move without great sacrifice, the lack of alternatives is called the **caging effect,** like being in a cage. Class systems arise when it is possible for one group to create a monopoly over a scarce resource such as fertile fields for agriculture or vital irrigation water, a condition that existed only where people were geographically caged. A monopoly over a strategic resource created opportunities for the collective power found in traditional societies that built edifices such as Stonehenge or the Easter Island monuments, as well as—and this is the novel feature—distributive power, by which some people control others (Mann 1986). It does not mean that people feel overtly oppressed. Modern society is caged—to have a decent living, people must take a job and at least minimally participate in social life. Even though they grumble about their jobs and there is no other realistic option for most people, few feel seriously oppressed.

The second condition for a class society is the existence of an **economic surplus**; that is, people must produce more food, clothing, and other necessities than they consume. The surplus provides the resources that upper classes use to perpetuate domination.

These conditions first developed in the part of the Middle East known as the "Fertile Crescent," the crescent-shaped area extending from the Nile Valley to the Tigris and Euphrates Rivers, spanning present-day Syria and Iraq. Deserts on both sides created a caging effect, while river-based ecologies generated enough surplus for a dominating class (Mann 1986).

One of the first class-based civilizations was ancient Mesopotamia, a society in the Fertile Crescent that had been originally organized along egalitarian lines. They developed an agricultural system based on irrigation canals by about 5000 B.C.E. and built the first cities in human history by about 4000 B.C.E. With at least half of the population living in cities of more than 1,000 people, caging was achieved. Cities can exist only on surplus product. People who grow food in agrarian regions must be able to grow enough for the people in the cities as well as themselves. By about 3000 B.C.E., writing appeared, another huge breakthrough in human history. In addition to the enrichment of the human condition through literature and poetry, writing also makes possible administrative structures that can regulate social life. The key was the irrigation system. Whether irrigation arose from cooperation or coercion, it offered an opportunity for some people to gain control over others. When people were dependent on irrigation, those who controlled water could control society. And when some people could control others, they formed groups that became constituted as classes. When one group established the right to control a resource such as irrigation or the land on which irrigated crops grow, it created a system of property. A new concept appeared—"ownership." In contrast to the majority of societies in which people make claims on resources by using them, ownership describes a system in which people control resources whether they use them or not. Irrigation systems permitted some groups to dominate other groups, which they described as a "right" of property, thereby forming classes.

Because the same surplus that makes class society possible also makes civilization possible, civilization first arose with class society. A **civilization** is a society with specialized institutions and occupations that creates art, music, literature, and other artifacts of an explicitly aesthetic nature. In most civilizations, the artifacts that constitute the grandeur served to symbolically represent the power of the ruling classes. Ruling classes tend to accumulate and display fine art, sculpture, architecture, music, and literature as evidence of their cultural and economic distinction.

Class civilizations arose spontaneously in only a handful of places. Nearly all the civilizations that have existed throughout human history have developed from contact with other civilizations. The Mesopotamian civilization influenced India to the east and Egypt to the west. Egypt influenced the development of ancient Greece, which kindled Rome; these were roots of modern Anglo-European civilization and its class structure. For the sake of brevity, I will skip over the rest of the ancient world and explore the origins of capitalism, the class system that has become virtually universal in the late 20th century, beginning with its germination in feudalism.

Feudalism

Feudalism was the set of economic and social relations that preceded capitalism in Europe. It was a complicated system with many variations across Europe, but here are the basic features: There were two major classes, the nobility and peasants. The nobility was organized around a

FIGURE 6.1

A Tenant Renews His Vows

SOURCE: *Sachsenspiegel*, early 14th century, Cod. Pal. Germ. 164. University of Heidelberg.

military government headed by a king (or occasionally a queen). Vertical chains of personal loyalty linked higher members, starting with the king at the top, to lower members. The higher members promised to protect the lower members, and the lower members promised to pay a portion of their goods as a tribute. The responsibilities went in both directions. Those above were responsible for protecting lower members from the frequent wars that were fought among the nobility, from the ravages of drought, and to feed them if illness disabled them. The "landlord" could not evict tenants if there was a formal bond of exchange (although in practice, this was often violated). The medieval drawing in Figure 6.1 depicts the ceremony by which a tenant renews his loyalty to his lord. Like the modern institution of marriage, one person made a pledge to another with vows that their relationship would be sacred and transcend all others. The nobility was also responsible for protecting the common lands. Common lands were areas where anyone could graze cattle or sheep, grow a garden, or hunt. Some land was set aside for individual families to cultivate food for themselves, but if they failed to use it, they lost control of it.

The king nominally owned the kingdom but gave the higher nobility practical control of large parcels as part of their exchange of protection for tribute. The higher nobility then split their parcels into smaller parcels and gave practical control to the lesser lords as part of the exchange of protection for tribute. And so forth down the line to the bottom, where the peasants were. Peasants or *serfs,* as they were sometimes called, were bound to the land; that is, they were legally caged. They were obligated to work the land and give a portion to the nobility immediately above them. If a new nobleman took control of the land, they were obliged to him. The major institution of feudalism was the **manor,** a settlement of a lord and peasants, often surrounding a castle, perhaps with a church. The lord of the manor had formal control over most aspects of life. It was not a comfortable life for anyone except royalty and nobility. Most people lived in small, shoddy cabins; dressed in homemade clothes; suffered from disease, sores, lice, and other vermin; and rarely had enough food to go around, even in good times. Many children died young, and those who did survive were lucky if they had both parents alive when they reached adulthood. Feudalism was the archetypal class society, in which all rights and privileges depended on what group you were born into. Those born into royalty remained royal, those born into nobility remained noble, and those born as peasants generally remained peasants. The trade that flowed through the few cities and the production of the few manufactured goods were peripheral to the way the system worked. The only important cities were the capital cities such as London or Paris where royal governments were housed. But the cities were autonomous, not under the control of the feudal nobility, which made them potential breeding grounds for new social systems and the new classes that arose with them.

Feudalism was organized around the dominant social institutions. One distinctive feature was that economic and political institutions were not separate from each other. Political power and economic power were inseparable from each other. The royalty, nobility, and peasantry were political as well as economic categories. Because the nobility was a warrior class with their own armies, ownership of land went hand in hand with military power. The king was the one with the biggest army and legal title to all the land. The vertical chain of power included judicial and other sorts of political power. If a peasant broke the law, his or her nobility decided guilt and meted out punishment. If a noble person broke the law, the higher nobility or king presided. Kings made the law, so they were accountable only to God, a doctrine known as the "divine right of kings."

Religion was the only other highly developed institution. Though the church often conflicted with kings and nobility over power, it was part of the same structure. The pope, as head of the Roman Catholic Church, was like a king, with the bishops similar to nobility—and typically born into the noble class—and parishioners analogous to peasants. Not only was the hierarchy of the Church similar to the feudal hierarchy, but the Church also reinforced secular class relations. Ideologically, the Church preached that God created the world as a hierarchy in which each person is to know his or her place. Because the authority of kings was legitimated by the divine right of kings, they had to be approved by the pope and were typically coronated by a bishop. Socially, the Church assisted in controlling the lower classes, defining insubordinate behavior as a sin, and helping the nobility mete out punishment. Economically, the Church was a major landlord, and politically it had its own armies.

Other institutions were weak or nonexistent. No one attended schools, and there were only a few universities for the privately tutored children of the higher nobility. The few doctors, midwives, and witch doctors hardly constituted a coherent institution. And there was no mass media because all writing was in the church or royal household. The institutional unity of the system, the advances in agricultural productivity, and the high centralization of military power meant that the dominant classes were able to become very wealthy.

English royal kings in the 14th century had annual incomes of £135,000, which was about 85% of the combined income of the entire noble class, in a society in which most peasants lived close to starvation (Sanderson 1999:113).

Capitalism

After 1000, European feudalism entered a prolonged period of crisis. Periodic bouts of the "Black Plague," a deadly disease spread by the fleas on rats, decimated the population. More people moved to cities, where they were protected against feudal law, creating a cycle in which the new artisans made and merchants traded more goods, making the cities more appealing to those wanting to escape the feudal system. Economic development in civilizations such as India and China expanded world trade in arousing nobles to wring more wealth from the peasants. The resulting conflict between peasants and nobles provoked attempts to find new economic arrangements. Instead of the old arrangement of swapping protection for tribute, nobles and peasants began to rent land for cash or pay cash for labor.

What emerged were the two fundamental characteristics of capitalism and of capitalist class relations. First, rather than producing goods and services primarily to consume, people produced to sell on the market. Capitalism is a market system. In feudalism and earlier systems, there were always markets, but they were peripheral to the main activity by which people collected or grew their own food, made their own clothes, constructed their own homes, and exchanged tribute for protection. People used markets mainly for the things they could not supply for themselves such as salt or, for the wealthy, luxuries. When commodities such as grain were traded locally, it was considered morally wrong to charge as much as people could afford. A seller was supposed to charge a traditional "fair" price, even if supplies fell, as during a drought, or if demand increased. In contrast to capitalism's market economy, this was a **moral economy,** which meant that prices were set by standards of morality, not by the market itself (Thompson 1971). During the transition period between feudalism and capitalism, local merchants who violated the moral economy by charging the market price or hauling their grain to cities before offering it to local folks at the "fair" price were often forcibly detained by crowds, their grain sold to locals, and the money turned over to the original merchant (Tilly 1971). When the moral economy is replaced by a market economy, a person's relationship to the market, primarily based on how much money he or she has, is a major dimension of class structure. Rich and poor have different relations to the market.

The second major feature of capitalism is that the great majority of people have to sell their labor power to a few people who buy it; that is, most people have to work for a living. **Selling labor** means that some people exchange their time and effort for money, that is, taking paid employment. Others buy it by employing people. This is the difference between capitalists and workers (which includes not just factory workers but everyone who must work for a living). In advanced capitalism, this is of course more complicated than this caricature depicts, but there is still a systematic difference between the people who live primarily from the profits of others and those who live by wages and salaries.

Like buying and selling land (discussed in Chapter 3), buying labor was incomprehensible to precapitalist mentalities. Labor is something you do, not a "thing." What people "buy" when they buy labor—when they hire someone—is a set of rights, entitlements, and responsibilities, which the "seller" is giving up for money. Most centrally, the buyer is buying the right to control the seller's body—and at least part of his or her mind—for a fixed period of time. The employer (buyer) can dictate that he or she wants the employee (seller) to flip hamburgers, attach a door panel to a car on an assembly line, smile to customers, prepare a legal brief, or give reading lessons to children. The buyer is entitled to whatever the seller produces. Whether it is the hamburger that the cook flips or the new computer chip invented by a scientist, the employer owns it. The buyer also has responsibilities—most specifically, to pay the employee the agreed-on wage. More specific rights, entitlements, and responsibilities have been hammered out in different times and places, but all within the basic framework of making labor a commodity.

From today's vantage point, one might assume that peasants would have gladly given up their miserable existence for the freedom of paid employment. But many did not. Rather than moving voluntarily to paid employment, many were forced off the land and had no choice but to take paid employment. **Proletarianization** is a form of class formation whereby people's alternative means of a livelihood are taken away until the only option is a job for wages. Landlords were increasingly requiring money rents for land, so many tenants began taking part-time jobs. Younger sons who could not take over land farmed by their fathers had to look for jobs that paid cash wages. And the common lands that had been available for grazing or gardens were increasingly enclosed. So more and more, people had to work in the coal mines, textile factories, or commercial farms. In doing so, they not only lost a familiar way of life but also the paternal responsibilities that lords had previously owed peasants. They became caged in the working class.

Property

At the heart of any class system is the property system. The common-sense notion of *property* is that of ownership and that all societies have a concept of ownership. People might own a toothbrush, clothes, a car, and perhaps a house, meaning that only they can use it and can authorize when and how anyone else can use it. But such a view of property is specific to Anglo-European society. In other societies, the rights, entitlements, and responsibilities that come with property are quite different.

Variation of Property Systems

First, societies vary in how the use of things is allocated. Do you get to use the land that your parents used? Do you get a hut to live in because you won it in a fight? Does everyone get to graze their sheep on a pasture? Is hunting in the forest first come, first served? Does marriage mean you get access to the land of the bride? Are people compelled to farm land because their parents were conquered?

Second, societies differ in the kinds of rules that govern who gets the fruits of labor. Does someone else automatically get half of what you grow? Are people with more food obliged to share it with those with less? Are you forced to farm for someone else who gets everything except what they give you for meals?

Third, societies differ in how people can transfer things from one person to another. Can you easily exchange things for money? Are their moral standards for how much you can charge people? Are you required to pass land on to your children even if you do not want to? If you do not use things, can other people come along and take them over? Are there traditions that restrict who you can transfer things to, for example, out of your clan, locality, or occupational group?

The Anglo-European notion of *absolute property,* which means that the person who owns something has all the rights, entitlements, and responsibilities relative to that object, is rare among human societies. Developing over several centuries but culminating in the 19th century, absolute property is a particular, historically constructed mode of property that must be explained, not taken as a natural quality (Vandevelde 1980). Besides the economy itself, the institution that played the most important role in the development of the concept of absolute property was the state. Many people associate the absolute notion of private property with limited government power, as extolled by the ideology of **laissez-faire** (French for "let it be"), the doctrine that government should have as few activities as possible, being reduced primarily to enforcing property rights. However, the freedom of people to use their property as they wish required that governments develop enough power to restrain other institutions from regulating property. As Anglo-European states expanded after 1500, communities, guilds, churches, corporate bodies of nobles, clans, and other groups surrendered traditional authority over property relations. Like the traditional rights that communities had to common lands, guilds could restrict how products were made or what price they could be sold for, and churches could limit the interest on loans. States used their growing power to let owners decide how property was to be used and replaced traditional duties to supply armies to the king with property taxes (Horwitz 1977). As the state became the ultimate guarantor of property rights, it increasingly prohibited other institutions from enforcing traditional rights, entitlements, and responsibilities. The rights that people had to graze their sheep or cattle on common lands were nullified as owners were named and given exclusive control. Traditional fair prices were defined as contrary to the rights of owners to sell grain at whatever price the market would bear. The expectation that young men could farm the land their fathers had farmed could be dashed for whatever reason fathers chose to exclude the sons from their wills. It was ironic that the absolute notion of property extended state power under the banner of freedom from state intervention.

What Societies Treat as Property

The meaning of property also varies in terms of what different societies treat as property. As discussed in Chapter 3, most societies have not treated land as property. Precapitalist European societies treated some land as personal property but restricted what the owner could do (for example, making it very difficult to sell land for money). Anglo-European societies have a concept of intellectual property, which treats inventions and ideas as property. Patent laws allow inventions to be treated as property, including the right to buy, sell, or rent them. Copyright laws treat words, music, and pictures as property, allowing the creator to sell them to others, although changing technologies and cultural change are making it more problematic (Buranen and Roy 1999). A century ago—much to the chagrin of European literary circles—American publishers brazenly pirated and reprinted European books because there was no international copyright law. Now—much to the equal chagrin of American software manufacturers—foreign companies in places such as China copy and distribute American software. In contrast, other societies have treated things as property that Anglo-European societies do not. Many societies have treated people as property; it was called slavery. As discussed in Chapter 4, slavery has existed in very different forms, with slave holders having very different rights, entitlements, and responsibilities, but only American chattel slavery, based on Anglo-European notions of absolute property, gave slave owners such extreme control of slaves, including not only their work also but their sexual favors, the right to buy and sell them, and ownership of their children. The French, before their 1789 revolution, treated political offices as property. People would purchase for money a position such as tax collector or food inspector and then sell it to someone else or pass it on to a son as an inheritance.

The kinds of "things" defined as property help structure what sorts of classes are found in a society. Where only land is treated as property, as under feudalism, the main classes are the landed and unlanded, that is, nobility and peasantry. Where labor is bought and sold as a commodity, there are employers and employees or capitalists and workers. When ideas become a major form of property, as some people describe the emerging postindustrial society, those with educational certificates such as college degrees become a "new class" (Konrad and Szelenyi 1979). The more things are commodified and exchanged for money, the more money itself becomes a basis for class differences. For example, in traditional English society, the upper class expanded to the newly wealthy. Money could not buy entrance into elite schools, clubs, or marriages. The nobility looked down on the nouveau riche as uncultured, greedy, and crass. But as the nobility declined, many sought rich young sons of manufacturers to marry their titled but no longer wealthy daughters. Increasingly, prestige is accorded to those with money and the things that money can buy, such as time, clothes, and vacations. At the same time, poverty is interpreted as a stigma in itself; people are degraded just for being poor. The concept "respectable poor" is now virtually unheard of.

Personal Versus Productive Property

Another distinctive feature of Anglo-European society is that it lumps together **personal property,** in which a person has the right to exclusive control of something for personal use, such as toothbrushes and clothes, and **productive property,** in which ownership gives a person the right to arrange with other people to use it for the benefit of the owner. With productive property, property is more of a social relationship between people relative to things than it is between people and things. Many societies have some notion of personal property, where people have exclusive use of items for themselves. But fewer societies allow people to own productive property. Only capitalism allows it on a large scale, and in capitalism, it is the key to how the system works and how classes are formed. There is a distinct split between the people who own factories, stores, farms, and offices and collectively make up the capitalist class and those who produce things, sell, grow, and administer things and who make up the broadly conceived working class. The particular rights, entitlements, and responsibilities that come with owning productive property set the context for how employers and employees relate to each other around work, an issue at the very core of class relations. Under what circumstances can the employer hire or fire a worker? How are wages and salaries set? If workers get upset and go on strike or occupy a factory, will the government protect the owner's property in all circumstances? If the employee gets hurt on the job, who is responsible? When the concept of absolute property is adopted, all these things tilt to the owner's side. Few question the owner's authority to control because, of course, it is his or her property—he or she has the "right" to do what he or she wants with it.

Cultural Boundaries

The taken-for-granted realities of class include not only structures and practices that allocate people into positions with more or less access to material things. They also include the ways in which some things or social positions are seen as "high" or "low." If "high" can mean more of some things such as money or less of others such as the number of people in a club, and if some things that are not even countable are ranked as high, how do things become defined as high or low in the first place? Why, in some parts of the country, is it considered upper class to refer to your parents as "faathaa" or "muhthaa" rather than "fatherrr" or "motherrr"? Why is pale complexion considered high class in some times and places but low class in others? Why is ballet more cultured than bowling? Why is the violin chosen more often by upper-class students and accordions by lower classes? Why are string quartets classier than string bands? Why is counterpoint considered a higher musical form than country and western?

These examples all refer to **status symbols**: objects, titles, manners, and activities that members of a society interpret as bestowing prestige on the people who have or do them. Because the mass media so emphatically accentuate status symbols, most members of Anglo-European societies can decipher status symbols with skill and subtlety.

Boundaries

While some status symbols are just ranked along a gradual continuum from high to low, many create boundaries, a sense of "us" versus "them" in which those with the "higher" culture look on the "lower" orders as uncultured, coarse, or unrefined, and the "lower" sorts feel that the "higher" classes are effete, vain, or ostentatious (Bourdieu 1984; DiMaggio and Useem 1978; Gans 1974; Lamont and Fournier 1992). Not surprisingly, these things vary dramatically from one culture to another. For example, Americans see money as a key to personal freedom, so many in the upper class feel no restraint about flaunting their wealth with fancy cars, pretentious homes, or idle talk about how much they spend. In contrast, the French strive to be above money and equate "classy" with refined tastes, cultivated poise, and sophisticated discernment. Whereas upper-class Americans value practical knowledge and down-to-earth common sense, the French elite have developed a cult of language in which they relish rhetorical skill and elegant eloquence (Lamont 1997).

Highbrow and Lowbrow Culture

Nonetheless, Americans draw sturdy boundaries between highbrow culture and lowbrow culture. **Highbrow culture** refers to art, music, literature, and other aesthetic forms that are considered refined, lofty, and high status. **Lowbrow culture** is art, music, literature, and other forms of popular entertainment considered ordinary, common, unrefined, or low status. It is synonymous with popular culture. Bach, Braque, and Balzac are highbrow. Boogie, baseball, and *Baywatch* are lowbrow. Opera, abstract art, ballet, and classical music are definitely associated with the upper class, while blues clubs, representational art, ethnic dance, and country and western music are more often considered lower class (not lower class like the very poor, but lower relative to the upper class) (DiMaggio 1982b; Gans 1974; Lamont and Fournier 1992). This does not mean that all the upper class or only the upper class enjoys high culture or that all the lower classes or only the lower classes enjoy low culture (Halle 1993; Peterson and Simkus 1992). It means that the upper classes have self-consciously defined "high culture" as their culture, legitimating their status in society as more refined than "greedy fat cats." As DiMaggio (1982b) explains it, "Particularly in the case of a dominant status group, it is important that their culture be recognized as legitimate by, yet be only partially available to, groups that are subordinate to them" (p. 303). J. Paul Getty is now known as a world-class art museum in Los Angeles, not one of the world's richest oil barons. Andrew Carnegie is more known for his concert halls, foundations, libraries, and university than as being the richest man in the world at one time.

The distinction between highbrow and lowbrow culture did not always exist in this country. Early in the nation's history, the democratic spirit repudiated European high culture and affirmed popular music, arts, and dance, making little distinction between high culture and popular culture. A concert might include a violin solo by Brahms, a fire-eater, a soliloquy from Shakespeare, a couple of comedians in blackface, and a devotional song. Museums included fine art, bearded ladies, mutant animals, and Chinese curiosities.

Not only did the elite embrace popular culture, but also ordinary people consumed what today would be considered high culture. One of the most popular varieties of entertainment in 19th-century America was parodies of Shakespeare, like the spoof taken off from "all the world's a stage" in *As You Like It*:

> *All the world's a bar,*
> *and all the men and women merely drinkers;*
> *They have their hiccups and their staggering. . . .*

Levine (1988:4)

Such satires were virtually universal in all regions, cities large and small, and for all classes. And in contrast to today, when parodies of Shakespeare have been reduced to only a few scenes in a plays such as the balcony scene in *Romeo and Juliet*, minor scenes from virtually all his plays were ridiculed. Parodies are possible only when there is widespread knowledge of the original. Only the Bible was found in more homes than books of Shakespeare's plays.[37] Theaters, along with churches and schools, were among the important social institutions found in new towns and white settlements spread westward. Along with Shakespeare and the satires on his plays, such theaters would have magicians, dancers, acrobats, and minstrels. Audiences included a microcosm of American society from the rich to the rabble, there to enjoy culture —not high culture or low culture—just culture, because that distinction meant little (Levine 1988). By the early 20th century, the American upper class successfully created a boundary between highbrow and lowbrow culture in terms of both content and organization. The local elite of

---

[37]Levine (1988) gives several clues for why it may have been easier for 19th-century readers to understand his plays than it is for people today. First, it was a very oral or, more strictly, oratory culture. People were used to listening to sermons, political speeches, and lectures for hours at a time, and schools generally taught public speaking (homiletics) along with reading, writing, and numbers. Second, most culture of the period was very melodramatic, so the audiences then were more accustomed to what modern audiences would consider rhetorical excess. Shakespeare was usually understood by audiences in moralistic terms based on "lessons" of the melodrama. Third, the melodramatic acting style then in fashion made the considerable humor of Shakespeare more accessible to common folks. All three of these factors faded in the 20th century, facilitating the elevation of Shakespeare to the novel category of high culture.

Boston created the Boston Museum of Fine Arts in 1870. At first, they balanced the display of art for connoisseurs with public education, admitting the public for free at least one day a week and working with public schools. But education, which reached across class boundaries, receded as the trustees aspired to eminence. Said one leader,

> The museum is dedicated to those who come, not to be educated, but to make its treasures their friends for life and their standards of beauty. Joy, not knowledge, is the aim of contemplating a painting by Turner or Dupre's "On the Cliff," nor need we look at a statue or a coin for aught else than inspiration and the pleasure of exercising our faculties of perception. (DiMaggio 1982a:307)

Explicitly mimicking the museum and the orchestra, theaters adopted the nonprofit corporation and separated themselves from lowbrow culture (DiMaggio 1992). Theater declined in general, especially with the rise of film, splitting into the higher "legitimate" theater and the lower popular theater. Upper-class theatergoers were not only making negative comments about the "coarse" acts that distracted from the increasingly sacrosanct Shakespeare but also complained about the riffraff that frequented theaters. They wanted higher culture for higher people. Besides, it was said, the masses did not understand Shakespeare anyway. When the *New International Shakespeare* was published in 1903, it included two sets of notes, one for the scholar and one for the average reader, explicitly dividing the readership into higher and lower, sophisticated and simple. Shakespeare was canonized as a genius, his plays the epitome of refined taste, and he disappeared from commercial theaters.

Opera also followed the same process from mass culture to highbrow culture. Earlier, operas had performed in English, in all regions to all classes. Most people had a thorough knowledge of the major repertoire. At mid-century, P. T. Barnum, the famous circus entrepreneur best known for exhibiting midgets and Siamese twins, was hired as manager of the New York Opera because he understood that opera was for common folks. But by the end of the century, it took on upper-class connotations. The New York Academy of Music was developing as an elite venue, for the people with "old money," but when several of the newly rich could not obtain box seats, they banded together and created the Metropolitan Opera, which gave box seats to anyone who could afford one. Critics increasingly insisted that opera should be enjoyed only by those with the breeding, refinement, and knowledge to truly appreciate it. By the 20th century, it was performed mainly in Italian for upper-class audiences (Levine 1988). As the 19th century gave way to the 20th, the

American mass media increasingly made invidious comparisons between the entertainment of the upper and lower classes.

Pure Versus Commercial Culture

The organizational vehicle for separating high culture from popular culture was the nonprofit corporation, which had a board of trustees com-
posed of wealthy benefactors and a professional staff who made artistic
decisions. In the late 19th century, groups of urban elites created nonprofit corporations to oversee museums, orchestras, and theaters, while
popular music, theater, and other forms of popular culture remained under the aegis of profit-making companies. Nonprofit corporations
funded by voluntary donations could keep orchestras, museums, and
theaters free from the constraints of the market, allowing the culture to
be artistic rather than commercial. Supporters often commend high culture because they consider it more artistically pure than popular culture,
which is blown by the winds of the market. But this relationship between
the stature of culture and the market is relatively new. Thus, the higher
culture of the higher classes involves not only those groups making
claims to "their" art, music, or theater but also a different logic of aesthetic standards. Popular culture is judged by the standards of the market, in which successful culture means commercially successful. It is not
at all uncommon that movies, television shows, and popular music are
received very differently by critics than by audiences. Some highly ac-
claimed works bomb, and some of the biggest commercial successes are
panned by critics. But both audiences and producers celebrate the works
that sell, regardless of what the critics say. Everyone agrees that
Baywatch, Titanic, and Madonna are momentous. In contrast, highbrow
culture adopts aesthetics based on complexity, taste, and refinement.
Only those with the training, discernment, and acclamation of their
peers are given the authority to judge the artistic merits of high culture
because it is considered ineffable and sublime, beyond the reach of objective validation or the understanding of the common person (DiMaggio
1982a). This means that the process of evaluation remains within the control of a small group with close connections to those who produce fine
arts.[38]

---

[38]This does not mean that commercially successful culture never measures up to
the standards of high culture, though some arbiters of taste seem to think so.

However, is highbrow culture inherently more complex and nuanced than lowbrow culture? All culture requires knowledge to understand its complexities and subtleties. Are fine art and classical music criticism more sophisticated than the complicated ruminations of a baseball announcer pondering the best pitch a right-handed pitcher should deliver to a left-handed .230 hitter with a runner in scoring position and a 3-2 count when the batting team is one run ahead? High culture differs from popular culture more in its institutional setting. Institutions of formal learning teach highbrow culture. Schools teach Rachmaninoff but not rock 'n' roll; Shakespeare, not *Shakespeare in Love*; ballet, not boxing. Part of that education is the mystification that these art forms are beyond full comprehension, that only the connoisseur can appreciate them. When equally complex cultural formations must be learned by other means, it becomes "common sense" that high culture is more complex and elusive, accessible only by the most accomplished practitioners. Thus, the knowledge needed for high culture is explicitly recognized as learned. People come to believe that high culture is inherently different from low culture because the tastes for high culture must be acquired and because its forms are more complex (Gans 1974). Opera, string quartets, and ballet are acquired tastes, like broccoli or Brussels sprouts. However, high culture is explicitly learned because it is more bound within specific institutions, while the knowledge needed to understand popular culture permeates throughout the society. Children spending hundreds of hours watching television shows can "read" the nuances in a situation comedy the way a music major can interpret a symphony.

Since the 1960s, in part because of the antielitist movements of that period, the boundary between highbrow and lowbrow culture has softened, although a debate continues between those who would like to further erode it and those who would like to retrench the differences. Conductor Michael Tilson Thomas, then a rising young star in the classical music world, wrote in 1976,

> There has been altogether too much separation of different types of music, such as so-called "classical" and "rock". . . . There's no reason why a person can't be ardently into rhythm-and-blues and chamber music as well—they're so different, yet beautiful human realities. (Levine 1988:243-44)

In the 1990s, jazz trumpeter Wynton Marsalis crossed over from the other direction, making several classical albums and, as New York Philharmonic conductor Leonard Bernstein did in the 1950s, lecturing to young people about the joys of classical music. Reuniting Shakespeare with P. T. Barnum, a production of *The Comedy of Errors* in the 1980s included juggling, acrobatics, rope walking, tap dancing, unicycling, and baton twirling. Andy Warhol, the father of "pop art," which even in its title reached beyond highbrow art to a popular audience, not only made representations of ordinary objects such as a Campbell soup can into art but also mass produced them, following the technique, not just the look, of popular culture. These attempts to bridge the boundary between highbrow and popular culture sparked the so-called "culture wars" of the 1980s and 1990s. A best-seller by literature professor Alan Bloom (1987) echoes the arguments made in the late 19th century to justify a solid boundary between highbrow culture and lowbrow culture. Alarmed by an intellectual crisis of the highest magnitude (cited in Levine 1988:250), Bloom lamented that classical music, which once differentiated between the cultured and uncultured, has died in the younger generation. Culture, which should be a heritage created by the few for the few, has been debased by the tasteless public.

Although the outcome of the "culture wars" is still up for grabs, America is unlikely to return to the heterogeneous diversity of the 19th century when Shakespeare and sword swallowers shared a stage before audiences that included notables and nobodies. Nonetheless, it is likely that culture will continue to represent class differences, although perhaps in a new form. David Halle (1993) found very little relationship between Americans' social class and the kind of art they had in their homes, concluding that the difference between those with abstract art and those with representational art was less a difference between the upper class and the middle or lower classes than between a small part of the upper class and everyone else. Most people, regardless of their class, typically displayed landscapes, although upper-class people were more likely to have original paintings, while others had reproductions. Moreover, upper-class people did not necessarily interpret art any differently from others. Peterson and Simkus (1992), in a survey of musical tastes, found that the main difference between higher-class and lower-class respondents was not as much that higher classes listened to classical and lower class to popular music but that higher-class listeners enjoyed many types of music, including classical, country and western, and blues, while lower-class listeners tended to listen to only one or two types. The "cultured" then become defined as those who can equally expound on Shostakovich and Springsteen. Culture continues to be organized on class lines, but the modality is new. If culture serves more to create boundaries between classes than to legitimate the social position of the upper class, class pluralism may serve the purpose. The "higher" people are those who can appreciate not only country and western and classical but also Chardonnay, Capra, and Cancun.

Conclusion

Classes in America are a contradiction. On one hand, people believe class makes no difference, that it does not matter whether your origins are humble or wealthy: Anyone can become what they set their minds to, marry whomever they fall in love with, go to whatever schools they have the talent for, and be as rich as their abilities let them. Most people feel that except for a few misfit poor and a few enterprising billionaires, it is a middle-class nation. And yet the stirring of class insecurity is everywhere. Middle-class parents hire consultants to help their children get into the "right" kindergarten. High school students judge each other on the basis of dress, cars, and who they hang out with. College students know that the hierarchy of schools is more than academic. Young adult professionals know that they need to drink the right coffee, eat at the right restaurants, and shop at the best stores, while they envy and resent those who can afford to do the "right" things. Middle-aged careerists learn the painful truth that they will not reach the aspirations they imagined when young, feeling like failures in a culture that values what job you have more than how well you perform whatever job you do have.

This chapter has offered two insights into how this contradiction might be eased. The first is that despite the pervasive ideology of individualism in America, classes are groups of people more than individuals, groups of people who are differentially rewarded for their efforts. While many people are acutely aware that races and genders are groups, the ideology of individualism blinds them to the ways that classes are groups. The competition for a comfortable and satisfying life is not an even playing field. Some children attend good schools, have parents who manage their education, complete college without having to work, speak Standard English, and "naturally" develop the easy confidence that signals competence. Other children attend schools with crowded classrooms and obsolete books, have to figure out the educational system alone, work their way through college if they ever get there, and make an impression only by bluster. To imagine that all children have an equal shot at achievement will condemn many of them to unfulfilled potential and adult misery. Second, although the reinforcement of class by so many institutions makes change difficult, the hierarchies discussed in this chapter are malleable because they are constructed. The relationships between employers and employees; the kinds of rights, entitlements, and responsibilities that define property; and the symbolism of high and low culture were created by human activity and can be changed by human activity. While most people know that these hierarchies are not natural in the biological sense, as race and gender are sometimes imputed, too many people, even when they see the problems, become resigned to "just the way things are." When people realize that the relations between employers and employees have always been a matter of negotiation, not just the purchase of a thing called labor, they can be empowered to reconfigure that relationship. When they realize that even ownership is a construction, they can emphasize some of the responsibilities that come with ownership or renegotiate such issues as the tension between environmental stewardship and property rights. When all kinds of art, music, and literature are accorded intrinsic dignity, and true social superiority is not achieved by displaying the kind of cultural knowledge that comes from elite institutions, everyone can enjoy their own tastes without pressure to swallow other people's judgments about taste.

7

Intersections Small and Large

One of sociology's biggest challenges is to untangle the complex, entangled causal web of social relations in which everything seems to be affected by everything else. The challenge becomes even more perplexing in a social constructionist view that many of the "things" often invoked to explain social life such as time, space, race, gender, and class must be explained. This chapter will attempt a more holistic approach than the individual chapters by examining three topics that illustrate the intersection of all five of our themes. These three topics span the sociological spectrum from micro to macro—the home, the city, and the nation.

The Home

Few aspects of social life are as personal as homes. While it is possible for many people to take a detached view of public policy, social problems, or economic trends, virtually everyone has strong feelings about their homes. As a private refuge from the pressures of the larger society, it would be the place where macrosociological relations such as race, gender, and class should have the least effect. However, Chapter 5 described how the sense of privacy that allows people to separate the home from the rest of society is itself a recent historical development. The separation of the public and private spheres arose with the physical separation between work and home. But the spatial dimension of the public and private life organized the physical setting of the home itself and intersected with gender, race, and class—especially gender. Not only have men and women occupied different spaces in the home, but spatial organization has also been fundamental to the creation of the modern gender order.

The Place of Gender

Home design organizes domestic activities such as cooking, sleeping, relaxing, and entertaining. Insofar as those activities are gendered, spatial design can reinforce or ameliorate gender differences. The American middle-class Victorian ideal home had a drawing room for women, with billiards, libraries, and smoking rooms for men, the height of domestic spatial segregation. Women were supposed to enter the male areas only to clean, and men would rarely enter women's areas except to pass through. Architecture since then has become more egalitarian as single-purpose, gender-segregated rooms, libraries, or billiards rooms have given way to multipurpose gender-integrated rooms such as living rooms. Recently, even the distinction between living rooms and dining rooms has become blurred. Kitchens have become larger to have social as well as cooking functions and allow joint cooking (Spain 1992). But the most fundamental kinds of gender segregation in homes continue.

Nineteenth-century middle-class, mostly white feminists and other social reformers created new designs for living arrangements to create more opportunities for women by bridging the gap between public and private space. Reasoning that the confinement of doing housework and child care unduly restricted women and their talents, feminists sought to change social arrangements by altering the spatial layout of homes. If housework and child care could be more of a community task, individual women would be free to express their talents in other ways. As long ago as the early 19th century, communitarian[39] Robert Owen, an English textile manufacturer, used his wealth to create a community in New Harmony, Indiana, with community kitchens and a child care center. Another communitarian, Frenchman Charles Fourier, declared that the private dwelling presented one of the greatest obstacles to women, whose freedom was the key to progress of the civilization. These two reformers inspired nearly 50 experimental communities in America. Careful to clarify that they did not intend to eliminate privacy or independence but to enrich it, most designers reserved private space for each family. For example, the North American Phalanx, a New Jersey group of about 125 families founded in 1843, had a communal kitchen, laundry, and bakery

---

[39]Communitarians are people who believe in the fundamental importance of the community, in contrast to individualists who believe that all other levels of social organization should be subordinated to individuals. Many communitarians have advocated and participated in self-conscious communes organizationally and physically designed to embody their principles.

built near private apartments. Motivated by increased efficiency as well as freedom for women, they aimed to bring the advantages of the factory to the kitchen and laundry (then done by hand with heated water toted in large iron kettles). Many of these groups proudly adopted the latest technologies, including their own inventions. For example, the Shakers, a Christian religious group that came to America from England, invented the common clothespin, the flat broom, the removable window sash, and an apple peeler (Hayden 1984).

Women activists wistfully hoped that redesigned homes would allow jobs previously done by women to be done collectively. One model proposed small clusters of kitchenless living units around the periphery of a block, with a common kitchen, laundry, and child care facility in the middle. Collective organization could replace the inefficient redundancy of each family separately doing cooking, cleaning, and taking care of children. Few plans proposed entirely eliminating a gendered division of labor by having men perform domestic chores but assumed that those women who enjoyed domestic work could continue. Those who wanted other options would be free to pursue them.

One of the most widely publicized examples of cooperative housekeeping was at the 1893 World's Columbian Exposition in Chicago. Ellen Swallow Richards, an instructor of sanitary chemistry at MIT, designed the "Rumford Kitchen," a collective kitchen capable of serving 10,000 people. A small house looking like a residence, it was filled with the latest scientific equipment customized to maximize nutrition and conserve energy. The meals were served in an attractive dining room at low prices, with complimentary analyses of fat, protein, and carbohydrates. Richards's ideas were highly touted in home economics and social work, two emerging fields that were stressing collective solutions to women's problems and the use of experts to deal with domestic life. Richards and Mary Hinman Abel, an expert on nutrition, put the ideas into effect, creating the New England Kitchen in Boston where they sold affordable, nutritious meals to the poor. They made lunches for poor children at school and took lunches to women working in factories. But their inability to attract more funding prevented expansion.

In the decades around the turn of the century, there were at least 33 cooperative food experiments, including 13 community dining clubs, nearly all in small towns, and 20 cooked food delivery services, mostly in large cities. The *Ladies Home Journal*, hardly a feminist voice, enthusiastically supported them in a 1919 article that confidently predicted that "the private kitchen must go the way of the spinning wheel, of which it is the contemporary" (Hayden 1984:2). These were not utopian ideas but were tried widely. Specific projects sometimes failed due to interpersonal problems but more often faced opposition from mortgage lenders or government agencies. The entire movement, however, was not strong enough to withstand the pressure of most dominant institutions to keep women in the home doing "women's work." However, as more women have taken full-time jobs, it will be interesting to see the extent to which home designs facilitate new domestic divisions of labor or reinforce old ones.

Homes and Race

The typical American home combines the micro intersection of space and gender with the more macro intersection of race and space created by residential segregation. People of different races live in neighborhoods but enter each other's homes within the framework of class and gender categories. While some racial minorities visit the homes of white people as equals, more often, they visit to service the homes of middle- and upper-class whites. Minority women typically come as domestic helpers and child caregivers, while minority men come as gardeners, repairmen, or construction workers. Mirroring the homeowners' gendered division of labor, minority women work in the homes' more private spaces, spending more time cleaning the kitchens and bathrooms than the living and dining rooms, while minority men spend more time in either the homes' public spaces, such as the yard or the uninhabited places to fix the plumbing, electrical wiring, or roofing. One of the consequences is that poor minorities often have a fuller picture of how middle- and upper-class whites live than vice versa. Minority women in particular thus gain a unique insider-outsider perspective on social life from their vantage of working inside white homes as outsiders with lived experience in poor minority homes (Collins 1990).

In contrast, while some whites visit minority homes as social equals, more often they visit them from positions of authority, as landlords, social workers, police officers, or insurance sellers. The gendered division of labor in minority homes links to the gender differences among whites who visit. Predominantly male landlords, police officers, and insurance salespeople connect to minorities in the more public aspects of their homes, while predominantly female social workers become involved in more private aspects such as child care and marital issues.

The intersections of race, gender, and class relations not only reflect the ways that these categories are reconstructed but also reflexively reproduce them. White middle-class couples can enhance their class position when affordable domestic help and child care make it possible for the women to work in paid jobs and live up to the image of modern femininity—managing a household while maintaining good looks, a successful career, and community activism. The property values and prestige of middle- and upper-middle white neighborhoods are bolstered by the army of minorities that trek there in aging pickup trucks and public transportation to cheaply manicure the lawns, paint the houses, and fix the roofs.

On the other side of the coin, the whites who visit minority homes are part of the system that sustains racial inequality. The social workers or insurance agents may not be central actors in reproducing racial inequality, but landlords still charge rents that eat up a large proportion of poor minority incomes, or police equate "criminal" and "dark" in their minds.

Homes for Workers

The most successful spatial reorganization of the home intersected with class more than gender. After the First World War, workers' groups spearheaded the development of large-scale cooperative living arrangements. In 1918, the United Workers Cooperative Association began a project that would eventually include 750 units in New York, including an auditorium, a library with 10,000 books, a school, a combined nursery and kindergarten open from 7 a.m. to 7 p.m. each day, and a cooperative laundry, butcher shop, tailor, grocery, newsstand, and cafeteria. Although it reflected a visionary dream, the buildings were architecturally conventional, reflecting functional need more than aesthetic refinement. And unlike many of the reform experiments of the 19th century that were run by and for middle-class members, all residents of the New York co-ops were workers. Their commitment to workers got them into financial trouble during the Great Depression, when they refused to evict people for missing rent. Taken over by private ownership in 1943, they still exist and continue to have a collective feel (Hayden 1984).

Cities

The most visible and vivid intersection of class and space is in the organization of cities. While cities are the sites for all sorts of activities from factories to florists, apartments to art galleries, banks to boutiques, subways to sandwich shops, or parks to parking lots, one dynamic force that underlies the growth of cities has been called the "growth machine" (Logan and Molotch 1988; Molotch 1976). The growth machine is the coalition of real estate industry, banks, commercial interests, local newspapers, city governments, and civic groups that depend on continued growth of an urban area. They not only require that the city thrive but that it also grow and expand. Land is at the center of this process. The real estate industry cannot prosper unless the value of land is increasing. Banks earn much of their income from mortgages on land and buildings (along with loans to businesses that need growing markets). Similarly, most newspaper revenues come from the sale of advertisements to local retailers. City governments depend on tax revenues, primarily property taxes based on the value of property. Civic groups such as museums, orchestras, or charities all depend on revenues from these other groups. So the owners, managers, and proprietors of all these groups cooperate to ensure growth. Without steady growth, they all stagnate. The growth machine ensures that airports are built and expanded, that public transportation gets people to work and back, that good schools attract talented employees to the city, that arenas and stadiums are built so professional sports franchises locate in the city, and that the city has an identity, an image that give its residents a sense of belonging. These people participate mostly directly in local government, mobilized through organizations such as the chamber of commerce, the business council, and other business-dominated citizens groups. While few quarrel with the concept of growth itself, several problems illustrate how the growth machine fosters the intersection of race, gender, and class.

The first is that the costs and benefits are allocated along class and race lines. The middle class and working class of all races pay most of the taxes and spend a higher proportion of their income on housing. The white upper classes, based in real estate, banking, commerce, and newspapers, glean most of the economic benefits. When boosters talk of the millions of dollars in revenue that a new professional sports franchise will pump into the economy if a new arena or stadium is built, they rarely mention that the people whose taxes subsidize the arena are not the same people who profit from the new revenues. When city officials justify the construction of a business park and generous tax breaks for new businesses in terms of the number of jobs that will be created, they do not mention that city residents will have to pay higher property taxes on their more valuable homes or higher rents in a tighter housing market. When public leaders ceremoniously cut the ribbons on new freeways or urban transit, local newspaper accounts rarely show how poor and minority communities are underserved.

In addition to the monetary costs, lower classes and minorities disproportionately suffer reduced quality of life due to greater traffic congestion, increased pollution, crowded schools, and depleted city services. Over the past few decades, American cities have mushroomed while streets, sewers, schools, parks, and libraries have crumbled. The lower the class of residents and the higher percentage of minorities, the more neighborhoods have deteriorated. In cities that have grown the fastest, where the growth machine has been most dominant—regions such as Houston, Los Angeles, Long Island, the Silicon Valley, and South Florida—growth has been virtually unregulated, creating boundless expanses of tract housing, mini-malls, congested freeways, and dirty air. With little thought given to the development of schools, parks, cultural facilities, or public transportation, children are bussed long distances to sit in crowed classrooms and find their recreation at the mall, perhaps not even aware of the parks or cultural facilities that would give them richer experiences.

The intersection of space with class and race is most damaging to the **underclass,** the group of people trapped in the decaying cores of large American cities, who experience long-term unemployment, disproportionately engage in street crime or other illegal activities, and experience long-term poverty (Wilson 1987:8). Sociologist William Julius Wilson has emphasized how the decline of heavy industry in American cities and the relocation of other jobs to suburbs, coupled with the low education level of many lower-class urban residents, have created a mismatch between the jobs available and the skills of residents. As these changes in the spatial organization of jobs create unemployment, families are increasingly disrupted, young men turn to illegal means to gain a livelihood, and the residents become even more cut off from the opportunities for a better life. Poverty becomes concentrated in the urban core, and the urban core begets more poverty. Growth has been organized spatially, building up new areas and abandoning the central city.

Even though the white upper classes benefit from the urban growth machines, they also have unique opportunities to escape from the negative effects of growth. In the past few decades, a counterforce has arisen in affluent communities, the antigrowth coalition. Often attracting people of similar class position as the growth coalition, antigrowth coalitions have used political means to limit growth in their residential neighborhoods, regulate development, and use the techniques of urban planning to create more congenial environments for themselves. Small municipalities set in large urban areas—places such as San Marino near Los Angeles, White Plains in the New York City area, Highland Park just outside Dallas, or the towns along the Main Line outside Philadelphia—have strictly restricted growth to sustain a high-quality environment. Using techniques such as strong zoning laws to regulate what activities can be done on any given property, property taxes to support public services, and careful attention to match employment opportunities to the available labor force, these elite enclaves contain the excesses of the growth machine but primarily for whites at the upper end of the class structure (Logan 1976).

Nation

One of the most politically volatile intersections of race, gender, and class with time and space is in the social relations of the nation. From the "ethnic cleansing" of Native Americans by whites or Albanians by Serbs to the exclusion of immigrant women from welfare and the debates over women in combat, conflict over the social composition of nations and the appropriate rights of citizenship fuels conflict and propels political change. **Nations** are groups of people who claim a common heritage and history, a sense of "us" or an imagined community that distinguishes them from other groups and gives them claim on territory, typically in the form of a state (Anderson 1991). **States,** on the other hand, are territorial entities in which a bureaucratic central government claims ultimate authority over anyone inside its boundaries, claims a monopoly on violence, extracts resources through taxes, and interacts with similar organizations (Tilly 1975). Though analytically separate, nations and states have so often united in nation-states that people think of them as interchangeable. In the modern world, most states have associated nations, such as the English, German, Russian, or Chinese nations. But the relationship is far from perfect. All states have people of many nations within their borders, sometimes peacefully, but too often contentiously. Some nations, such as the Palestinians or Kosovar Albanians, actively seek to create a state of their own.

While nations and races often coincide, the extent to which groups define themselves as nations or races can be fiercely debated and changeable. Some national groups think of themselves as races, the most extreme case being German Nazis, who sought to exterminate non-German races in the areas they controlled. The English during the colonial period saw themselves as a race, different not only from Africans and Native Americans but also the Irish, who were physically very similar to themselves. In the past several decades, conflict has intensified over the "Englishness" of nonwhites who migrated to England from former colonies such as India or the West Indies (Gilroy 1992).

As discussed in Chapter 4, the U.S. Congress, shortly after the Revolution, equated the American nation with the white race by granting the right of citizenship only to white immigrants. For much of the period since then, many people have believed that to be fully American means to be white. One site where this racial view of the American nation has been most hotly contested has been language. The use of the hyphenated "American" to refer to groups at one time excluded from the American nation—African Americans, Irish Americans, Chinese Americans, and others—unifies categories once considered incompatible, deracializing the meaning of the American nation. The recognition of hyphenated Americans has the racial meaning of space. When nation is a racial concept, only the members of the dominant race "belong" in that nation's state. When only whites were "true" Americans, blacks, Latinos, Asians, or even those whose families have been here for centuries were treated as outsiders. America was "not their land."

Other countries unite racial meanings of nation with citizenship more explicitly. Unlike the United States, where all immigrants now have the legal right to citizenship regardless of race, Germany accords citizenship rights to only those of German ancestry. People who are considered non-German, even if they, their parents, and grandparents are born in Germany, do not have a right to citizenship (though they may apply for approval). But people of German ancestry, even if they and their parents and grandparents were born outside Germany, have a right to German citizenship. So Germanness is considered in racial rather than territorial terms (Brubaker 1992).

The demise of the Soviet system in Eastern Europe has allowed an especially virulent form of nationalism to emerge in the past decade or so. Even though the USSR and its satellites adopted an official policy of ethnic equality, actual practices were based on ethnicity. Certain jobs were regularly assigned to people of one ethnicity or another, kindling the fires of ethnic resentment (Brubaker 1996). As communism disintegrated, ambitious and often unscrupulous politicians have ignited the simmering resentments to build their own power. The most notorious has been Slobodan Milosevic, former president of Yugoslavia, who has repeatedly used the tactic of "ethnic cleansing" to eliminate everyone except his own Serbian nationals from some former provinces of Yugoslavia. In "ethnic cleansing," soldiers or paramilitary groups enter a village, round up people of some ethnic groups, and either kill or expel them. In the early 1990s, this tactic was used against Croatians and Muslims in Bosnia, Croatia, and Slovenia. However, after the peace settlement in 1995, legitimating Bosnia-Herzegovina and Croatia as separate countries, ethnic cleansing was used against Serbians. Milosevic then attempted to "cleanse" the Yugoslav province of Kosovo of Albanians, whose Kosovo Liberation Army was seeking independence. After several months of bombing by the combined forces of the United States and European powers under NATO supervision, Milosevic agreed to withdraw his troops and set up a NATO protectorate. Many observers expect that these kinds of nationalistic conflicts over territory will intensify in coming decades, but few foresee the possibility that national/ethnic boundaries and state territorial boundaries will ever match. A multicultural society will require that the linkage of nation and territory be severed and that people of different ethnic, racial, and national identities live in a common space.

Nations and Time

Nations also intersect time with race, gender, and class. Nations are groups set in time. All nations have historical narratives that glorify how they became a unified group and how they have survived threats to their existence. These histories not only describe the past but also define the nation. Without the history, there is no nation. The national history defines the boundaries (determines who is in and who is out of the nation) and legitimates their right to a state. Nations have traditions, and traditions create nationhood. Whether Palestinians and Jews in the Middle East, Serbs and Albanians in Kosovo, Native Americans and European Americans in North America, or Indians and Pakistani in Kashmir, groups legitimate their claim to territory by attempting to show that they have existed as a distinct group and have been there a long time. Conflicts among groups are discussed not just in terms of grievances experienced by living individuals but also by their ancestors, that is, by people related to them in time. Palestinians and Jews argue that they have been groups since biblical times and that conflicts of the current era are only the latest chapter of a very long book. If groups fail to effectively portray their existence and the conflict as very ancient, many participants in the conflict, including those now willing to die for "their people," might suspend their commitment, and other states might reconsider their support. Similarly, Native Americans and African Americans have demanded reparations for atrocities committed hundreds of years ago, invoking a relationship in time to enhance solidarity within their groups and reinforce boundaries with other groups.

While claims to groupness are made on the basis of history, recent scholarship has shown how much these histories are socially constructed. It is less that the histories are entirely made up of lies, although that occasionally happens, than that groups rediscover, select, repackage, and mythologize events, some of which may have been previously forgotten. In other words, they invent traditions. "Memories" that seem ancient are often quite recent in origins (Hobsbawm and Ranger 1983). For example, folk songs, one of the more effective devices for creating a sense of belonging, are often written by those hoping to build solidarity. The Scottish tartans, the plaids that denote "ancient" clans and are now a symbol of Scottishness, were mostly adopted in the 19th century. Some African Americans have donned African clothes, learned African songs, and learned African history that is entirely unknown to their parents and grandparents, declaring a link to an African past for very contemporary goals. This is not necessarily bad. Traditions are invented by powerful and subordinate groups alike, used on behalf of domination and liberation.

Nations, like races, ethnicities, and other categories, do not just arise. They are built. Indeed, nation building has been one of the most far-reaching processes of the modern era. After the American Revolution, the leaders of the new country faced the daunting task of uniting the people of 13 disparate and competing colonies into a single whole. People did not think of themselves as Americans but as Virginians, New Yorkers, or Georgians. Historians helped build the new American nation by creating national historical myths such as Columbus's discovery of America, the romance between John Smith and Pocahontas, and the Boston Tea Party. These events were real but became part of the American national memory only by conscious effort. National holidays commemorating historical events were created, including Thanksgiving and Independence Day. In the wake of the Civil War, citizens publicly extolled the nation in everything from small-town statues of soldiers to the glorification of Lincoln's Gettysburg Address. Lincoln's remarks were not a major event at the time but just a few brief comments to remember the soldiers who died in the ghastly combat, but after his assassination,

American opinion leaders enshrined the address as a symbol of American nationhood. Thus, American schoolchildren, like schoolchildren everywhere, learn their nation's history and who they are.

But why should common ancestry create social boundaries? If my great-great-grandparents were on the opposite side of a boundary from yours, why should you and I be on opposite sides? Fiction and drama often ask the question about two young lovers from feuding families, the best known being Romeo and Juliet, who paid the ultimate price of death for their passion. While most people agree that the genetic differences between different nations or different races are superficial at best, they still talk about "blood" differences. But what is passed down in ancestry? Is it culture, or is it merely a socially constructed set of categories that get reified as biological?

This is not to say that history is meaningless, that people should forget that some groups have oppressed others, often for hundreds of years. Rather, we must specify how time makes a difference and what the mechanisms of historical continuity are. Group boundaries and the kinds of social relationships that happen between groups are reproduced. Whites still have more opportunities than blacks or Latinos. It may be appropriate for blacks to remember 300 years of slavery both to create the solidarity they need for collective action to improve their opportunities and to remind whites that there is still inequality to overcome.

The Spread of Nationalism

Although nationalism thrives throughout the world, it has not arisen anew in each country. Once reified as a "thing," it has spread from one country to another, especially to newly independent societies. For example, nationalist sentiments were propagated throughout the British Empire in Asia and Africa, via schools established to "civilize" colonial peoples, exposing native children to Western understandings of the nation-state. In societies where most people thought of political authority as loyalty to a person and felt identity with people from their village or kin group, children in colonial schools learned that authority was organized spatially and that they belonged to imagined communities defined by the territorial boundaries of administration. These ideas took root, and as these children aged, many discovered that the imaginary community they belonged to had a legitimate right to participate in governance. Revolutionary movements called for the end to colonial rule and the establishment of European-style nation-states.

For many colonial subjects, the notion of the nation-state was so real that they strove to establish their own even at great costs, often along arbitrary criteria. For example, the national movements to create separate nation-states for Hindus and Muslims during the final years of British rule in India were based on newly created imaginary communities. About half of the land area of the United States, the area colonized as India, had been home to hundreds of languages, numerous religions, and a wide variety of political entities. As the British prepared to withdraw, influential Muslim leaders such as the British-educated Muhammad Ali Jinnah believed that Indian Muslims constituted a separate nation and required their own state, Pakistan. Radical Hindu leaders similarly believed that Hindus constituted a separate nation requiring their own state, Hindustan. Mahatma Gandhi, leader of the anticolonialist movement, was against dividing India up into separate states and questioned the logic behind it. As he pointed out, the ethnolinguistic differences between these two religious groups were not great, and most Indian Muslims had Hindu ancestors (Wolpert 1997). Furthermore, the two religions had generally coexisted peacefully prior to the arrival of the British. However, both factions grew and became increasingly violent; the departing British caved to the pressure to divide their former colony into two separate nation-states. The resultant division of the Indian subcontinent had immediate and explosive consequences: Some 10,000,000 people who found themselves on the "wrong" side of the border gathered up their belongings and moved en masse. Along the way, many were attacked by angry mobs consisting of the opposing "nationality." Trains filled with dead Muslims arrived in Pakistan; trains filled with dead Hindus arrived in India. All in all, more than 1,000,000 people did not survive the trip across the newly established borders. When Gandhi tried to stop the conflict, he was assassinated by a Hindu fanatic. The conflict has continued for more than half a century. The two countries continue to kill each other's citizens over the disputed territory of Kashmir, and both developed nuclear weapons in the 1990s.

Conclusion

In physical intersections, streets, roads, and thoroughfares come together. This book has emphasized that we are not on a single path from the past to the future. History matters, but it is not destiny. We have come to the present along paths, passing intersections, forks in the road, and detours. Had we taken other routes, the present would be very different. The Anglo-European sense of time might not have been so linear, its sense of space not so angular. People might not understand the concept of buying time or space. The notion of race—that a person's skin color signals a core characteristic of the person himself or herself—might have never occurred to anyone. A person's genitals might have been thought to affect only his or her role in reproduction but not his or her place in society. People might have more material possessions, prestige, and power more because of their abilities and aspirations than because of their systematic relationship to social institutions. I am not harkening back to some imagined Garden of Eden where none of these things existed. There never was such a time or place. Nor is there any guarantee that things would be better than today's world if other roads were taken. In retrospect, we can see intersections and forks leading to more equality, democracy, and material comfort for all. Slavery that made the members of one race the property of another has ended, and the descendants of slaves rallied to end legal segregation a century later. Women have moved across the gap between the private and public spheres to demand their rightful place in major institutions. In the past century, for the first time, technological achievements have created enough food to feed everyone in the world, eliminating any excuse for continuing starvation anywhere.

However, many of the categories constructed on the path to the present continue to prevent people from seeing the path to a more just society. Like a horse wearing blinders, they do not know that different paths could take them to a better destination. Aware only of the path that brought them to the present, too many people assume that it is the only path. Harried in busy lives, people only think about finding more time, not realizing how "time" is a language to describe social relations that might be renegotiated. Believing that inequality is individual, not social, they ignore how the geography of poverty and race physically separates aspiring indigent African Americans and other poor people from opportunities for a better life. Cognizant of enduring racism, too many people only hope for more opportunities for minority races while still assuming that skin color reveals an essential quality of people. Similarly, they attribute social differences between men and women to genetics without questioning why different genitals should result in such momentous social differences. And they proclaim a classless society because feudal, hereditary nobility has nearly disappeared, ignoring how institutions help reproduce vast inequality in wealth and opportunities from one generation to the next.

On the other hand, it is misleading to blithely proclaim, as do some postmodern writers, that because things such as time, space, race, gender, and class are socially constructed, they can be transformed or swept aside by simply "changing our minds." Socially constructed reality is as real as it gets. The social relations framed in terms of time can be very compelling; you cannot tell your boss that promptness entails only socially constructed time. The bleak conditions of the ghetto have resisted many attempts at reform and in many places are deteriorating. Simply studying the history of race will leave many problems unchanged. White teachers can still assume that African American or Latino students are less intelligent than their white counterparts. White college students can still believe that their minority classmates were admitted only through affirmative action. People of all races can describe some friends of other races with racial adjectives, whites describing their "black friends" or Mexicans their "Anglo friends." The need to clean house and raise children remains when women enter formerly all-male occupations. And the rich continue to have the material resources and access to institutions they need to ensure that their children remain among the privileged, while the poor lack the same resources and access their children need to climb out of poverty.

Awareness of social construction only fosters knowledge that change is possible, if we can imagine another way. Imagination has been a powerful historical force, a quality shared by revolutionaries in America and China alike, by inventors such as Louis Pasteur or Jonas Salk and by visionaries such as Martin Luther King, Jr., Susan B. Anthony, and Mahatma Gandhi. But as the most prolific inventor in world history, Thomas Alva Edison, said, "Invention is one-tenth inspiration and nine-tenths perspiration." Realizing how reality is constructed only begins to rattle the shackles of the past. It still takes a collective effort to wrest them free. Then perhaps we can walk together down a new path to a future we can now only dimly appreciate.

References

Agnew, John. 1996. "Time Into Space: The Myth of 'Backward' Italy in Modern Europe." *Time and Society* 5 (1): 27-45.

Allen, Theodore W. 1997. *The Invention of the White Race: The Origin of Racial Oppression in Anglo-America.* London: Verso.

Almaguer, Tomas. 1994. *Racial Fault Lines: The Historical Origins of White Supremacy in California.* Berkeley: University of California Press.

Andersen, Milton L. 1994. "The Many and Varied Social Constructions of Intelligence." Pp. 119-38 in *Constructing the Social*, edited by T. R. Sarbin and J. I. Kitsuse. London: Sage.

Anderson, Benedict. 1991. *Imagined Communities.* New York: Verso.

Auden, W. H. 1966. *About the House.* New York: Random House.

Austin, Alfredo Lopes. 1997. *Tamoanchan, Tlalocan: Places of Mist.* Translated by Bernard R. and Thelma Ortiz de Montellano. Boulder: University of Colorado Press.

Aveni, Anthony F. 1995. *Empires of Time: Calendars, Clocks and Cultures.* New York: Basic Books.

Banton, Michael. 1998. *Racial Theories.* 2nd ed. Cambridge, UK: Cambridge University Press.

Basedow, H. 1929. *The Australian Aborigine.* Adelaide, Australia: Preece and Sons.

Bederman, Gail. 1995. *Manliness and Civilization: A Cultural History of Gender and Race in the United States, 1880-1917.* Chicago: University of Chicago Press.

Berger, Peter L. and Thomas Luckmann. 1966. *The Social Construction of Reality: A Treatise on the Sociology of Knowledge.* New York: Anchor.

Biernacki, Richard. 1995. *The Fabrication of Labor: Germany and Britain, 1640-1914.* Berkeley: University of California Press.

Bloom, Alan D. 1987. *The Closing of the American Mind.* New York: Simon & Schuster.

Boorstein, Daniel J. 1985. *The Discoverers: A History of Man's Search to Know His World and Himself.* New York: Vintage.

Boswell, John. 1994. *Same-Sex Unions in Premodern Europe.* New York: Villard.

Bourdieu, Pierre. 1984. *Distinction: A Social Critique of the Judgement of Taste.* Edited and translated by Richard Nice. Cambridge, MA: Harvard University Press.

Brubaker, Rogers. 1992. *Citizenship and Nationhood in France and Germany.* Cambridge, MA: Harvard University Press.

———. 1996. *Nationalism Reframed: Nationhood and the National Question in the New Europe.* New York: Cambridge University Press.

Buranen, L. and A. M. Roy, eds. 1999. *Perspectives on Plagiarism and Intellectual Property in a Postmodern World.* Albany: State University of New York Press.

Burns, Lee. 1993. *Busy Bodies.* New York: Norton.

Casper, Lynne M. and Ken Bryson. 1998. *Current Population Reports: Household and Family Characteristics: Population Characteristics. March 1998 (Update).* Washington, DC: U.S. Bureau of the Census.

Charrad, Mounira M. 1999. "Bringing in Tribe: Beyond a State/Class Paradigm." *Newsletter of the Comparative & Historical Sociology Section of the American Sociological Association* 11 (3): 1-3.

Chojnacki, Stanley. 1994. "Subaltern Patriarchs: Patrician Bachelors in Renaissance Venice." Pp. 73-90 in *Medieval Masculinities: Regarding Men in the Middle Ages*, edited by C. A. Lees. Minneapolis: University of Minnesota Press.

Collins, Patricia Hill. 1990. *Black Feminist Thought: Knowledge, Consciousness, and the Politics of Empowerment.* Boston: Unwin Hyman.

Connell, Robert W. 1995. *Masculinities.* Berkeley: University of California Press.

Cooper, Susan F. 1870. "Female Suffrage: A Letter to the Christian Women of America." *Harper's Magazine* 41:438-46.

Cope, Edward D. [1888] 1985. "The Relations of the Sexes to Government." Pp. 210-16 in *Men's Ideas/Women's Realities: Popular Science, 1870-1915*, edited by L. M. Newman. New York: Pergamon.

Cornell, Stephen and Douglas Hartmann. 1998. *Ethnicity and Race: Making Identities in a Changing World.* Thousand Oaks, CA: Pine Forge.

Cott, Nancy F. 1977. *The Bonds of Womanhood: Women's Sphere in New England, 1780-1835.* New Haven, CT: Yale University Press.

Cowan, James. 1982. *The Mountain Men.* French Forest, New South Wales: A. H. and A. W. Reed.

Cronin, Vincent. 1964. *Louis XIV.* London: Collins.

Danziger, Sheldon and Peter Gottschalk. 1995. *America Unequal.* Cambridge, MA: Harvard University Press.

DeParle, Jason. 1994. "Better Work Than Welfare? But What If There's Neither?" *New York Times*, 18 December, Section 6, p. 44.

Dilke, O. A. W. 1985. *Greek and Roman Maps.* Ithaca, NY: Cornell University Press.

———. 1987. "Maps in the Service of the State: Roman Cartography to the End of the Augusta Era." Pp. 201-211 in *History of Cartography: Vol. 1. Cartogra-

phy in Prehistoric, Ancient, and Medieval Europe and the Mediterranean, edited by J. B. Harley and David Woodward. Chicago: University of Chicago Press.

DiMaggio, Paul. 1982a. "Cultural Entrepreneurship in Nineteenth-Century Boston: Part II. The Classification and Framing of American Art." *Media, Culture, and Society* 4:303-22.

―――. 1982b. "Cultural Entrepreneurship in Nineteenth-Century Boston: The Creation of an Organizational Base for High Culture in America." *Media, Culture, and Society* 4:33-50.

―――. 1992. "Cultural Boundaries and Structural Change: The Extension of the High Culture Model to Theater, Opera, and the Dance, 1900-1940." Pp. 21-57 in *Cultivating Differences: Symbolic Boundaries and the Making of Inequality,* edited by M. Lamont and M. Fournier. Chicago: University of Chicago Press.

DiMaggio, Paul and Michael Useem. 1978. "Cultural Democracy in a Period of Cultural Expansion." *Social Problems* 26:179-97.

"Dred Scott v. Sanford." [1857] 1995. Pp. 322-25 in *Race, Class, and Gender in the United States: An Integrated Study,* edited by P. S. Rothenberg. New York: St. Martin's.

Dubbert, Joe L. 1980. "Progressivism and the Masculinity Crisis." Pp. 303-20 in *The American Man,* edited by E. Pleck and J. H. Pleck. Englewood Cliffs, NJ: Prentice Hall.

Durkheim, Emile. 1995. *The Elementary Forms of Religious Life.* New York: Free Press.

Elias, Norbert. 1992. *Time: An Essay.* Oxford, UK: Blackwell.

Evans-Pritchard, E. E. 1939. "Nuer Time-Reckoning." *Africa* 12:189-216.

Faderman, Lillian. 1991. *Odd Girls and Twilight Lovers.* New York: Penguin.

Faludi, Susan. 1991. *Backlash: The Undeclared War Against American Women.* New York: Anchor.

Ferrante, Joan and Prince Brown, Jr. 1998. *The Social Construction of Race and Ethnicity in the United States.* New York: Longman.

Filene, Peter G. 1998. *Him/Her/Self.* 3rd ed. Baltimore: Johns Hopkins University Press.

Fischer, Claude S., Michael Hout, Martin Sanchez Jankowski, Samuel R. Lucas, and Kim Voss. 1996. *Inequality by Design: Cracking the Bell Curve Myth.* Princeton, NJ: Princeton University Press.

Foucault, Michel. 1987. *History of the Present.* Berkeley: University of California Press.

Fraser, J. T. 1987. *Time: The Familiar Stranger.* Amherst: University of Massachusetts Press.

―――. 1990. *Of Time, Passion, and Knowledge.* Princeton, NJ: Princeton University Press.

———. 1994. "Calendar: Western." Pp. 75-80 in *The Encyclopedia of Time,* edited by S. L. Macy. New York: Garland.

Gans, Herbert J. 1974. *Popular Culture and High Culture.* New York: Basic Books.

Gardner, Carol Brooks. 1994. "Out of Place: Gender, Public Places, and Situational Disadvantage." Pp. 335-55 in *NowHere: Space, Time and Modernity,* edited by R. Friedland and D. Boden. Berkeley: University of California Press.

Gardner, Howard. 1983. *Frames of Mind: The Theory of Multiple Intelligences.* New York: Basic Books.

Gilmore, David D. 1990. *Manhood in the Making: Cultural Concepts of Masculinity.* New Haven, CT: Yale University Press.

Gilroy, Paul. 1992. *There Ain't No Black in the Union Jack.* London: Routledge Kegan Paul.

Glenn, Evelyn Nakano. 1999. "The Social Construction and Institutionalization of Gender and Race: An Integrative Framework." Pp. 3-43 in *Revisioning Gender,* edited by M. M. Ferree, J. Lorber, and B. B. Hess. Thousand Oaks, CA: Sage.

Gough, E. Kathleen. 1974. "Nayar: Central Kerala." Pp. 298-384 in *Matrilineal Kinship,* edited by D. Schneider and E. K. Gough. Berkeley: University of California Press.

Gould, Stephen Jay. 1981. *The Mismeasure of Man.* New York: Norton.

Granovetter, Mark. 1974. *Getting a Job: A Study of Contacts and Careers.* Cambridge, MA: Harvard University Press.

Gress, David. 1998. *The Idea of the West and Its Opponents: From Plato to NATO.* New York: Free Press.

Hacking, Ian. 1999. *The Social Construction of What?* Cambridge, MA: Harvard University Press.

Hale, Grace Elizabeth. 1998. *Making Whiteness: The Culture of Segregation in the South, 1890-1940.* New York: Pantheon.

Hall, Edward T. 1969. *The Hidden Dimension.* Garden City, NY: Anchor.

Halle, David. 1993. *Inside Culture: Art and Class in the American Home.* Chicago: University of Chicago Press.

Haney Lopez, Ian F. 1996. *White by Law: The Legal Construction of Race.* New York: New York University Press.

Hannaford, Ivan. 1996. *Race: The History of an Idea in the West.* Baltimore: Johns Hopkins University Press.

Hansen, Karen V. 1991. "'Helped Put in a Quilt': Men's Work and Male Intimacy in Nineteenth-Century New England." Pp. 83-103 in *The Social Construction of Gender,* edited by J. Lorber and S. A. Farrell. Newbury Park, CA: Sage.

Hantover, Jeffrey P. 1998. "The Boy Scouts and the Validation of Masculinity." Pp. 101-08 in *Men's Lives,* 4th ed., edited by M. S. Kimmel and M. A. Messner. Boston: Allyn & Bacon.

Harris, Cheryl I. 1993. "Whiteness as Property." *Harvard Law Review* 106:1707-91.

Harvey, David. 1989. *The Condition of Postmodernity: An Inquiry Into the Origins of Cultural Change.* Cambridge, UK: Basil Blackwell.

Hayden, Dolores. 1984. *The Grand Domestic Revolution: A History of Feminist Designs for American Homes, Neighborhoods, and Cities.* New York: Norton.

Herdt, Gilbert. 1993a. "Introduction: Third Sexes and Third Genders." Pp. 21-84 in *Third Sex Third Gender: Beyond Sexual Dimorphism in Culture and History,* edited by G. Herdt. New York: Zone.

———. 1993b. "Mistaken Sex: Culture, Biology and the Third Sex in New Guinea." Pp. 419-46 in *Third Sex, Third Gender: Beyond Sexual Dimorphism in Culture and History,* edited by G. Herdt. New York: Zone.

Herrnstein, Richard J. and Charles Murray. 1994. *The Bell Curve: Intelligence and Class Structure in American Life.* New York: Free Press.

Hewlett, S. A. (1986). *A Lesser Life: The Myth of Women's Liberation in America.* New York: Warner.

Hobsbawm, Eric J. and Terence Ranger. 1983. *The Invention of Tradition.* Cambridge, UK: Cambridge University Press.

Hochschild, Arlie Russell with Anne Machung. 1989. *The Second Shift: Working Parents and the Revolution at Home.* New York: Viking.

Holstein, James A. and Jaber F. Gubrium. 1994. "Constructing Family: Descriptive Practice and Domestic Order." Pp. 232-50 in *Constructing the Social,* edited by T. R. Sarbin and J. I. Kitsuse. London: Sage.

Horwitz, Morton. 1977. *The Transformation of American Law, 1780-1960.* Cambridge, MA: Harvard University Press.

Ignatiev, Noel. 1995. *How the Irish Became White.* New York: Routledge Kegan Paul.

Jacobson, Matthew Frye. 1998. *Whiteness of a Different Color: European Immigrants and the Alchemy of Race.* Cambridge, MA: Harvard University Press.

Jurczyk, Karin. 1998. "Time in Women's Everyday Lives: Between Self-Determination and Conflicting Demands." *Time & Society* 7 (2): 283-308.

Kain, Roger and Elizabeth Baigent. 1992. *The Cadastral Map in the Service of the State: A History of Property Mapping.* Chicago: University of Chicago Press.

Kimmel, Michael S. 1987. "The Contemporary 'Crisis' of Masculinity in Historical Perspective." Pp. 121-53 in *The Making of Masculinities: The New Men's Studies,* edited by H. Brod. Boston: Allen & Unwin.

———. 1993. *American Manhood: Transformations in Masculinity From the Revolution to the Modern Era.* New York: Basic Books.

———. 1996. *Manhood in America: A Cultural History.* New York: Free Press.

Konrad, George and Ivan Szelenyi. 1979. *The Intellectual on the Road to Class Power.* New York: Harcourt Brace.

Konvitz, Josef. 1987. *Cartography in France 1660-1848: Science, Engineering and Statecraft.* Chicago: University of Chicago Press.

Labov, William. 1994. *Principles of Linguistic Change.* Cambridge, MA: Blackwell.

Lamont, Michèle. 1997. "Money, Morals, and Manners." Pp. 224-40 in *Sociology: Exploring the Architecture of Everyday Life,* edited by D. M. Newman. Thousand Oaks, CA: Pine Forge.

Lamont, Michèle and Marcel Fournier. 1992. "Introduction." Pp. 1-20 in *Cultivating Differences: Symbolic Boundaries and the Making of Inequality,* edited by M. Lamont and M. Fournier. Chicago: University of Chicago Press.

Landes, David. 1983. *Revolution in Time.* Cambridge, MA: Harvard University Press.

Laqueur, Thomas. 1990. *Making Sex: Body and Gender From the Greeks to Freud.* Cambridge, MA: Harvard University Press.

Leccardi, Carmen. 1996. "Rethinking Social Time: Feminist Perspectives." *Time & Society* 5 (2): 169-86.

LeGoff, Jacques. 1980. *Time, Work, and Culture in the Middle Ages.* Chicago: University of Chicago Press.

Levine, Lawrence W. 1988. *Highbrow, Lowbrow: The Emergence of Cultural Hierarchy in America.* Cambridge, MA: Harvard University Press.

Lewis, Martin W. and Kären E. Wigen. 1997. *The Myth of Continents: A Critique of Metageography.* Berkeley: University of California Press.

Logan, John R. 1976. "Industrialization and the Stratification of Cities in a Suburban Region." *American Journal of Sociology* 82 (2): 333-48.

Logan, John R. and Harvey L. Molotch. 1988. *Urban Fortunes: The Political Economy of Place.* Berkeley: University of California Press.

Lorber, Judith. 1994. *Paradoxes of Gender.* New Haven, CT: Yale University Press.

Mann, Michael. 1986. *The Sources of Social Power: A History of Power From the Beginning to A.D. 1760.* Cambridge, UK: Cambridge University Press.

Martin, Thomas. 1996. *Ancient Greece: From Prehistoric to Hellenistic Times.* New Haven, CT: Yale University Press.

Marx, Anthony W. 1998. *Making Race and Nation: A Comparison of the United States, South Africa, and Brazil.* New York: Cambridge University Press.

Massey, Douglas S. and Nancy A. Denton. 1993. *American Apartheid: Segregation and the Making of the Underclass.* Cambridge, MA: Harvard University Press.

McLeish, John. 1992. *Number.* New York: Fawcett Columbine.

McNamara, Jo Ann. 1994. "The *Herrenfrage*: The Restructuring of the Gender System, 1050-1150." Pp. 3-29 in *Medieval Masculinities: Regarding Men in the Middle Ages,* edited by C. A. Lees. Minneapolis: University of Minnesota Press.

Messner, Michael. 1987. "The Meaning of Success: The Athletic Experience and the Development of Male Identity." Pp. 193-209 in *The Making of Masculinities: The New Men's Studies,* edited by H. Brod. Boston: Allen & Unwin.

Molotch, Harvey. 1976. "The City as a Growth Machine: Toward a Political Economy of Place." *American Journal of Sociology* 82:309-32.

More, Hannah. 1787. *Sacred Dramas: Chiefly Intended for Young Persons: The Subjects Taken From the Bible: To Which Are Added: Reflections of King Hezekiah, and Sensibility, a Poem.* Philadelphia: Printed for Thomas Dobson.

Mundy, Barbara. 1996. *The Mapping of New Spain: Indigenous Cartography and the Maps of the Relaciones Geograficas.* Chicago: University of Chicago Press.

Myers, Fred R. 1986. *Pintupi Country, Pintupi Self: Sentiment, Place and Politics Among Western Desert Aborigines.* Canberra: Australian Institute of Aboriginal Studies.

Naidis, Mark. 1970. *The Second British Empire: 1783-1965.* Reading, MA: Addison-Wesley.

Newman, David M. 2000. *Sociology: Exploring the Architecture of Everyday Life.* 3rd ed. Thousand Oaks, CA: Pine Forge.

O'Malley, Michael. 1990. *Keeping Watch: A History of American Time.* New York: Viking.

Omi, Michael and Howard Winant. 1994. *Racial Formation in the United States: From the 1960s to the 1990s.* 2nd ed. New York: Routledge Kegan Paul.

Opperman, Renee, et al. 1984. "Prehistoric Cosmology in Mesoamerica and South America." Pp. 4-16 in *Occasional Publications in Anthropology.* Greeley: University of Northern Colorado Press.

Oyèwùmí, Oyeronke. 1997. *The Invention of Women: Making an African Sense of Western Gender Discourses.* Minneapolis: University of Minnesota Press.

Paolucci, Gabriella. 1996. "Time Shattered: The Postindustrial City and Women's Temporal Experiences." *Time & Society* 5 (3): 265-81.

Pateman, Carole. 1989. *The Disorder of Women: Democracy, Feminism and Political Theory.* Stanford, CA: Stanford University Press.

Patterson, Orlando. 1982. *Slavery and Social Death: A Comparative Study.* Cambridge, MA: Harvard University Press.

Peterson, Richard A. and Albert Simkus. 1992. "How Musical Tastes Mark Occupational Status Groups." Pp. 152-86 in *Cultivating Differences: Symbolic Boundaries and the Making of Inequality,* edited by M. Lamont and M. Fournier. Chicago: University of Chicago Press.

Poggi, Franco. 1978. *The Development of the Modern State: A Sociological Introduction.* Palo Alto, CA: Stanford University Press.

Polanyi, Karl. 1957. *The Great Transformation.* Boston: Beacon.

Polanyi, Livia. 1997. "Interview With Deirdre McCloskey." *Challenge* 40 (1): 16-29.

Pollner, Melvin. 1987. *Mundane Reason: Reality in Everyday and Sociological Discourse.* New York: Cambridge University Press.

Pred, Allan. 1990. *Making Histories and Constructing Human Geographies: The Local Transformation of Practical Power Relations and Consciousness.* Boulder, CO: Westview.

Roediger, David R. 1991. *The Wages of Whiteness: Race and the Making of the American Working Class.* New York: Verso.

Rossum, Gerhard Dohrn-van. 1996. *History of the Hour: Clocks and Modern Temporal Orders.* Chicago: University of Chicago Press.

Rotundo, E. Anthony. 1983. "Body and Soul: Changing Ideals of American Middle-Class Manhood." *Journal of Social History* 16 (4): 23-38.

————. 1993. *American Manhood: Transformations in Masculinity From the Revolution to the Modern Era.* New York: Basic Books.

Rutz, Henry J. 1994. "Primitive Time-Reckoning." Pp. 496-97 in *Encyclopedia of Time,* edited by S. L. Macey. New York: Garland.

Ryan, Mary P. 1981. *Cradle of the Middle Class: The Family in Oneida County, New York, 1790-1865.* New York: Cambridge University Press.

Sacks, Karen Brodkin. 1998. "How Did Jews Become White Folks?" Pp. 78-102 in *Race,* edited by S. Gregory and R. Sanjek. New Brunswick, NJ: Rutgers University Press.

Samson, Basil. 1974. "Economic Structures of the Bantu." Pp. 135-175 in *The Bantu Peoples of Southern Africa,* edited by W. D. Hammond-Tooke. London: Routledge Kegan Paul.

Sanderson, Stephen K. 1999. *Macrosociology: An Introduction to Human Societies.* 4th ed. New York: Longman.

Schivelbusch, Wolfgang. 1986. *The Railway Journey: The Industrialization of Time and Space in the 19th Century.* Berkeley: University of California Press.

Schwartz, Barry. 1983. "George Washington and the Whig Conception of Heroic Leadership." *American Sociological Review* 48 (1): 18-33.

"Scientists Say Race Has No Biological Basis." 1995. *Los Angeles Times,* 20 February, A1.

Sennett, Richard. 1974. *The Fall of Public Man.* New York: Vintage.

Shaw, Margaret. 1974. "Material Culture." Pp. 85-126 in *The Bantu Peoples of Southern Africa,* edited by W. D. Hammond-Tooke. London: Routledge Kegan Paul.

Simmel, Georg. 1955. *Conflict and the Web of Group Affiliations.* New York: Free Press.

Simon, Joel. 1997. "Prophecy, Plague and Plunder." *Amicus Journal* 19:28-34.

Smedley, Audrey. 1993. *Race in North America: Origin and Evolution of a Worldview.* Boulder, CO: Westview.

Smith, Anthony D. 1983. *Theories of Nationalism.* London: Duckworth.

Soja, Edward W. 1994. "Postmodern Geographies." Pp. 127-63 in *NowHere: Space, Time and Modernity,* edited by R. Friedland and D. Boden. Berkeley: University of California Press.

Sorokin, Pitirim and Robert K. Merton. 1990. "Social Time: A Methodological and Functional Analysis." Pp. 56-66 in *The Sociology of Time,* edited by J. Hassard. New York: St. Martin's.

Spain, Daphne. 1992. *Gendered Spaces.* Chapel Hill: University of North Carolina Press.

Standage, Tom. 1998. *The Victorian Internet.* New York: Walker and Company.

Standbury, Peter. 1977. *The Moving Frontier: Aspects of Aboriginal-European Interaction in Australia.* Sydney, Australia: Charter.

Stimson, Henry A. 1904. "The Small Business as a School of Manhood." *Atlantic Monthly* 93 (557): 337-40.

Stuard, Susan Mosher. 1994. "Burdens of Matrimony: Husbanding and Gender in Medieval Italy." Pp. 61-71 in *Medieval Masculinities: Regarding Men in the Middle Ages,* edited by C. A. Lees. Minneapolis: University of Minnesota Press.

Takaki, Ronald. 1990. *Iron Cages: Race and Culture in 19th Century America.* New York: Oxford University Press.

Thomas, William I. and Dorothy Swaine Thomas. 1928. *The Child in America.* New York: Knopf.

Thompson, E. P. 1971. "The Moral Economy of the English Crowd in the Eighteenth Century." *Past and Present* 50 (February): 76-136.

Thrift, Nigel. 1996. *Spatial Formations.* Thousand Oaks, CA: Sage.

Thrower, Norman J. W. 1996. *Maps and Civilization: Cartography in Culture and Society.* Chicago: University of Chicago Press.

Tilly, Charles, ed. 1975. *The Formation of National States in Western Europe.* Princeton, NJ: Princeton University Press.

——. 1998. *Durable Inequality.* Berkeley: University of California Press.

Tilly, Louise. 1971. "The Food Riot as a Form of Political Conflict in France." *Journal of Interdisciplinary History* 2:23-58.

Trachtenberg, Alan. 1981. *The Incorporation of America: Culture and Society in the Gilded Age.* New York: Hill and Wang.

Turner, A. J. 1994. "Instruments of Time Measurement to Ca. A. D. 1275." Pp. 304-12 in *Encyclopedia of Time,* edited by S. L. Macey. New York: Garland.

Vandevelde, Kenneth J. 1980. "The New Property of the Nineteenth Century: The Development of the Modern Concept of Property." *Buffalo Law Review* 29:325-67.

Whitman, Edward. 1952. *World Time Differences.* London: Whitman.

Wilford, John Noble. 1982. *The Map Makers.* New York: Vintage.

Williams, Raymond. 1983. *Keywords: A Vocabulary of Culture and Society.* New York: Oxford University Press.

Willoughby, W. C. 1923. *Race Problems in the New Africa.* Oxford, UK: Clarendon.

Wilson, William Julius. 1987. *The Truly Disadvantaged: The Inner City, the Underclass, and Public Policy.* Chicago: University of Chicago Press.

Wolf, Eric. 1982. *Europe and the People Without History.* Berkeley: University of California Press.

Wolpert, Stanley. 1997. *New History of India.* London: Oxford University Press.

Woodward, C. Vann. 1969. *Tom Watson: Agrarian Rebel.* New York: Oxford University Press.

Wyckoff, William K. 1989. "Landscapes of Private Power and Wealth." Pp. 335-54 in *The Making of the American Landscape,* edited by M. P. Conzen. New York: Routledge Kegan Paul.

Yerkes, R. M. (Ed.). (1921). *Memoirs of the National Academy of Sciences: Vol. 15. Psychological Examining in the United States Army.* Washington, DC: Government Printing Office.

Zerubavel, Eviatar. 1979. *Patterns of Time in Hospital Life.* Chicago: University of Chicago Press.

———. 1985. *The Seven Day Circle: The History and Meaning of the Week.* Chicago: University of Chicago Press.

———. 1991. *The Fine Line: Making Distinctions in Everyday Life.* New York: Free Press.

Glossary/Index

D

Darwin, Charles, 89

Descartes, René, 62-63

Dimorphism the notion that there are two kinds of bodies, male and female, 113-114

Dominant institutions institutions in society that wield the most power, that is, that most profoundly influence other institutions and affect people's lives, 22-23

Domination, types of, 27

Dred Scott v. Sanford, 95

E

Economic class material possessions such as income or wealth, 159

Economic surplus food, clothing, and other necessities in excess of what a society consumes for subsistence, 166

Education and class, 159, 162-163

Egalitarian values, 85-86

Enclosure movements a set of activities during the transition from feudalism to capitalism by which governments removed peasants (often forcibly) and gave land to individual nobles for commercial use, 67

English societies, 86-87, 175, 193

Enlightenment, 37, 63-64

Essentialist perspective a point of view that assumes that everything that we *see* and *touch* is a manifestation of a deeper essence, 8-10

Ethnic cleansing, 194

Ethnic groups, 79

Ethnicity, 76

Euclidean geometry, 56

F

Family:
  and class, 161-162
  and gender, 132-133
  category of, 16-18

Femininity. *See* Gender

Fertile Crescent, 166

Feudalism the economic and social system that preceded capitalism in Europe, organized by a hierarchical chain in which individuals exchanged tribute for protection, 66-67, 86, 167-170

Forster, John, 115

Fourier, Charles, 186

Fowler, Rev. Philemon, 125

France, 37-38, 62-67, 174

Freedom, concept of, 96-97

French Revolution, 36

G

Galen, 118

Galton, Francis, 3

Gender kinds of social relations commonly attributed to differences between males and females, 112-113
  and homosexuality, 140-143
  and masculinity:
    and sex, 112-113
    character of, 128-129
    concept of usefulness, 131-133
    earlier European meaning of, 129-130
    in America, 131-136
    physical character, 134-136
    rise of the state and, 130-131
    the crisis of, 136-140
    the "self-made man," 133-134
    today's tough men, 136
  categories of:
    changes in Anglo-European society, 23
    concluding thoughts on, 152-155
    cross-cultural variations, 114-115
    dimorphic genders, 113-116
    historical construction of, 23, 111-112
  history of sex and:
    kinds of bodies, 117-119
    prehistoric societies, 116-117
    public and private spheres, 122-125
    women before femininity, 119-122
    women's voting rights, 125-128
  intersections of:
    homes and, 186-188

intersections of:
  affirmative action, 106-108
  gender and, 151-152
  homes and, 188-189
  identity, 104
  nations and, 192-194
  preracial categories, 81-84
  racial segregation, 72, 104-106
  reflexivity of, 21-22, 101-103
  socialization, 103-104
  worldview of, 80-81
legal validation, 94-96
physical differences, 77
ranked hierarchically, 79-80
Races groups of people who are assumed to (1) have particular physical characteristics in common, especially skin color; (2) fall into distinct and sharply bounded groups; (3) inherit their racial status; (4) share behavioral characteristics that are imputed to their physical qualities; and (5) are ranked hierarchically, 76
Racial segregation, 72, 95-96, 104-106. *See also* Race
Rank society a society in which some positions have higher status and authority but without material advantages, usually with strong norms against using privilege for material gain, 165
Reality. *See* Social construction of reality
Reflexive a logical relationship in which factors explain each other, like the proverbial chicken and the egg, 31-32
Reification a process by which "facts" that were originally merely someone's ideas, speculations, or theories take on a reality of their own, 18-20
Relationship to an institution the title a person occupies in organizations, the connections to other people, and the rights, privileges, and responsibilities that come from his or her position, 161
Religion:
  and class, 163, 169-170
  and race, 82
  and time, 36-38

Residential segregation, 188-189
Reverse discrimination, 101
Rights, notion of, 64
Romance languages, 33
Romans, 33, 34, 57-59, 142
Romantic friendships, 141-142
"Rosie the Riveter," 146
Russian Revolution, 36

S

Sacred spaces, 52-53
Savagery, concept of, 86-88
Science and race, 88-93
Segregation:
  racial, 72, 95-96, 104-106
  residential, 188-189
Selling labor some people exchange their time and effort for money by taking paid employment, 171-172
Semai, 115-116
Serfs (peasants), 159, 169
Seton, Ernest Thompson, 138
Seven-Day Circle, The (Zerubavel), 32
7-day week, origins of, 32-33
Sex biological differences between the male and female of the human species, 112-113. *See also* Gender
Shona culture, 12
Sieyes, Abbe, 65
Siuai of Bougainville, 165
Slaves and slavery:
  and racial inequality, 21-22, 101-102
  as indentured servants, 83-84
  as property, 84, 174
Social construction of reality historical process by which our experiences become put into categories and treated as things, 5-18
  and intelligence, 1-5, 24-26
  concluding thoughts on, 28-29
  constructionist perspective, 10
  defining reality:
    categories and language, 11-14
    concluding thoughts on, 197-199
    consequences of categories, 16-18